HOMER TO BRECHT

Homer to Brecht

The European Epic and Dramatic Traditions

edited by

Michael Seidel

and

Edward Mendelson

New Haven and London, Yale University Press
1977

Designed by Susan McCrillis Kelsey
and set in Selectric Journal Roman type.
Printed in the United States of America by
The Murray Printing Company,
Westford, Massachusetts.

Published in Great Britain, Europe, Africa, and Asia
by Yale University Press, Ltd., London.
Distributed in Latin America by Kaiman & Polon, Inc.,
New York City; in Australia and New Zealand by Book & Film
Services, Artarmon, N.S.W., Australia.

Library of Congress Cataloging in Publication Data
Main entry under title:

Homer to Brecht.

    1. Epic literature—History and criticism—Addresses,
essays, lectures. 2. Drama—History and criticism—
Addresses, essays, lectures. I. Seidel, Michael A.,
1943-   II. Mendelson, Edward.
PN56.E65H6   809   76-25014
ISBN 0-300-02028-7

CONTENTS

PREFACE

The sixteen essays in this book constitute an introduction to the epic and dramatic traditions in European literature from Homer to Joyce, from Aeschylus to Beckett. Six essays treat epic action and epic structure, detailing the transformations of epic heroism from the plains of Troy to the streets of modern Dublin. Ten essays concentrate on the varying worlds of dramatic action, from the disintegration of the House of Atreus to the closed family of *Endgame.*

Part of the excitement of discovery or rediscovery of literary works is the recognition that they remain integral with their own time and culture while building toward a tradition that is larger than anything a single work can encompass. We have tried to provide a sense of the large, self-correcting, and cumulative traditions that great works of literature generate, alter, and maintain.

Although each essay is, we hope, a contribution to the critical literature on its subject, each is primarily an introduction to the work at hand. This book's emphasis is therefore literary and historical, placing works that have become timeless in the context of the literary acts and historical choices that precede and follow them. For readers in the present, past literature displays the qualities of both *strangeness*—its forms and substance are unique to its own age—and *immanence*—its problems remain universal and compelling for all time. While respecting the timelessness, and therefore the contemporaneity, of great literature, we have tried to observe the particularity of the worlds in which great works originate. Readers may recognize in the prolonged warfare of the *Iliad* grim conditions that recur throughout history, but they will find it equally instructive to discover in the poem the unique expression of a heroic Greek culture whose values, like its warriors, live and die around the walls of a Troy doomed to an irrevocable fall.

While commemorating the past, we are aware of our debts in the present. We thank Margaret Anbar, Wanda Fiak, and Doris Nelson for timely help on many occasions, and we thank our editors Ellen Graham and Lynn Walterick for unfailing encouragement and good sense.

These essays are based on lectures given during the past several years in a Yale College humanities course originally devised by A. Bartlett Giamatti, to whom the editors gratefully dedicate this collection.

M. S.

E. M.

THE EPIC TRADITION

THE *ILIAD*

James Nohrnberg

I

The *Iliad* has deep roots in what I will call the strife epos, that is, narratives about fighting—lays about border clashes, cattle raids, clan feuds, military exploits, the razing of settlements and cities, and deeds of exceptional physical courage in battle. We are told that such materials have their historical origins in wars of migration; presumably quest epics and epics of colonization are differentiated out of the same substrate as well. The heroic construction is put upon the strife epos when the protagonists are imagined as greater than ourselves, and when their contests are assigned to a "heroic age," most likely the memory of a turbulent, marauding baronial class idealized as a model of manhood and valor by a more settled and less ambitious successor culture. A vanished ideal age is close to the conception of heroism itself, which, not being found in ordinary life, or the present, has to be located somewhere, such as an "earlier" or parental world where the figures are larger and the sense of possibility greater. Homer's war is heroic in another sense also: it is noble. There is no torture, no slaughter of innocents, and no treachery. Exceptions may be found, but by far the greatest number are in the night raid of book 10, the Doloneia, which has a somewhat subversive relation to the rest of the poem and espe-

3

cially to the unavailing "statesmanship" of the embassy in the book which precedes it.

Although the heroic code and the tale of strife have epic potential, they do not by themselves make an epic. There are at least two formal or generic requirements. One is the concept of a total action[1] —every epic has this—and the other is a nearly determinative relation to a culture. On the latter account, the epic shows a tendency to become a "scripture" of its culture. Such a poem is in fact not so much a cultural production as a cultural producer. Helen says that the things that have happened to her happened because she and Paris were destined to become a song for ages to come. It seems a singularly vain and complacent thing to say, but it is second nature to Helen to be the subject of song and story: people *will* talk, and she gives them something to talk about. The bard, however, means that the events of his poem, in the mind of the culture it forms, are indistinguishable from the poem about them. In the epic, the fall of Troy is destined to be—it is part of the poem's "total action." In the culture that the epic expresses, the epic itself seems equally "destined to be." Such an epic is one of the things that a culture, in its quest for self-definition, *intends.*

Apart from pure prowess, the organizing ideas of the strife epos are offense and reprisal. These are obviously useful to the storyteller because they make things happen, especially fights. They provide the negative basis for the heroic code. The positive basis is heroic obligation: the hero's obligation to be heroic. To this are added rules of heroic deference and demeanor. A rich source of ideas here is heroic giving: generosity to inferiors, yielding to superiors, restitution for wrongs, appeasement of those in the right, and even giving way to

1. The nature of this "total action" in the epic form is described by Northrop Frye in *The Return of Eden* (Toronto: University of Toronto Press, 1965).

superior force on the battlefield or yielding gracefully to old age—another's, or one's own.

The theme of the Iliadic example of the strife epos is not so readily intellectualized, but it ought to derive from the generative ideas just summarized. Homer's poem takes the mechanism of offense and reprisal and brings it to bear on a single warrior. The relations of Agamemnon and Achilles are obviously governed by this mechanism, but Achilles' retaliation for the offenses done him by Agamemnon offends not only Agamemnon but also offends Achilles' own status as a warrior. And his retaliation ultimately widens to encompass the death of his best friend.

Homer begins in book 1 by showing us the wrath subject in a state of fission, as Greek fights with Greek over a woman; by book 9 he has also achieved a kind of fusion, or rather an introversion of the wrath subject, as Achilles angrily confirms his withdrawal from warrior society, and continues at war with himself. From the start the hero divides himself from the sources of his heroism on the battlefield. Room is thus made for a variety of Achilles figures to step into the place of the leading player, especially the flamboyant but loyal Diomedes, the company man or team player for the offense, and the dependable but blockish shield hero Ajax, the corresponding figure for the defense. Meanwhile, Achilles persuades the fatherly Phoinix to join him in his tent; this instance of the introversion movement is reversed in the final book, when Achilles opens his tent to Priam, the father figure from the side of the enemy.

The introversion of the wrath subject throws the emphasis on character, that is, on angry persons, rather than on actions taken in anger. Homer's characters are always unified, or consistent with themselves. They somewhat lack an "inside," but not a single one lacks character. Their lifeline, however, is their connection to other people, and they define themselves in terms of the good or evil they cause to others, or the approval or disapproval or loyalty they secure from

others. As Helen herself said, her essential existence will
consist in just such a legend as she leaves upon the lips of
others.

II

Teachers of the *Iliad* usually direct attention to Sarpedon's
speech on the heroic code, which is crucial for any discussion
of the hero's motivation. In the middle of the poem, Sarpedon
turns to Glaukos and tries to justify the drive toward glory.
He says that he and Glaukos obtain their place of honor
among men because they have embraced the obligation to be
heroic: they lead into the fighting, and they are therefore
treated like immortals. Then he considers the alternative:

> Man, supposing you and I, escaping this battle,
> would be able to live on forever, ageless, immortal,
> so neither would I myself go on fighting in the
>   foremost
> nor would I urge you into the fighting where men
>   win glory.
> But now, seeing that the spirits of death stand
>   close about us
> in their thousands, no man can turn aside nor escape them,
> let us go on and win glory for ourselves, or yield
>   it to others.

[12.322–28]

In the underlying train of ideas here, battle glory is a substitute for an otherwise unattainable immortality. At the same
time, it crosses Sarpedon's mind that if he could just get
away from the coercive battle situation in which he finds
himself, he would not have to argue that winning glory was
the only real choice. Ordinarily, a warrior accepts just this
premise—the spirits of death always stand close about him,
it's do or die, and one heroically takes one's chances for the
sake of glory. Sarpedon's defense of valor is paradoxically a
consequence of his exposed position.

A decidedly different speech on the subject of valor belongs to the Achilles of book 9. Achilles claims that his acceptance of the standard heroic obligation has not, in fact, made any difference in the honor (or consideration or glory) that he has been accorded:

> Fate is the same for the man who holds back, the same
>   if he fights hard.
> We are all held in a single honour, the brave with the
>   weaklings.
> A man dies still if he has done nothing, as one who
>   has done much.
> Nothing is won for me, now that my heart has gone
>   through its afflictions
> in forever setting my life on the hazard of battle.
>
> [9.318–22]

Achilles almost equates Agamemnon, who will not honor him, with Fate or Death. Both treat all men the same, no matter what any *one*, as an individual, may have done to distinguish himself. Like Death, Agamemnon denies Achilles an immortality.

Achilles then announces to the embassy that he carries with him two sorts of destiny, between which he has a choice. One destiny is the everlasting glory entailed in an early death at the battle of Troy. The alternative destiny is a long life after his return to his fatherland—a long life without glory. This inglorious alternative, which Thetis did not bother to mention in book 1, reminds us of Sarpedon's idea of escaping the battle and living on forever, a possibility he rejected as strictly hypothetical. Since Achilles says that he would win everlasting glory if he stayed at Troy, he seems to contradict his previous assertion that the valorous and cowardly get the same reward, though perhaps this assertion is only addressed to a temporary aberration from the proper norm. Nonetheless, it has obviously occurred to Achilles that death in the vanguard might not be all that glorious after all, despite the official line peddled by good soldiers like Sarpedon. Of course Achilles thinks the alternative home-keeping destiny also ignoble: he does not in the least want to be a swineherd like the home-keeping Eumaeus of the *Odyssey*, or a clod breaker like the one he cites as an example of minimal life in the later poem's representation of the afterlife. In the river episode of the *Iliad* he specifically dreads being drowned like a common swineherd, swept away while trying to ford a storm-swollen torrent. Achilles' contempt for the alternative life has thus left his self-esteem no place to turn.

Achilles and Sarpedon are agreed that glory is to be won only in the hazarding of life in the forefront of the fighting—except that Achilles fears that it is not really won even there. Thus Achilles' speech does not so much want to take issue with Sarpedon as with some larger framing of the case. The dead hero and the dead coward—are they so different, are they the only choices? Death, in a way, dishonors them both. Agamemnon's insults are no longer the only heart's afflictions for Achilles. Odysseus, after all, has offered to rectify the problem of the just distribution of honors: there has merely been a little delay—nothing to get huffy about. Achilles, however, is not really speaking to Odysseus's offer but rather to the relation between his own personal destiny and the conventional heroic code. If there are no real alternatives inside the code, might he not still be able to find a destiny outside it? And yet he is unable to get much beyond the terms of the argument as Sarpedon proposed them. Achilles says that Fate is the same for the hard fighter and the hesitant one. Just what Sarpedon would say: Fate is the same, but glory can be different, so die for glory rather than die in shame. Achilles recognizes this difference; he can hardly criticize Agamemnon's alleged equation of the brave man and the cowardly one unless he can appeal to someone's recognition that each deserves a different treatment. Once Achilles admits that someone recognizes the difference, even though both hero and coward are fated to die, well, that is just what Sarpedon urges. Perhaps Achilles has sought his quarrel with Agamemnon in order to have the leisure to think these things out.

Let us suppose that Sarpedon has stated the traditional view of the warrior society, and that Achilles wants somehow to dissent from this view, but without losing title to his un-cowardly nature. Then it appears that in using the warrior society's typical language about destiny, honor, and ever-lasting glory, Achilles ends up unable fully to differentiate an argument from the traditional view. The Achilles of book 9 is the prisoner not only of his camp but also of his terms.

Achilles is intuitive, and apparently he intuits that the heroic formulas are not working for him. He can only state this negatively, by recurring to the formulas deconstructively, or inarticulately. Sarpedon tells the warrior to become a man of destiny, to assume personally the thrust of battle. Thus Sarpedon sees a world in which there are not very many possibilities. Achilles would like to see a different world, but the effect of the embassy is to show us that Achilles needs Troy in the way that a "bonus baby" needs the Big Leagues or the world champion needs the National Association of Boxing: he may want it on his own terms, but he cannot do without it. Achilles asserts that he has an alternative back in horse-pasturing Phthia; but like the pastoral scenes depicted in many of Homer's epic similes, the alternative is only hypo-thetically there. Entertaining ideas about an alternate self is of course part of self-consciousness as a whole, but a totally self-invented life would be quixotic at the least, if not just plain mad.

Achilles withdraws from one possibility, without any hope of developing another to replace it. As a result, he is denied the chance to be a conventional hero during the greater part of a poem thronged by conventional heroes. Likewise, he is excluded from the poem's title, even while a syllable of his name lurkingly survives there. Achilles' poem is named after the city of his official enemies; correspondingly, he is a self-divided man. As the overlapping assonance can suggest to us, Achilles is both in the *Iliad* and out of it.

Sarpedon, on the other hand, finds himself in the thick of it, and his counsel is to face the music. In a way, the very mechanics of the epic meter,[2] with its fixed places for certain names and identifying epithets, promotes this adaptation to the given arrangement, to the formulas of the code, the preordained measures on the dancing floor of the battlefield, and the compulsions of the collective will. In current parlance, Sarpedon is unlikely to hear a different drummer.

We can also see a character like Helen as "locked in" in this way. When she puts up a fuss about Paris's regular impulse toward the bedroom, Aphrodite tells her that she had better get going. Helen is enslaved, as Andromache will someday be, to the mechanical rhythm of another man's loom.

The gifts of the gods do not free, they compel—even the gift of Aphrodite. The same is true of the gift of the Muse. If your name links with *dios*, by god, you'll be *dios* ("godlike" or "brilliant"), even if you do not happen to be capable of anything very brilliant at the time. Thus the epithets create a somewhat hollow world of convention, where a man is called a king of men even though he is actually behaving like a snivelling bully—and where, in a shame culture, Agamemnon's power over Achilles seems to depend mainly on his being almost completely shameless.

III

Achilles' own "brilliance" is in many ways related to his apartness from his society. Achilles' withdrawal looks like Homer's model for that self-division whereby consciousness comes to know itself as distinct from the things it contemplates. This individuation of the subject is accompanied by the corresponding individuation of the object from which

2. A good explanation of these mechanics—discovered by Milman Parry—is G. S. Kirk's *The Songs of Homer* (Cambridge: Cambridge University Press, 1962).

the subject is withdrawing. Hence the paradox that what we call subjectivity—the subject's preoccupation with himself—is something like a necessary prerequisite for objectivity. Although Achilles is the most self-involved of Homer's characters, he is also the most objective about the war, because he has begun to develop a self apart from it. Nonetheless, while the isolation of consciousness is the inaugural act of a philosophical mind, for a participating hero it is an experience akin to a confrontation with pure meaninglessness. If the war cannot be in some way his war, why has the warrior been fighting at all?

Achilles argues, in so many words, that under Agamemnon the Greeks have become an anti-heroic society, one that hates heroism and willingly degrades the hero. Book 2 of the *Iliad* offers him much support in this. It shows us an army, to borrow a joke, commanded by General Ineptitude, backed up by Major Disaster, Corporal Punishment, and Private Interest. In the following books, Diomedes is particularly offered to us as a refutation of the Greeks' appearance of selfish incompetence, but Agamemnon is even stupid and arrogant enough to insult this model communal spirit. Under Agamemnon, Achilles' *nature* is too big for his *fortune*, and this makes Achilles rebellious; but so long as Agamemnon is to retain his authority as the order figure in the Greek camp, things must remain as they are—Achilles too big for his britches, and Agamemnon vainly trying to fill Zeus's shoes.

Of course, where Agamemnon's fear of impotence makes him tyrannical and *dis*orderly, he is subject to a kind of nemesis; but the dislocation of Achilles does not, in fact, cause the collapse of the Greek effort as a whole. It makes for more of a stalemate, but after nine years of fighting that only means more of the same.

For a time Achilles appears to be the victim of a father figure determined to emasculate him, but after he is offered restitution and refuses to accept it we can see that the quarrel has become a device for opening up a larger subject, namely, the uniqueness of an Achilles in *any* society, and not merely in one where he stands out because the people around him are petty and repressive.

Achilles might well strike us as having a unique kind of self-respect: he cannot be bought. But the mind of the poem does not really see it that way. As Phoinix's allegory about lame Supplications hobbling after swift-footed Ruin shows, Achilles is understood by Homer as merely a profoundly alienated man, and hence a man in great need of reconciling.

Of course, Achilles is a different man to start with. Heroes in Greek religion are literally a race apart, and when they die their passion causes obscure convulsions in the deeper reaches of nature. We know that Achilles comes from far away: coming from horse-pasturing Phthia is apparently a little like coming from New Zealand. Patroclus accuses his friend of having Mount Pelion and its waters for his parents rather than a man and a sea nymph—Achilles is cold and hard. He is surrounded with a mysterious entourage of Myrmidons, almost another species, like Captain Ahab's private crew of Mohammedans. On the verge of battle, Achilles' horse turns and talks to him: to talk with animals is given to certain preternatural characters in folk and fairy tale. Achilles is fed with nectar and ambrosia, and apotheosized with a ring of fire. So much is he the elemental force that the only effective opposition he is offered in the poem is the phantasmagoric flooding of the River Scamander, which becomes half-human as Achilles becomes half-fire. When this unique spirit passes out of nature, as the choral lamentation of the mother goddess Thetis reminds us, nature will lose no little portion of herself.

Achilles overreacts in his difference with Agamemnon, in the sense that he reacts to something larger than what we see. He is faced with the tremendous and anxious mystery of his own death: to die for Agamemnon is not enough. His deepening preoccupation is not, therefore, with Agamemnon, even if he thinks it is. To understand his concern we must invoke the whole process of his individuation.

The opening events of the poem recall the myth of a Titan's rebellion, within a divine confederation, against authority; or a cataclysmic separation within a divine family. The same events suggest that vast meiosis whereby the individual comes to know his own separateness from the parent body of his society. Milton's *Paradise Lost*, for example, begins with just such a myth, namely, the fall of the proud, divisive Satan, out of which emerges the poem's profound reflection upon the limits of human liberty. Homer seems to offer other, occasional indications of the split between the private person and the collective reflex. He says that the captive women as a group wept for Patroclus, but actually each wept for her own woes. Likewise, when Achilles weeps with Priam over Hector, Homer says that in his heart Achilles was weeping for his own father and Patroclus.

To us Achilles looks like the conscientious person who can resist the impulses embodied in the group. But the conscience of one who is participating fully in the group is simply the group will. We might deem that kind of conscience a traitor within our gates, since it cooperates with the unindividualized will outside. But to the fully participated being, our kind of conscience is a dangerous schismatic. At any rate, the circumference of the group forms a sort of moral frontier. That is why Achilles, estranged from the Greeks, sets up a small or private Troy for himself, representing the fact that the estranged man must be his own society. Achilles' tent has the lyre songs, lovemaking, and domesticities that are otherwise Trojan in the poem.

You cannot call your soul your own—if we can put it this way—until you have in fact done so. There is something necessarily antisocial in such an act: one divides from the common stock or stream of being one's own portion of it, and there is a sense in which that portion, like a mortified limb, cannot long survive its separation. Individuation makes each of us a small Troy, brooding within the tent of the self and approached by suppliants and aggressors from without. And like the greater one, this lesser Troy is doomed to fall.

IV

If the *Iliad* has a major initiative in the individuation of
Achilles, we ought to ask how the poem's *construction* reflects the hero's isolation, even while telling a story that
involves a number of other characters—Patroclus not the least
among them—in a common fate. The withdrawal-and-return
motif is obviously the means whereby Homer detaches
Achilles from the society of the other characters and at the
same time compounds the isolated hero with his participating
friend Patroclus. It is to this "compounding" that I wish to
address myself.

There is a phenomenon in the *Iliad* that one might call
"Homeric duplex." Examples of it are the twin gates of sleep,
for false and true dreams; the two jars of Zeus, for good and
evil destinies; the two springs outside Troy, one warm and
one cold; the simultaneous birth of Hector and Polydamous,
one brave in battle and one wise in council; the two names
for the river outside Troy, one used by men and one by gods;
and the two Ajaxes, one big and one little. All structure is
compound, and so Homeric duplex is in some way elemental
to the creation of any structure whatsoever. Considering the
vast recoil of revenge that prevails in the *Iliad* overall, we may
also suspect that Homeric duplex contains a rudimentary
principle of structures specifically Homeric. The compound
wrath, or compounding of Achilles' wrath, is a case in point.

To see the elements of the Iliadic compound in a somewhat
decomposed state, one may compare the plot of the non-
Homeric *Aethiopica*, an epic poem supposedly the sequel to
the *Iliad* but, as close scholarly scrutiny has revealed, also a
kind of double for it. The hero of the *Aethiopica* is Memnon,
a late arrival at the Trojan War, who comes from Ethiopia to
help the Trojans. He is able to kill several Greek heroes, and
among his victims will be Antilochus, who has joined the
Greek army late in the siege, over the objections of his father
Nestor. Achilles, at any rate, befriends the eager boy, and
successfully sues with Nestor to get him into battle. Then, on

a day when his sponsor happens to be absent from the field, Antilochus is slain. Thetis tells her son of this, and Achilles thereupon plunges into the fighting to avenge the death of his young friend. Zeus weights the unequal fates of Achilles and his friend's killer, and Achilles then puts Priam's Ethiopian ally to death.

The *Aethiopica* is a looser version of the *Iliad*: Achilles is partly responsible for the death of a friend whom he then goes on to avenge. However, since both Memnon and Antilochus are latecomers to the war, their connection to the subject of Troy is not so strong as their connection to each other. Achilles is Antilochus's sponsor, but not his guardian (someone else is assigned the job). And Memnon, the Trojan hope, has not all along been the chief mainstay of the city. Antilochus is therefore less tied to Achilles than Patroclus is, just as Troy is less dependent on Memnon's help than on Hector's. By having Achilles avenge his dearest friend (rather than his young protégé), Homer makes Achilles the fullest possible party to the reprisal in question: Achilles in a sense avenges not only another but also himself. Homer also pre-cipitates the fall of Troy into a foregone conclusion, while nonetheless keeping it beyond the scope of the actual poem.

It is the withdrawal-and-return motif that replaces the late-arrival theme of the *Aethiopica*; Patroclus and Hector come into their own somewhat latterly, precisely because of the unprecedented vacuum created by the absence—the late arrival—of the benched Achilles. Achilles' absence from the field in the *Aethiopica* contains the germ of his Homeric withdrawal, for it leads to the death of the friend. But where-as Nestor, in the *Aethiopica*, is finally unable to protect his son from death (Antilochus actually dies trying to protect his father), Homer's Achilles is very nearly an accomplice in the death of his charge Patroclus.

We can now appreciate the importance of Achilles' pro-tracted disaffection with the war. His absence emboldens Hector and, in turn, Patroclus. By staying out of the war,

Achilles sets in motion the very train of events that will force him to rejoin it. Homer saw how the two linked subjects of the *Aethiopica* could be reduced to a single compound of action and reaction. Achilles is no longer merely the pre-destined link between the stories of two latecomers to op-posite sides of the Trojan War. He is now the central subject, and it is his all-important destiny that the two flanking desti-nies serve to illustrate. Antilochus died because Achilles was not around to protect him; but Patroclus dies because he as-sumes Achilles' own arms. Memnon died because he killed Achilles' friend; but Hector dies because he kills Achilles' alter ego. Thus Homer makes Achilles avenge the death of the once and future Achilles.

V

In a simpler poem Achilles would have returned in the nick of time to save the Greek cause. He rejects this opportunity for glory not once but twice. Achilles will return, but the Greek cause is not hopeless when he does; it is actually worse when Patroclus goes into battle in Achilles' place. And when Achilles does make his return, it is too late to help the only Greek about whom he has given evidence of caring. Phoinix has warned in book 9 that something like this would happen: he spoke of the hiatus between Prayers and Ruin. We can now see this hiatus as obtaining throughout the poem. It opens up in the sequence of offense and reprisal (or amends) and in the sequence of withdrawal and return. It is this hiatus which has made tragic the glorification of Homer's hero. The poet shows the lesser hero returning and being de-feated, while the greater hero prolongs the period of supplica-tion, the taking of vengeance, and the rejoining of battle. He returns only after glory and victory have lost their meaning. Patroclus has fallen before his time, and therefore the swift-footed Achilles has stayed too long.

When Achilles is rolling around in the dirt and symbolical-ly abasing himself for the death of his friend, Odysseus tries to bring him round and get him to eat; but Achilles refuses. This is not so much an example of the heroic dedication to winning glory; on the contrary, it shows Achilles' inability to rehallow his existence. Achilles does not finally enter the battle possessed by Sarpedon's idea of not yielding glory to others, but rather by something akin to the death wish. We cannot miss, in Achilles' speeches to his victims, his weariness with his own life. They are flat and numb with a cruel indifference: "So friend, you die also. Why all this clamour about it?" Because of these speeches, we may well feel that the poem never closes the gap between the warrior who merely risks his life and the warrior who merely despises it. The ideal consecration is always implied; perhaps it can never quite be shown.

The word *friend*, in the address just quoted, was an inspired choice on Homer's part, for it is both cynical and disinterested. It even has a kind of vinegar-sponge compassion about it. Achilles has spared this unfortunate character once in the past; in an odd anticipation of the end of the poem, he almost thinks that this is the man's ghost come back to haunt him. And since Achilles showed him mercy, they really were friends, once.

The river fight shows us a reaction to Achilles like our own. Nauseated with the death and destruction radiating from the hero and at the same time engulfing him, the River Scamander rises up to assert some natural limit. Achilles, equally nauseated by life, and caught up in a truly cannibalistic frenzy, is almost the mirror of his mighty opposite, "muttering in foam and blood and dead bodies." If this is indeed an immortal frame of mind, weaker stomachs may feel that the immortals can have it.

It is the comparison of Achilles to the Dog-star, near the opening of book 22, that epitomizes the hero's transformation into god and brute, with the consequent loss of the intervening mediation of the human. In a dog-eat-dog world, the sweep of this sign across the heavens spells disaster for

Hector—he can no longer escape the scavenger-like demon that gapes for a warrior at his death. Hector says it is these same death-spirits that bore the ships of the Greek "dogs" in their sweep against his city in the first place.

We must note—with Charles Rowan Beye—that we do not feel any great miscarriage of justice in the death of Hector. We have known all along that he is not the better warrior, and when Patroclus predicts Hector's death in book 16, we are not reassured by Hector's tendency to whistle in the dark. Achilles, when he is in the same situation, shows himself to be much more realistic, which here means fatalistic and accepting. All of the similes warn us that the combat is unequal. Hector has told Andromache that he has *learned* to be valiant, and in the moment of crisis it is possible to forget what one has merely learned. The predetermined course of the battle reminds us of a certain sinister kind of sports event that turns a defender into a victim: a contestant known as a gentleman, through the undermining of his psyche, becomes a sitting duck for a contestant known for his "killer instinct." There are no deals between lions and lambs, as Achilles tells Hector when it is too late for the knowledge to do him any good. "The lion only lies down with the lamb when the lamb is inside it,"[3] and book 24 tends to confirm this deduction.

At the onset of Achilles' second wrath, Zeus tells all the gods to go down into the field. This invitation sounds the authentic cataclysmic-eschatological cadence, for the coming out of the gods is a standard feature of stories about the beginning and the end. The poem becomes quite hallucinatory from this point to the death of Hector. In the aftermath, the brutalized hero drags the corpse of his victim around the walls of the city, a little like Joshua circling Jericho in order to dispel the *temenos* or magic ring of an impregnable fortress.[4]

---

3. In its original context, this phrase belongs to Northrop Frye, speaking on Blake.

4. I owe this idea to George Lord, who compares the circling of Troy with the city-founding and city-binding rituals and the Troy games described in the *Aeneid*, and refers to Fustel de Coulanges's examples in *The Ancient City*.

Troy's fate is symbolically sealed by this gesture, and the episode that begins with Priam's appeal to his genitals and Hecuba's to her breasts ends with Andromache raising her terrible lament over the destiny of the fatherless son. The description of the psychological plight of the orphan is so grim —and perhaps overdrawn—that one who has children does not always willingly reread it.

The sequence that leads up to the death of Hector is *the* major piece of Homeric construction, and it can be described as an example of Homeric duplex writ large. The duplex derives from the dissociation of Achilles into an "identity" and a "similitude." The similitude is Patroclus, who is interpolated for the hero by having him adopt Achilles' armor. We may therefore study the compounding of Achilles by studying the fortunes of his arms.

First, Patroclus wears the arms. Once he is in them he exhibits unprecedented ferocity and forwardness, which carry him beyond the limits Achilles sets for him, and even to his death. Patroclus enters the arms, but the arms also enter Patroclus. With the Patrocleia as its prologue, two-thirds of the way through the text, *Achilles'* poem, we sense, has at last begun. But Patroclus in the arms is only *like* Achilles: he is not really an Achilles himself.

It is a key irony of the poem that Hector strips the arms of Achilles from his victim, and that Hector himself is wearing these same arms when he encounters his nemesis. Thus the fighter opposite Achilles is one that Achilles himself has armed and compelled. One can imagine a kind of shadow-boxing theme here: Achilles is profoundly out of favor with himself, and it is not inappropriate that his old armor stand up against him. Some readers will find here an image of the mutual destructiveness of war; others may think of Achilles as both having transcended the limits implied by the old arms and still having to come to terms with those limits. Hector, on the other side, is a marked man, for he is subject to the same limitations as the last person who wore the armor, the overextended Patroclus. Like Patroclus, Hector has cast him-

self in the role of a similitude Achilles. But Patroclus and
Hector are only human. In his fast, and in the totality of his
commitment to revenge, Achilles has put to death what is
merely human in him; both Patroclus and Hector seem to be
casualties of the process.

In the meantime, Achilles has acquired new arms. These include his famous shield, an art work within an art work.
Homer's description of the shield is recessively symmetrical.
On the periphery, at the beginning and end of the description, is found the cosmogenic milieu (elemental bodies; and
Ocean River "whence men and gods arose"). Next come civic
institutions—on one side the cities at peace and war, on the
other the human (or design-producing) arts of architecture
and choreography. At the center are the georgic and pastoral
arts, that is, the physical basis of life in the domestication of
nature. (The pattern is ABCCBA.) Overall, the shield depicts
life in its major ratios: war is only a fraction of the total
activity, whereas it is more or less Achilles' whole existence.
Thus it might seem that the shield is precisely the wrong
emblem for this erupting mankiller to be wearing. The shield
is more like an alternative to Achilles than a representation of
him. We notice the same paradox in the epic similes, which
adduce a single, striking similarity to something on the battlefield, and then go on to develop a picture rather more diver-
gent than parallel. The shield is attached to Achilles like an
enlarged epic simile. The similes take one feature from the
natural milieu that turns up in human warfare and restore it
to its natural context. Thus the similes catch the disturbing
connection in our experience between natural energy and
human violence: in the unrelenting biological compulsions
of the natural world there is an analogy for warfare, and the
same energies that run through the dancers at the harvest
festival may at some other moment be mobilized for making
war. The shield also serves to provide a minority report on
the majority opinion of the poem, namely, that war is man's
predominate natural condition. Like the similes, the shield

offers "epic relief"; it gives us another version of the alternative life back in horse-pasturing Phthia.

Our study of the armor sequence may be slightly extended. It is important that Patroclus, at the height of his *aristeia*, make a major killing, if he is to be in any way comparable to Achilles. The killing should touch upon human limits. The right victim is found in Sarpedon, the spokesman for the heroic code.

Sarpedon belongs to the first rank of the Trojan chivalry; those who defend his body sound like the essential Trojans, and Aeneas is the only one we are told will survive the war. Sarpedon, however, is not altogether a Trojan: he is an ally from far beyond the city, and thus stands in part for those who get drawn into the conflict in spite of themselves—as does Achilles himself. Like Achilles also, Sarpedon has one divine parent. Sarpedon is connected to the overall plan of the poem because this parent is none other than Zeus, the father of gods and men. Zeus, who holds that golden chain to which the whole sequence of creation is attached, allows his own son to perish, rather than pull him up out of the fighting. This divine deference to destiny is thereby symbolically enforced upon all the other persons in the poem.

Sarpedon's armor becomes the trophy of his slayer Patroclus. We do not hear any more about it until the penultimate book of the poem, where it turns up, like the ghost or after-image of the man who wore it, as a prize at the funeral games in honor of the man who slew him. Homer has not nodded. In point of fact, Sarpedon's armor is offered as second prize in a duel between Diomedes and Ajax: in this kind of contest of arms, second prize is also *last* prize.

VI

The disposal of the hero's arms is a suitable end topic for the military epic, as the *Aethiopica* might be adduced to illustrate—there Odysseus beats out Ajax again, winning Achilles' own arms. It is to the ending of Homer's poem that

I now wish to turn. Homer's last two episodes take up two loose ends from the killings of Patroclus and Hector, namely, the disposal of the bodies. This long coda, filling books 23 and 24, is both retrospective and remedial. In the course of it we are made party to something like the rehabilitation of Achilles, as opposed to his mere rearmament. Here we will be reminded of Aristotle's theory of the purging of the passions in tragedy: with Achilles, as with Aristotle's spectator, emotional rehabilitation is congruent with restoration of civic function. At the end of the poem we meet an Achilles who has at last achieved his independence and so is now free to stabilize his relation to society and even to fraternize with the enemy. And we meet an Achilles who has accepted his personal death —the price of his kind of individuation—and so is now free from his overriding preoccupation with himself: he is beyond his earlier self-pity and self-hate.

The ending of the poem begins with Patroclus's plea for a proper burial, an obvious indication in itself of a terminus. It is a fine irony: Achilles, in his wrath against the corpse of Hector, has forgotten about the corpse of Patroclus. Patroclus comes back to describe the unappointed soul wandering forever before the gates of Hades, and thus his appeal to Achilles roughly coincides with the poet's determination to lay his poem to rest. The exhaustion of Achilles' fury exhausts the poet's principal inspiration, which Plato was later to call a "fury" also. So ends the rhapsody of wrath.

Actually, the *Iliad* has a double ending. The heroic games of book 23 do not exactly use up the aggression in the poem—Patroclus's funeral pyre includes twelve live Trojans— but they do stylize and distance it. Games are related to art, and art works formalize their borders by allusions to their kind. In one last expression of exasperated community, the games begin with Achilles withdrawing from contention in a footrace where the first prize is a woman; they end with Achilles inviting Agamemnon to yield some glory to a warrior lower in rank.

Though an affirmation of heroic society, the games are also a funeral. There is apparently a connection between the celebration of youthful prowess and the elegy over the slain: Pindar's Eighth Olympian Ode, which treats the wrestling victory of one Alkimedon, concludes with the reflection that the family dead will doubtless hear about Alkimedon's accomplishment in the underworld, and soon be telling one another about it. In the *Iliad*, Achilles presides over the games honoring Patroclus, but Patroclus has specifically requested that his ashes and Achilles' be mingled in a common urn, and so the funeral over which Achilles presides is also in some sense his own. Thus the poem can end with Achilles in a kind of final repose, even while sparing us the spectacle of his forces finishing in their own ruin.

Because of the closures achieved by this first ending, the poem's *second* ending can almost seem to take place after the poem is over. It is a studied effect, I think, one that makes the "postlude" of the poem somewhat eerie and mysterious and unreal. "And you, old man," Achilles says to Priam, "we are told you prospered once." Achilles sounds concerned to be courteous here, but he also sounds rather sleepy, as if the discussion of former times were taking place upon some occasion after death. Just as Achilles has achieved a special measure of objectivity about the commitment to glory, so now he gains a similar objectivity about the nature of an enemy. The episode therefore constitutes a second embassy.

Once again, the scene is the tent of Achilles, that part of the Greek encampment where a Trojan might almost feel at home. Priam sets out to recover his son's corpse, and he and Achilles, between them, conclude what amounts to a separate peace. It is not the end of war for Achilles, but it is the end of his war with Priam's son. Patroclus has told us that the spirit whose body is without proper burial cannot be at peace, and so Achilles must surrender up any further vengeance upon his enemy. Achilles and Priam, young man and

old, will neither one live much longer, and Achilles' own
father Peleus will, like Priam, survive his son. Thus Achilles
and Priam now have a number of things in common, and
Achilles need no longer feel unmanned by the claims made
upon him by the father figure; he can yield to them without
loss of face. Achilles now has the objectivity toward which
he was groping during the first embassy. It is not a means of
keeping his fellows at bay, nor is it his indifference to his
victims on the field: it is statesmanlike, and self-possessed.

In his detachment from a personal interest Achilles seems
to join in the movement whereby the poem passes beyond
itself toward its own postmortem interpretation. Here we
may note the parallel between the events of book 24 and
book 1. This parallel is detailed in a way that makes such
symmetry seem like a new discovery on Homer's part, as
if the poet had found that a poem obtains its coherence from
a recognition of its own subject matter. We may take the last
book to be the poem's own effort of self-comprehension; it
also embodies the elegiac knowledge that the heroic poem
survives the thing it celebrates.

Like the first book, the action of the last derives from the
repatriation of a child to a suppliant old father. There are sufficient references to Achilles' manslaughtering hands to remind us of the danger Agamemnon ran in book 1 when he
almost goaded Achilles into drawing his sword. But pure
repetition in a design is indeterminate, unless the repeated
element is in some way able to bespeak not only its sameness
but also its difference. The differentiating factor here is em-
phatic: the child in book 1 was alive; in book 24 he is dead.

Let us review the events leading to Priam's recovery of his
child. These events are dignified by the intercession of the
gods, and the intervention of Zeus who sends Hermes, in
disguise, to see Priam on his way. There is considerable
humor in the encounter: a staple of comedy is the character
incognito who is badly underestimated by those he parlays
with. Hermes asks Priam leading questions, and Priam makes

remarks that are truer than he knows—as well as looking rather silly when he tries to bribe Hermes, the god of sharp practice. Here Hermes proves too scrupulous to accept the offer, which reminds us that one of the reasons the gods pay a visit to the earth in disguise is to test the piety of men. All of this seems beside the grander theme, however, which depends upon a deepening of the motif of the night journey.

First, Priam's wagon is loaded with a treasure that is being alienated from Troy forever. Hermes thus appears as a special custodian for a kind of inheritance. The entourage leaves at nightfall, and there are broad hints that Priam may not return. He passes the tomb of Ilos, the ancestor whose name the city of Ilium bears. He comes to the threshold represented by the River Scamander, which we have already encountered as a river of death. Hermes now appears to expedite the passage over the intervening no-man's-land: the space almost seems to stand for the difference between the known and the unknown. Hermes is traditionally the god of wayfarers; at the analogous end point of the *Odyssey* we find him guiding the departed suitors to the land of the dead. In short, in accepting the hazard of this journey, Priam has also reconciled himself to death. Hermes comes to Priam armed with the magic that closed the eyes of Argus, and he sends sleep upon the guards of the place where Hector's body lies. A little earlier the other Olympians had urged Hermes to steal the body from Achilles, and we can see how the god might have done it. Access to Achilles' enclosure is by way of a gate barred with a gigantic bolt that it takes three men to move, but it is no hindrance to the messenger deity. Although it may be later than Homer, the so-called Homeric Hymn to Hermes confirms the idea that is emerging here, for the Hymn says that Zeus appointed Hermes to be lord over all sleep, and "also that he only should be the appointed messenger to Hades, who, though he takes no gift, shall give him [Hades] no mean prize." Hermes takes no reward for bringing the dead to Hades, the god of the dead.

The yielding motif also confirms the idea that the visit to Achilles is a visit to Hades, for Achilles gives up the body as he was once urged to give up his wrath against Agamemnon. In book 9 Agamemnon says of Achilles: "Let him give way. For Hades gives not way, and is pitiless, and therefore he among all the gods is most hateful to mortals." When Odysseus repeats Agamemnon's appeal to Achilles, he judiciously omits the unflattering comparison of Achilles to Death, but the student of the poem is advised to let it stand. Thus Achilles appears in book 24 as a benign "lord of the dead," the very phrase he uses in the underworld of the *Odyssey*— of, by implication, his own position there. So Priam, in his ransoming of the dead body, accomplishes a shadowy liberation of Hector from one Hades, even while making it possible for Hector to find rest in another. Priam's last mission also solemnizes a compact between his own personal destiny and that of Hector's corpse. Priam stands on the doorsill of old age—elsewhere the doorways of death—and the text, following suit, inters itself in the last solemnities in Ilium. Thus the tomb of Ilos is very near the resting place of the *Iliad* itself.

The last mythological reference in the poem is also terminal in character. The allusion is to Niobe, whom Achilles compares to the destitute father Priam. Achilles keeps telling Priam that the bereaved mother remembered to eat, but the image of this royal figure, somewhere among the rocks in the lonely mountains, stone-still, brooding on the sorrows that the gods have given her—this image shows us that Niobe was well past eating. Paralyzed with grief, she is (in the idiom of *The Greek Anthology*) a monument who is become her own sepulchre. The surpassing bleakness of the description can hardly be meant to suggest a return to life.

Niobe's image introduces the three women back in Troy who lament the death of their protector, Hector. Hector's death creates the unanimity of his people in grief, and Achilles has already respectfully shared in this grief. Even the gods have concurred, in their protection of Hector's corpse. With the death of Hector one could truly say of Troy, as the Bible says of another Asian holy city, "How like a widow she is become, who was once great among the nations!"

The *Iliad* is a poem of strife which may be as old as the biblical Song of Deborah, one of the purest examples of the strife epos known to literature. Like the *Iliad*, the Hebrew example ends among the bereaved women in the city of the enemy, but they receive no part of the singer's sympathy: the last line of Deborah's poem is, "Thus always may the Lord do unto his enemies." The poem is still participating in the antagonism between Them and Us, and whoever first sang it was a kind of grim cheerleader for Our Side. Homer, on the contrary, is quite aware that men form a single party, however divisive by nature; and his hero has some claim to being the most Trojan of the Greeks.

The *Iliad* encourages us to consider concern and detachment as inseparable in a person who is a whole or just person. Conversely, blind passion and mere indifference may ultimately wear the uncomprehending and collective face. In making his peace with Priam, Achilles enjoys a unique elevation, seeming to preside over the late action of the poem rather than being merely caught up in it; the last two books present his experience as comprehended rather than only suffered. We have described Achilles as a benign Hades, for he ultimately promotes proper burial on *both* sides. The same healing disinterest emerges in the final turning of the poem toward Troy. The last line, "Such was their burial of Hector, breaker of horses," is a great one, but not only because it ends a great poem. It is great because the poem that began with "Pelean Achilles" does not end, as did that first sentence, with "brilliant Achilles," but rather with his enemy Hector. The fall of an enemy contains no less for fear and pity than the fall of a friend, and there can be no true tragedy where this idea has not first made itself felt.

BIBLIOGRAPHICAL NOTE

Precise dating of poetry that represents a traditional accumulation is impossible, but modern scholars often agree in assigning both the *Iliad* and the *Odyssey* to the second part of the eighth century B.C. Tradition derives both poems from a single author, and modern scholarship is sometimes comfortable with the notion that one man shaped masses of received material into two monumental poems much like the ones we now have. If Homer is one genius, however, the genius of the two Homeric poems is nonetheless very different. Insofar as it is not a language unto itself, the dialect of the poems suggests that the Homeric poems originated in Ionia off the coast of Asia Minor. Ancient tradition about "Homer" agrees, although, some modern scholars argue for a poet of Attic origins.

Citations are from Richmond Lattimore's verse translation, *The Iliad of Homer* (Chicago: University of Chicago Press, 1951).* It is widely used and widely respected, and its introduction is very helpful to beginners to the poem. A notable recent translation is that of Robert Fitzgerald (Garden City, N.Y.: Doubleday, 1975).*

My essay relies heavily on the ideas and formulations of Charles Rowan Beye's *The Iliad, the Odyssey, and the Epic Tradition* (Garden City, N.Y.: Doubleday, 1966);* and on Northrop Frye's *Fools of Time* (Toronto: University of Toronto Press, 1967)* for the overall conception of heroic society. Other notable debts are to Wolfgang Schadewaldt, *Von Homers Welt und Werk*, 3d ed. (Stuttgart: Koehler, 1959), on the Homeric reconstruction of the *Aethiopica* epic; Adam Parry, "The Language of Achilles," *Transactions and Proceedings of the American Philological Association* 87 (1956): 1–7; Cedric H. Whitman, *Homer and the Heroic Tradition* (Cambridge, Mass.: Harvard University Press, 1958);* Gabriel Germain, *Homer* (New York: Grove Press, 1961);* and F. M. Cornford, on the generation of the individual, in *From Religion to Philosophy* (London: Edward Arnold, 1912)*—to which one might add Eric A. Havelock, *Preface to Plato* (Cambridge, Mass.: Harvard University Press, 1963).*

Guidance on a variety of Homeric topics may be found in A. J. B. Wace and F. H. Stubbings, eds., *A Companion to Homer* (London: Macmillan, 1962). Two useful reader's guides are E. T. Owen, *The Story of The Iliad* (Toronto: University of Toronto Press, 1946),* and Malcolm M. Willcock, *A Companion to the Iliad* (Chicago: University of Chicago Press, 1976).

General works on Homer include W. F. Jackson Knight, *Many-Sided Homer* (London: Allen and Unwin, 1968), and C. M. Bowra, *Homer*

(London: Duckworth, 1972). S. E. Bassett's *The Poetry of Homer* (Berkeley: University of California Press, 1938) remains a remarkable study of Homer's mental habits as a poet.

Literary studies may be found in C. M. Bowra, *Tradition and Design in the Iliad* (Oxford: Clarendon Press, 1930); Rhys Carpenter, *Folk Tale, Fiction and Saga in the Homeric Epics* (Berkeley: University of California Press, 1946);* Gilbert Murray, *The Rise of the Greek Epic*, 4th ed. (Oxford: Clarendon Press, 1946);* Simone Weil, *The Iliad, or the Poem of Force* (Wallingford, Pa.: Pendle Hill, 1956);* D. L. Page, *History and the Homeric Iliad* (Berkeley: University of California Press, 1959); Albert Lord, *The Singer of Tales* (Cambridge, Mass.: Harvard University Press, 1964);* and James M. Redfield, *Nature and Culture in the Iliad* (Chicago: University of Chicago Press, 1976).

Important background material may be found in: M. P. Nilsson, *Homer and Mycenae* (London: Methuen, 1933); H. L. Lorimer, *Homer and the Monuments* (London: Macmillan, 1950); H. T. Wade-Gery, *The Poet of the Iliad* (Cambridge: Cambridge University Press, 1952); T. B. L. Webster, *From Mycenae to Homer* (London: Methuen 1958); G. S. Kirk, ed., *The Language and Background of Homer* (Cambridge: Heffer, 1964); and J. V. Luce, *Homer and the Heroic Age* (London: Thames and Hudson, 1975). See also *Homer: A Collection of Critical Essays*, ed. George Steiner and Robert Fagles (Englewood Cliffs, N.J.: Prentice-Hall, 1962).*

*Paperbound available.

THE *ODYSSEY*

Michael J. K. O'Loughlin

If he had smiled why would he have smiled?

Joyce, *Ulysses*

Just as all men were once said to be born either Aristotelians or Platonists, Northrop Frye has suggested that we may likewise be divided into Iliad critics and Odyssey critics. The distinction is a useful one for this occasion because it is my suspicion that most students today are more likely to be Iliad critics than Odyssey critics. The reason is probably the very existential bleakness of the earlier poem, the terrible honesty of the *Iliad*'s tragic sense of life. Take for example the lines in which Andromache comes to hear of Hector's death:

> So she spoke in tears but the wife of Hektor had not yet
> heard: for no sure messenger had come to her and told
> her
> how her husband had held his ground there outside the
> gates;
> but she was weaving a web in the inner room of the high
> house,
> a red folding robe, and inworking elaborate figures.
> She called out through the house to her lovely-haired
> handmaidens
> to set a great cauldron over the fire, so that there would
> be

> hot water for Hektor's bath as he came back out of the
> fighting;
> poor innocent, nor knew how, far from waters for
> bathing,
> Pallas Athene had cut him down at the hands of Achilleus.
> She heard from the great bastion the noise of mourning
> and sorrow.
> Her limbs spun, and the shuttle dropped from her hand
> to the ground.
>
> [22.437–48]

As the brutal fact from outside the gate penetrates to the inner room, we are wracked by the violation of those interior, feminine, civilizing forces whose fragility, even irrelevance, is so unendurably, but in this poem so undeniably, registered. There is the irrelevance of the shuttle that must be dropped, not only because of the shock to the hands that held it but because of the pointlessness of its very function, because the folded robe and its inwrought figures have lost the human reality which was to inform and substantiate the work of art. The body that was to be vested in this very emblem of civilization lies stripped and mutilated, far from the folded robe and the inwrought figures, far from the hot baths prepared for it. "Nearly all of the *Iliad*," writes Simone Weil, "takes place far from hot baths. Nearly all of human life," she continues, "then and now takes place far from hot baths." And this is what the Iliad critic brings to and finds in his poem.

When we turn to the *Odyssey*, on the other hand, it may not be too much to say that the quality of human life depicted there—even including the slaughter of the suitors—is never too far from hot baths. What Alcinous tells Odysseus of the Phaeacian way of life is but one conspicuous expression of a cultural ideal that seems to irradiate the entire poem:

> and all our days we set great store by feasting,
> harpers, and the grace of dancing choirs,

changes of dress, warm baths, and downy beds.

[8.249–51]

The *Odyssey* unfolds as a celebration of the fabric of civilization and of its artificers. "Courtesy," wrote Werner Jaeger,
"is the bloom on their lives." In provocative contrast to the
dropped shuttle of Andromache we might think of Penelope's
success in weaving the robe which preserves her inviolate in
her inner room. Indeed we might reflect still further on the
tactics of civilization in this typically "Odyssean" action, for
it is not so much in the weaving of Laertes' robe by day as in
its unweaving by night that Penelope is revealed as a consummate artist. It is paradoxically because of her artful dissolution
of her artifact that her artifice can sustain the time-defying
fiction that preserves her from the suitors' deadlines. These
are the kinds of meaning Odyssey critics seem to enjoy.

There are other paradoxical acts of "unweaving" in the
Odyssey that keep intact the fabric of its vision of civilization. And through these "unweavings" the poem may be
made available to those who are more likely to prefer the
tragic world of the dropped shuttle to the comedy and even
romance of the *Odyssey*'s unwoven, rewoven robe. My concern is not with the most familiar parts of the poem (the adventures in books 9 to 12) because I fear that to many they
are likely to be the *only* familiar parts of the poem. Instead,
I would like to consider those familiar episodes in the larger
structure of the emergent vision of the first half of the poem
—a vision of recivilization; then I would like to turn to the
attainment of that vision in the second half. The account of
the poem I propose might be epitomized in two feasts: first,
the hospitality which Odysseus enjoys in Phaeacia, which I
take as the consummation of the first half of the poem; secondly, the inhospitable festivity which Odysseus suffers from
the suitors in Ithaca. As part of the second "feast" I would
include the hero's triumph in that peculiarly festive frame of
reference that begins with Odysseus handling the bow just as
a harper plucks a new string on his instrument and ends with

his instructions to have the music playing after
so that passersby may take it for a wedding feast

I

When we turn to the first half of the *Odyssey*, we find that
it has continually anticipated the landing of the thirteenth
book by the recurrent image of the calm harbor sought from
the sea's flux. We might even say that the first twelve books
ask us not so much "How does a man define his identity?"
but rather, by the searching exploration of this governing
metaphor in a variety of contexts, "How does a man find his
proper harbor?" or, more radically, "What, if anything, constitutes the kind of harbor in which a man should rest?"
These are questions especially relevant to the human condition and our troubled awareness that we live both in and out
of time, that if we live "at sea" amid tides and tempests (the
very words are latent metaphors for time) we can also comprehend those intuitions of the timeless which we find, for
example, in what Shakespeare means in the plummetless
depths of his *Tempest* as a "sea change/Into something rich
and strange." In Homer's poems the enjoyment of a timeless
state is most evidently the privilege of the gods, who, according to the formula, are "those who live at ease." In the school-
boy's translation they are called the "blessed" gods, the
"happy" gods, and their bliss is the special kind of happiness
we call leisure or free time. In the *Iliad*, references to the
happiness of the gods often seem like ironic reminders of the
moral superiority of men, if only because men cannot, indeed
should not, "live at ease." On the other hand, the way in
which this condition might be man's as well seems to me to
be the great emergent issue of the first half of the *Odyssey*.

Our earliest version of this condition as a human possibility
is found, appropriately, in a description of the afterlife: the
Isles of the Blessed. It is worth noting that this myth, which
might have come from Egypt, never enjoyed the suffrage
accorded the legend of Hades. Odysseus will visit that gloomy

erworld and, in seeing its emptiness, see the emptiness of a heroic code that (as Achilles ruefully recalls) could inspire a man to be king of the dead rather than a humble farmhand who is still alive. But unlike Hades, the Isles of the Blessed offer a state where, according to Fitzgerald's modern translation, "all existence is a dream of ease." We might notice that Homer's Greek simply calls it the "life which is easiest for men"; compared to his matter-of-fact affirmation, the illusory and escapist connotations of the modern phrase tell us a good deal of our own cultural impoverishment, of how far we are from the integration of dream and reality which this poem comprehends. I would suggest that these islands of calm apart from the world of flux provide a *locus classicus* of the governing metaphor of the opening books. We see especially how their freedom from time is suggestively depicted by the use of seasonal motifs:

> As to your own destiny, prince Menelãos,
> you shall not die in the bluegrass land of Argos;
> rather the gods intend you for Elysion
> with golden Rhadamanthos at the world's end,
> where all existence is a dream of ease.
> Snowfall is never known there, neither long
> frost of winter, nor torrential rain,
> but only mild and lulling airs from Ocean
> bearing refreshment for the souls of men—
> the West Wind always blowing.

[4.559–68]

Significantly, this freedom from what Shakespeare called "the penalty of Adam, the seasons' difference" is the very aspect which the poet chose to emphasize in his description of Mount Olympus "where the happy gods spend all their days in pleasure":

> Never a tremor of wind, or a splash of rain,
> no errant snowflake comes to stain that heaven,

> so calm, so vaporless, the world of light.
>
> [6.42–45]

The notion that something like the happiness of these calm
and timeless realms might be located in man's temporal existence seems to me to be the great intuition of the *Odyssey.*
We can, I think, see this conception coming to life in the
early books, and in defining it we define the values which distinguish this poem from the *Iliad.* Indeed it is in the postwar
world of Menelaus, whose afterlife is described in the lines
just quoted, that we have our first hint of the free time of the
gods in this life. As we come to it with Telemachus in the
fourth book, the luxurious Spartan court is superbly festive
and graciously hospitable. While a double marriage is being
celebrated, Odysseus's son is welcomed, bathed, and fed.
"This is the way the court of Zeus must be," says Telemachus,
filled with wonder (4.74).

Sparta here contrasts noticeably with the less luxurious
home of Nestor that Telemachus visits in Pylos. Nestor is
found worshiping outdoors; Menelaus is presiding over a wedding indoors. Telemachus is welcomed with a collective shout
in Pylos, somewhat suspiciously viewed by a certain Eteoneus
in Sparta. Nestor lives without a wife, but surrounded by
many sons. Menelaus lives with Helen; their children are one
girl and one boy by a slave girl. Indeed one even has the impression that while Nestor's household retires to sleep at sun-
down, those in Menelaus's court stay up to all hours, spending
the time in conversation. The contrasts could be multiplied
but it does not take many of them before we will conclude
that in the less luxurious home of Pylos, Homer is suggesting
a norm to indict the good life at Sparta.

There is, I think, no better introduction to the ethos of the
Odyssey than the entertainment of this conjecture. For what
emerges soon enough from discussion is not only the absence
of any disvaluation of the wealth of Menelaus as such, but
indeed the positive pride of Nestor in his own portion of the
good life, his wealth, his artifacts. We remember, for ex-

ample, his insistence when Telemachus presumes to spend the
night on his ship instead of sharing Nestor's hospitality:

> Now Zeus forbid, and the other gods as well,
> that you should spend the night on board, and leave me
> as though I were some pauper without a stitch,
> no blankets in his house, no piles of rugs,
> no sleeping soft for host or guest! Far from it!
> I have all these, blankets and deep-piled rugs. . . .
>
> [3.353–58]

What Telemachus will find at the end of the poem is the fulfillment of these earlier visions of "the dream of ease," how
it is to be earned and authenticated not as a dream but as the
consummate reality of what we call civilization. For it seems
to me that what is symbolized in the hospitality of Nestor
and Menelaus is nothing less than what Yeats meant in that
celebration of "ancestral houses" which begins his "Meditations in Time of Civil War":

> Mere dreams, mere dreams! Yet Homer had not sung
> Had he not found it certain beyond dreams
> That out of life's own self-delight had sprung
> The abounding glittering jet. . . .

It is possible to argue, of course, that when we turn from
the opening books to the adventures of Odysseus, the ideal of
the life of leisure and art resists the main thrust of the poem.
The question is worth considering: after all, when in the next
book we first meet Odysseus on Calypso's island, he is preparing to leave an immortal existence of voluptuous ease that
is not unlike the Elysian pleasures promised to Menelaus and
anticipated in the delights of the Spartan court. We might
even recall how, bearing Zeus's instructions to Calypso,
Hermes surveys the lovely landscape so evocatively feminine
in its deep wood and exotic birds, its vine enclustered cave
and its bubbling springs. "Even a god who found this place,"
Homer tells us, "would gaze and feel his heart beat with de-

light" (5.73–74)—lines which may remind us of Telemachus's wonder at the palace of Menelaus. And yet Odysseus is to reject this beguiling existence.

To understand his motivation is, I believe, to understand the poem. Some are likely to applaud his departure because it manifests the restlessness of the omniverous seeker after experience. The reasons which Odysseus offers to Calypso, however, are far less glamorous. He resumes his *nostos* appropriately "nostalgic," homesick for a wife whose beauty he admits to be inferior to Calypso's, and who, in contrast to the immortal nymph, is doomed to die. At the same time, however, might it not also be true that, for Odysseus as for the rest of us, men are homesick for those values they regard as unchangeable, remote and irrecoverable though they may be? We sympathize immediately with Odysseus's nostalgia for we are left with the curious sense that it is the immortal nymph who is somehow ephemeral, that happiness on her terms would soon mean ennui for a man. To be "homesick" for Calypso would be unimaginable. Though Penelope is described as aging and fated to die, something timeless abides in her whose permanence evokes homesickness. Within time at the poem's end, with a wife growing old, Odysseus will achieve the sort of timeless content we find it hard to believe he ever enjoyed in the arms of Calypso. He leaves her island not because he restlessly prefers activity to *dolce far niente* but because he seeks the "dream of ease" not as an otherworldly gift but on his own terms as husband, father, and king. To put it another way, books 5 to 12 are about Odysseus's struggle to attain the good life which Menelaus has found at home in a land at peace. Indeed in the quality if not the quantity of his joys Odysseus will outdo the Spartan king, whose leisure is disturbed by the memories of family tragedy and lost comrades-in-arms (4.168–295). Unlike Menelaus, we might say, Odysseus need not look forward to the Isles of the Blessed in the afterlife. He need only look homeward, as indeed he does, soon after leaving Calypso, on the happy island of Phaeacia. For Odysseus's experience among the Phaeacians is more than an epic interlude providing the hero with an occasion to rehearse his adventures. It is a period of extraordinary repose which transfigures the overriding image of the journey and in which, while the voyage is interrupted, the hero and the reader seem momentarily to have escaped from the tides of time. It is a memorable dramatization of a civilization enjoying the fruits of leisure, where life is shaped by art.

We remember how Odysseus comes to this happy island after his raft has been battered and he has nearly drowned in the worst storm of his career. Gradually, however, the narrative shifts from this turbulent scene to a windless calm in which the shipwrecked wanderer swims to the smooth stones of a natural harbor. There in a protective grove he rests between two bushes; above him the intertwining branches close. They are so closely interwoven as to be impenetrable by the elements; covered with their fallen leaves Odysseus sleeps. We have left not only the storm, but the world where storms are possible (5.291–493).

Enacting the promise of this idyllic landscape, the shining Nausicaa comes to the shore playing and singing. So far the situation might seem analogous to what happened on Calypso's isle, but a difference emerges at the end of Odysseus's opening address to Nausicaa. Having praised her virginal beauty, and tactfully entreated for her succor, he prays the gods to grant her heart's desire, a husband and a happy home. There follows a famous declaration that nothing in the world is finer than when husband and wife share a house in one accord, a grief to their foes, a joy to their friends—"But all this they know best" (6.149–85). The speech, of course, is contrived to appeal to a young girl, but this should remind us of what in fact this young girl is, not an enchantress tempting to escapism, but the incarnation of those values which only gain an added poignancy in the light of Odysseus's struggle to restore them.

These values are manifest as the panorama of the Phaeacian way of life unfolds at the court of Alcinous. Once oppressed by the aggressive Cyclops, these people have founded a new world on this distant island "far from men who live by toil" (6.4–8). There they cultivate such arts of peace as weaving and shipbuilding and, as Alcinous tells his guest, they enjoy the fruits of leisure: feasting, singing, dancing, bathing. As was intimated in the figure of Nausicaa, this island is more than a *locus quietus* far from a turbulent world; the timeless calm has become the favorable climate for a special kind of human animation.

This transformation is superbly evident in the famous description of the gardens of Alcinous. The freedom from seasonal variation, the constant west wind which we found in the Isles of the Blessed, has become (quite literally) a fruitful condition:

> Fruit never failed upon these trees: winter
> and summer time they bore, for through the year
> the breathing Westwind ripened all in turn—
> so one pear came to prime, and then another,
> and so with apples, figs, and the vine's fruit
> empurpled in the royal vineyard there.

[7.117–20]

The passage is famous as one of the poem's detachable "beauties," but we miss its profoundly humanistic significance if we ignore the garden's relation to the rest of the story, especially to the expanding vision of Phaeacian life which it may be said to symbolize. For just as the perpetual fair weather nurtures the ever-fruitful garden, so the garden sustains and, as it were, invites us to the festivals which are the characteristic activity of this happy folk, and in which Odysseus now joins.

Among Homer's feasts, the banquets of the Phaeacians surely have the first place; what has generally been observed as to the significance of Homer's feasts is most vividly enacted here: sharing food renews the essential god/man bonds of civilization. It is, perhaps, more than a coincidence that having surveyed "the glorious gifts of the gods" in the gardens (7.132), Odysseus should next come upon the Phaeacian leaders pouring a last libation to Hermes (7.136–37). Nor are we surprised to learn that strangers here are welcomed as sacred to Zeus (6.207–08) or that the gods themselves often come to visit these celebrations (7.201–03). The leisure of the Phaeacians is the consummation of their innocence; holidays here are holy days too.

As Odysseus himself declares at the high point of the festival:

> Alkínoös, king and admiration of men,
> how beautiful this is, to hear a minstrel
> gifted as yours: a god he might be, singing!
> There is no boon in life more sweet, I say,
> than when a summer joy holds all the realm,
> and banqueters sit listening to a harper
> in a great hall, by rows of tables heaped
> with bread and roast meat, while a steward goes
> to dip up wine and brim your cups again.
> Here is the flower of life, it seems to me!
>
>   [9.2–11]

The "flower of life" (like "a summer joy") is an interpolation by the modern translator, yet, in terms of the interpretation I have been trying to advance, the phrase is happily emblematic of the convergence of the interrelated images of calm, garden, and festival. For what in the Greek is simply called "the fairest thing there is" (line 11) is the climactic enactment of all that the Phaeacian way of life has promised. It is also the fulfillment in human terms of that otherworldly "dream of ease" whose adumbrations we have observed in the Isles of the Blessed, Mount Olympus, and even the isle of Calypso. It looks back to the comforts of Menelaus's court, but it is achieved without the cost which experience has

exacted there. It looks ahead to the final blessings of Odysseus's restoration—the regeneration of peace and virtue and
their fruition in the life of leisure. The Phaeacian episode is
not so much a temptation to unearned ease for Odysseus as a
fabulous stimulus to the earning of free time in his own
world, the recreation there of what he so admires here.

That is why the poet will have Odysseus apparently contradict himself before this speech is concluded. As he gives his
name and rather poignantly describes the geography of his
native Ithaca (9.19–28), we are brought back to the world
across which he must toil and travel, a world where time is
anything but free. He recalls the sensuous delights of Calypso's captivity, but, again, this only deepens his nostalgia for
the domestic values he has gone so long without (9.29–33).
Soon, with another superlative, he seems to deny his praise
of the joys of the feast. Now, nothing is sweeter than the
sight of homeland and parents; even "a house of gold" in
far lands is no compensation (9.33–36). The "fairest thing
there is" ("the flower of life") has thus evoked its own dismissal. Here, as in the encounter with Nausicaa, the Phaeacian
way of life appeals to Odysseus by virtue of qualities which
turn his mind to how things might be in Ithaca. The leisurely
festival is eclipsed by a sense of the journey's urgency, yet,
paradoxically, the journey is urgent only because of its end,
the reconstitution of the good life such as Odysseus has
found here on this peaceful isle.

This paradox is nicely dramatized in a scene at the next
day's festival. It is after Odysseus has finished his narration
and his ship has been outfitted, and it is, we gather, much
like the feast of the previous night. Odysseus, however, is no
longer able to share in the delights he praised the day before.
The reason, as I have suggested, is that he is acutely conscious
of their true significance as a symbol of the goal he must
reach. While all around him make merry, and Demodocus the
minstrel sings again, Odysseus alone is distracted by his consciousness of time, his commitment to action, so he keeps

looking at the sun, waiting for it to set, eager for the voyage
home. The tension between the joys of the feast and the
longing for Ithaca is then condensed in this remarkable simile:

> Just as a farmer's hunger grows, behind
> the bolted plow and share, all day afield,
> drawn by his team of winedark oxen: sundown
> is benison for him, sending him homeward
> stiff in the knees from weariness, to dine;
> just so the light on the sea rim gladdened Odysseus. . . .
>
> [13.31–35]

It is an extraordinary analogy for the tenor of the comparison seems to contradict its vehicle: the lines say, in effect,
that in leisure Odysseus longs for work, just as the worker
longs for free time. Just as Odysseus is simultaneously aware
of the summons of the setting sun and the joys of the feast,
the simile holds the opposed attitudes of action and repose in
solution; it presents the burdens of time as momentarily
pressing, but it reminds us that we take up these burdens
only to be able to put them down. Like the action which it
describes, it suggests that we do without leisure only to have
leisure; like the episode which it concludes, it insists that
leisure is worth having.

II

If Odysseus's Phaeacian experience may be said to provide
the climactic vision of the good life toward which we voyage
in the first twelve books, it also provides the point of departure for the realization of that dream on Ithaca's rocky island
in the last twelve books. When the sun he had watched set
rises the next day, Odysseus, swiftly ferried over the waves
by his hosts, awakens on an Ithacan beach. Significantly,
however, the landscape is so lovely as to be unrecognizable
and he will suspect that once again he has been deceived:

> There, on the inmost shore, an olive tree
> throws wide its boughs over the bay; nearby

a cave of dusky light is hidden
for those immortal girls, the Naiadês.
Within are winebowls hollowed in the rock
and amphorai; bees bring their honey here;
and there are looms of stone, great looms, whereon
the weaving nymphs make tissues, richly dyed
as the deep sea is; and clear springs in the cavern
flow forever.

[13.102–09]

The landscape may indeed seem more like Phaeacia's calm harbor than what we—and Odysseus—have come to expect at Ithaca, but in its fusion of art and nature (the shade of the olive trees, the winebowls hollowed in rock, the looms of stone where the artifacts woven by the nymphs have also the natural beauty of the sea's color) it also looks ahead to that restored and transfigured Ithaca whose perfect symbol is the olive tree which Odysseus identifies to Penelope as the stock of his bedpost and the organic foundation in which his whole house is literally `rooted. Indeed it is worth noting that, following that revelation of the bed in book 23, Odysseus and Penelope will embrace in a fashion which is not only the best dramatic explication of that symbol but also a reminder of the scene of Odysseus's arrival here in Ithaca or shortly before in Phaeacia:

As the sunwarmed earth is longed for by a swimmer
spent in rough water where his ship went down
under Poseidon's blows, gale winds and tons of sea.
Few men can keep alive through a big surf
to crawl, clotted with brine, on kindly beaches
in joy, in joy, knowing the abyss behind. . . .

[23.233–38]

Odysseus's task in the last twelve books is thus to realize the promise of this last harbor, to realize it not as he first sees it as some other place too lovely to be his destination, but as the rooted Ithacan reality which he will share with Penelope.

What interests us most in these last books will be the unlikely kind of heroism by which Odysseus makes the Phaeacian dream figured in this first scene come true. The question has a special urgency because even before Odysseus awakens to this lovely landscape we are reminded that the Phaeacians themselves cannot, so to speak, make their own dream come true. Outraged by their hospitality to Odysseus, Poseidon avenges himself by turning their ship into an island of stone and forcing Alcinous to vow to welcome no more castaways in the future. The fate of the Phaeacians is doubly poignant for they are not only vulnerable because of their most attractive qualities, but the result of their defeat is the denial of the validity of those qualities, which Odysseus had celebrated so memorably at the banquet a few nights before. The Phaeacians suffer the perennial embarrassment of civilized men who must cope with a world that does not play by the rules of their dream.

By what rules then will Odysseus play—and win the dream? He plays—and the metaphor of game or drama is most appropriate here—in a way that is never more artful or civilized than when it seems least so. To return to my opening analogy, Odysseus, like Penelope, is saved from having to drop the shuttle (which we might say Poseidon forced the Phaeacians to do) through the art of his unweavings.

I find it useful here to compare two episodes in which Odysseus appears transformed by Athena's craft into a work of art. We recall how upon his landing at Phaeacia Athena had first changed Odysseus so as to render him attractive to his hosts and especially to Nausicaa:

> . . . making him seem
> taller, and massive too, with crisping hair
> in curls like petals of wild hyacinth,
> but all red-golden. Think of gold infused
> on silver by a craftsman, whose fine art
> Hephaistos taught him, or Athena: one
> whose work moves to delight: just so she lavished

beauty over Odysseus' head and shoulders.

[6.229–35]

But now consider what happens when Odysseus meets Athena on the beach at Ithaca. After some give-and-take as to their identities and location, she reveals herself to him as a woman "tall and beautiful and no doubt skilled at weaving splendid things" (13.288–89). Significantly, however, the effect of her art this time is, as it were, to "unweave" the very qualities she had heightened on Phaeacia:

> Speaking no more, she touched him with her wand,
> shriveled the clear skin of his arms and legs,
> made all his hair fall out, cast over him
> the wrinkled hide of an old man, and bleared
> both his eyes, that were so bright. Then she
> clapped an old tunic, a foul cloak, upon him,
> tattered, filthy, stained by greasy smoke,
> and over that a mangy big buck skin.
> A staff she gave him, and a leaky knapsack
> with no strap but a loop of string.

[13.429–38]

The fascination of the second half of the *Odyssey* lies precisely in the way in which we define the relationship between these two disguises or fictions. Which fiction, we might ask to begin with, is closer to the "real" Odysseus?—as if we knew that unlike the rest of us he was anything more than the maker and creature of fictions. Perhaps the better question is, How is the "truth" of the first fiction (which also serves to anticipate the poem's happy ending) translated into the "truth" of the second, "unwoven" fiction? The answer, in the exact sense of an often carelessly used term, is "ironically." Odysseus is our first, perhaps our greatest, ironic hero, and his example reminds us of the extent to which irony represents the only way in which the civilized sensibility can cope with and comically triumph over a world where Phaeacian ships get turned to stone.

Irony traditionally involves a self-deprecating *eiron*, with his secret truth which we share, and an *alazon* or overstater whose vaunted knowledge we know to be false from our "ironic" perspective. The rising comic rhythm of the second half of the *Odyssey* springs generally from our shared awareness of the secret of the hero's vitality and forthcoming restoration, so that we can laugh at those mechanical and smug denials that, properly understood, confirm our secret truth, ranging from Eumaeus's dismissal of his "guest's" report that Odysseus is alive ("Why must you lie, being the man you are?" 14.364–65), the vaunting of Melanthios and Irus, and finally the suitor's scorn for the "beggar's" handling of the bow ("Maybe he has one like it at home" 21.398). Within this shared ironic perspective on the typical events of the second half of the poem, I would like to suggest some specific issues for discussion in Odysseus's encounters with Eumaeus, Telemachus, and Penelope, and then consider the peculiar kind of ironic unweaving with which the poem itself ends.

If the meeting with Eumaeus provides us with a patent first instance of Odysseus's ironic concealment of his heroism, it is also one which continues to reward meditation on what is really being "concealed" not only in this exchange but in the poem as a whole. It is first of all the kind of quid pro quo which we see often enough in the movies and television (the "boss" disparaged unknowingly in his presence); yet the pattern has its memorable versions too, for example in Henry V's conversation with Captain Fluellen or in Richard the Lion-Hearted's reception by Robin Hood. The special complexity of Odysseus's exchange with Eumaeus, however, is that while the faithful servant, like Fluellen and Robin Hood, may not recognize his lord as such, he does perceive something essentially true in his guest's very capacity for deception:

> Well, man,
> His lady and his son will put no stock

in any news of him brought by a rover.
Wandering men tell lies for a night's lodging,
for fresh clothing; truth doesn't interest them.

[14.122–25]

At the same time, however, we might well ask how much of a
lie in fact *is* the tale that Odysseus tells. For it is tantalizing
to reflect that after all the fantastic adventures that Odysseus
tells the Phaeacians (and which were, strictly speaking,
"true" stories), we finally have the feeling that we are coming
to grips with reality in this account of a Cretan wanderer's
moving through the realistically depicted world of human
history, with all its restlessness, greed, and betrayal, the
world indeed which Odysseus is about to enter. Significantly,
too, Eumaeus believes in the grim burden of his Cretan
guest's history; it is, ironically, only the true part, the promise of Odysseus's return, which he dismisses as a product of
the stranger's fictive propensities—something too good to be
true in the historical world which he inhabits. Imagine if
Odysseus had in fact told him all the details of his fabulous
voyage! We smile knowingly at the naiveté of the swineherd's
belief only in the probable historical data, for we are confirmed in our ironic secret that "as a matter of fact" a dream
is about to come true. We never stop to reflect that "the
matter of fact" exists only in the book we hold in our hands.
Who is the more naive, the swineherd hearing Odysseus's tale
or the reader reading Homer's poem?

Because it is the enemy of overstatement and illusion, irony
is usually regarded nowadays as the servant of realism. In the
episode before us, however, and in all those where the disguised Odysseus is measured "realistically" or "historically"
it is the realist who is the alazon. The second half of the
Odyssey is that rare moment in Western literature where
irony exposes realism and serves to authenticate romance.
Here and later the singular effect of the realistic fictions told
by the unromantic wanderer is to confirm us in the truth of
the fabulous secrets we share. If the first half of the *Odyssey*

weaves together the fabric of an ideal, the second half understates this dream. We believe it is more likely to come true because it is embodied in a beggar, not the handsome creature Athena presented to the Phaeacians. The ideal is unwoven that it may be rewoven.

There is another supreme ironist in the *nostos* of the *Odyssey*: Penelope herself. In her many "interview" scenes of the later books, it is hard to resist the suspicion that Penelope already knows the answers. Indeed it is probably misleading to speak of Penelope's irony in the same way that we have applied the term to Odysseus, for in her case there is no explicit secret shared between her and the reader, there is only the reader's intuition that she knows more than she says. And, speaking of intuition, that might also be the best description of the only way that she herself "knows." We know, for example, what Theoclymenus has told her: Odysseus is on the island. Her reply is, in effect, "If only this came true" (17.185–91). Is this, then, why she seems so interested in the stranger who has just arrived, or would she have sensed who he was anyway, or does she sense it at all? If she does, why suddenly talk of marriage and show herself to the suitors? Why tell Odysseus that she feels that her husband will never return? After all, he has no way of knowing what she has just heard from Theoclymenus. It is hard to resist one's own intuition that it is the intuitive Penelope who is the most adroit ironist in the tale, especially in her interview with her husband. Of course it is she who proposes the stringing of the bow, and whether as a test or a tactical suggestion to the stranger, or both, his own intuition will make it his secret strength.

As our attention centers on the suitors' feast we witness the poem's fullest exploitation of the ironic strategy we have been tracing since Athena first disfigured Odysseus on the Ithacan beach. The slaughter of the suitors is just a necessary disfigurement: the ironic repudiation of one kind of festivity in order to make possible in an authentic way the Ithacan equivalent of the good life which Odysseus had praised at the Phaeacian banquet. In one way this latent affirmation is symbolized for us in the festive motifs which, as I have noted, begin and end the slaughter. Here we might also notice the expansive sense of a liberation from time that animates these books. The suitors, we recall, had been enjoying a "holiday." As Antinous tells Eurymachus, it is "no day to sweat over a bowstring" (21.268–69), but, instead, a holiday. Of course that condition will not be theirs, but his who slowly turns over the old bow in his hands checking for termite holes, and then, having strung the bow like a harper, and won the contest, proclaims that the suitors' time has run out. It is now his free time:

> I did not miss, neither did I take all day
> stringing the bow. My hand and eye are sound,
> not so contemptible as the young men say.
> The hour has come to cook their lordships' mutton—
> supper by daylight. Other amusements later,
> with song and harping that adorn a feast.
>
> [21.424–30]

We remember how at the close of the Phaeacian banquet Odysseus grew aware of the setting sun, but here in the carnage that is the unlikely means of realizing the previous ideal there is a pervasive air of leisure which may help to explain the comic detachment we have from the suffering of the slain. Consider, for example, the way in which the suitors, running in fear from the aegis of Athena, are serenely contemplated under the free time of the poem's imminent happy ending:

> And the suitors mad with fear
> at her great sign stampeded like stung cattle by a river
> when the dread shimmering gadfly strikes in summer,
> in the flowering season, in the long-drawn days.
> After them the attackers wheeled, as terrible as falcons

> from eyries in the mountains veering over and diving down
> with talons wide unsheathed on flights of birds,
>
> .   .   .   .
>
> and farmers love to watch those beaked hunters.
>
> [22.296–306]

Similarly, after Odysseus has identified the bed in the olive
tree to Penelope, and the two embrace, there is an extraordinary transfiguration of human duration, an apprehension
of the timeless even on a cosmic scale:

> The rose Dawn might have found them weeping still
> had not grey-eyed Athena slowed the night
> when night was most profound, and held the Dawn
> under the Ocean of the East.
>
> [23.241–44]

And yet—and this cannot be stressed too much—it must
also be granted that one of the most striking features of the
Odyssey is precisely our sense that this couple will again become subject to time. They do not quite "live happily ever
after." The poem itself seems unwoven at the end. Yet nothing could be more consistent with the example of Penelope
that began this essay. For the *Odyssey* too is unwoven that it
may be rewoven, it yields to time to sustain a vision of free
time not as "happiness ever after" but as the transfigured
moment within time. So even here while Athena slows the
night's passage for a while, Odysseus confesses that he has
one more trial to undergo, but he insists it is too late to talk
about that. Penelope, however, cannot rest until she is told
the prediction of Tiresias that Odysseus must travel overland
with his oar until men who have never seen the sea ask about
the "winnowing fan" he is carrying: then he will plant his
oar and propitiate Poseidon. Though this is the germ of the
legend of the wandering Odysseus, we notice how different
is Homer's inconclusiveness—one is tempted to say how conclusive it is. For if Homer unweaves this conclusion he inti-
mates a further reunion. And if that reunion too is someday

to be "unwoven" with the death of Odysseus, we can only observe that what is true of the end of this poem is also true of the end of this life: its unweaving is the condition of its woven perfection, and finally the two are inseparable:

> Then death will drift upon me
> from seaward, mild as air, mild as your hand,
> in my well-tended weariness of age,
> contented folk around me on our island.

[23.281–84]

By yielding to time, the hero's career, like the *Odyssey,* realizes its own kind of timeless fulfillment. As the hero's life and the poem's conclusion become "unwoven" and fade before us, the fading itself becomes but a sea change into something rich and strange: a life fulfilled in death, a work of art fulfilled in life.

BIBLIOGRAPHICAL NOTE

For dates of the Homeric epics see the bibliographical note to James Nohrnberg's *Iliad* essay in this volume. I have used Robert Figzgerald's translation, *The Odyssey of Homer* (Garden City, N.Y.: Doubleday, 1961).* For the *Iliad* I have used Richmond Lattimore's translation. Fitzgerald's translation of the *Odyssey* is the most lively and satisfactory one available. Although I occasionally indicate some misleading connotations in Fitzgerald's translation, I would still commend it as the best contemporary rendition. Lattimore has also translated the *Odyssey* (New York: Harper and Row, 1967),* as has Albert Cook (New York: Norton, 1967;* reprinted with useful background material and a collection of essays, New York: Norton Critical Editions, 1974).* W. H. D. Rouse's prose translation of the *Odyssey* (New York: New American Library, 1938)* is useful for its introduction and appendices. Somewhat inconsistently, perhaps, I have referred to characters in the Homeric poems by their familiar Latinate names (e.g., Menelaus for Menelaos), though Fitzgerald and Lattimore give Greek ones. The line numbers I cite refer to the Greek text of the poem conveniently available in A. T. Murray's Loeb Classical Library edition.

This essay is variously indebted to the following works: M. I. Finley, *The World of Odysseus* (London: Chatto and Windus, 1956);* Philip

Whaley Harsh, "Penelope and Odysseus in *Odyssey XIX*," *American Journal of Philology* 71 (1950): 1–21; W. B. Stanford, *The Ulysses Theme*, 2d ed. (New York: Barnes and Noble, 1964);* *Essays on the Odyssey*, ed. Charles H. Taylor, Jr. (Bloomington: Indiana University Press, 1963),* especially essays in this collection by Anne Amory, "The Reunion of Odysseus and Penelope," William S. Anderson, "Calypso and Elysium," George Dimock, "The Name of Odysseus," George deF. Lord, "The Odyssey and the Western World," and Charles H. Taylor, Jr., "The Obstacles to Odysseus' Return"; Simone Weil, *The Iliad, or the Poem of Force* (Wallingford, Pa.: Pendle Hill, 1956);* Cedric H. Whitman, *Homer and the Heroic Tradition* (Cambridge, Mass.: Harvard University Press, 1958).*

In addition to those general studies on the Homeric poems listed in James Nohrnberg's bibliographical note to the *Iliad*, I recommend Erich Auerbach's essay on the *Odyssey* in *Mimesis* (Princeton: Princeton University Press, 1953)* and A. B. Giamatti's study on versions of paradise in the epic, *The Earthly Paradise and the Renaissance Epic* (Princeton: Princeton University Press, 1966).*

*Paperbound available.

THE *AENEID*

Traugott Lawler

This essay is an attempt to define major aspects of the *Aeneid*, first through a brief discussion of a charge often raised against Virgil—that his poem is a piece of propaganda for Imperial Rome—and then through examining all the implications of the passage at the end of book 5 in which Virgil tells of the death of Palinurus, Aeneas's pilot. My approach owes much to Michael Putnam's brilliant book *The Poetry of the Aeneid.* In the course of his analysis of book 5, Putnam illuminated and clarified for me the figure of Palinurus, who had always loomed obscurely in my imagination as a pivotal figure in the poem. As a pilot, Palinurus is literally pivotal, and his appearance in, and disappearance from, the *Aeneid* provides a measure for Virgil's sense of epic structure and theme.

In many ancient manuscripts the *Aeneid* begins:

> Ille ego qui quondam modulatus avena
> Carmen et egressus silvis vicina coegi
> Ut quamvis avido parerent arva colono,
> Gratum opus agricolis: at nunc horrentia martis
> Arma virumque cano. . . .

> I am the one who made his music once on the slim reed-
> pipe, then left the woods and forced the nearby fields to
> obey the developer, no matter how greedy—a work farmers
> liked: but now I sing the hair-raising arms of Mars and the
> man. . . .

Early witnesses claimed the lines were written by Virgil but
rejected by his literary executors. They are surely inappropriate to the tone of the *Aeneid*, and yet they have the value
of reminding us that the right place to begin understanding
the *Aeneid* is at its connection with Virgil's earlier books, the
ten pastoral poems that comprise the *Eclogues*, and the
poetic manual of farming, the *Georgics.* Virgil's fame was so
overpowering in the later Roman period and the Middle Ages
that the idea of working from pastoral through domestic to
epic poetry became a sacred pattern for poets, a pattern that
both Spenser and Milton still found meaningful. Of course
the pattern had no such sacred meaning for Virgil; there is
no clear evidence, though there are hints, that the *Aeneid* had
occurred to him at all when he wrote the *Eclogues.* Nor has
any poet ever followed the pattern altogether strictly: neither
Spenser nor Milton produced anything really comparable to
the *Georgics.*[1] Still, Virgil obviously had fairly vast poetic
ambitions fairly early, and certainly he regarded the *Eclogues*
and *Georgics* to a degree as his literary apprenticeship.

The *Georgics*, in fact, have a very basic relevance for the
Aeneid, wide as the gulf seems to be that divides a treatise on
farming from an epic on the founding of Rome. The whole
thrust of the *Georgics* is domestication, the taming of recalcitrant nature, the establishment through labor of order out of

1. Both imitated the "Ille ego" quatrain. See the first stanza of *The Faerie
Queene* ("Lo, I the man, whose Muse whilom did mask . . .") and the first sentence of *Paradise Regained* ("I who erewhile the happy garden sung . . ."). Though
neither wrote a manual like the *Georgics*, neither ignores the basic Georgic notion
of working the earth: Adam and Eve are gardeners; *Paradise Regained* is about
"Eden raised in the waste wilderness"; and the hero of Spenser's first book is
St. George, brought up "in ploughmans state to byde" (1.10.66).

disorder. *Labor omnia vicit improbus*: "hard work, undignified though it may be, has overcome everything"—through hard work one can *recreate* fertility, redeem fruits from a recalcitrant earth. And the *Aeneid* too deals with recreating through hard labor from the ashes of Troy a new and fertile civilization whose mission is in turn to impose political order and fruitful peace on the whole world. "Such a struggle/It was to found the race of Rome," Virgil says at the very start of the poem; and when Aeneas is about to descend to the underworld in book 6, the Sybil once more lays emphasis on the struggle of the return to life: "But to climb again,/To trace the footsteps back to the air above,/There lies the task, the toil." *Hoc opus, hic labor est.* Aeneas's heroic mission has its unheroic side: his job is hard work, and *labor* is *improbus*; hard work is not very dignified, not very heroic.

What the hard work will achieve is related near the end of book 6, when Anchises foretells the future glory of Rome, and in particular the golden age of Augustus Caesar, who was emperor while Virgil was composing the poem, and was his patron:

> One promise you have heard
> Over and over: here is its fulfillment.
> The son of a god, Augustus Caesar, founder
> Of a new age of gold, in lands where Saturn
> Ruled long ago; he will extend his empire
> Beyond the Indies, beyond the normal measure
> Of years and constellations, where high Atlas
> Turns on his shoulders the star-studded world.

[6.791–97]

But Roman glory faded, and the golden age proved to be alloyed with tin and even tinsel; and so Virgil has frequently been charged with using his sacred poetic gift to serve the empty pomp of a tyrant. Since poets nowadays exercise their public function, when they do so at all, apart from, or in opposition to, established political powers, the political dimension of the *Aeneid* gives all modern readers trouble, and needs to be faced squarely. Was Virgil merely a propagandist for Augustus?

Here a short review of some familiar Roman history can bear significantly on our understanding of the poem. Augustus only took that name ("the august one," "the holy one") in 27 B.C.: his real name was Octavian; he was Julius Caesar's adopted son. He had been engaged in civil wars sporadically from 43 to 31 B.C.—first with Antony against Brutus and Cassius, then twice, in 41 and again in 32, against Antony himself. His defeat of Antony at the battle of Actium in 31 (a memorable scene in Shakespeare's *Antony and Cleopatra*) finally brought peace to Rome. Virgil himself, who, as Dante would emphasize, is above all a religious poet, had long had a charismatic sense that the world was laboring toward a golden age of peace and fruitfulness—in the Fourth Eclogue he had celebrated the paradoxically imminent yet distant arrival of just such a golden age. Its apparent realization in the Augustan peace gave Virgil precisely the sense of culmination, finality, and fructification after long toil that the future-looking movement of his poem needed.

In the Homeric epic, action is rarely teleological. The world of the *Iliad* is not directed toward a definable goal; it is a world of constant flux that has no apparent grand purpose. We are only rarely reminded, for example, of the purpose of the Trojan War itself, and even when we are, the Greeks seem largely to have abandoned it: Menelaus does not long for Helen, as we might expect him to. The night raid that Odysseus and Diomedes make in book 10 has no tactical value, and such slight purpose as it does have they abandon in order to steal some horses and commit some utterly gratuitous killings. In the *Odyssey*, Odysseus himself has a clear goal, but his civilization does not. Homer characteristically refrains from imposing large meanings on the fluid surface of life.

Virgil does just the opposite. The *Aeneid* has absolutely nothing in it that is not artistically connected, either positively or negatively, with his characters' purpose of founding Rome. Furthermore, Rome itself has a purpose, a teleology, and one of Virgil's chief aims was to demonstrate that purpose, an aim he could accomplish better if he could show the purposed end as actually realized, as already historically palpable. Thus it was poetically right to reveal the golden age, because it fulfills an expectation that the poem itself engenders. Virgil did not necessarily believe that Augustus was the perfect emperor, nor his age the millennium; as long as Augustus seemed to fulfill in a general way Roman aims as they are described in the poem, he fit its poetic purposes. The poetic rightness of the golden age is what should be important to us, and it is right not only because it answers an expectation set up in the poem, but because golden ages were traditionally a fit subject for poetry; historical reality is a secondary concern. Aeneas's labor needed a tangible end to give it definition; the Augustan peace seemed to provide that, and Virgil seized on it.

Furthermore, Virgil does more than celebrate the end of labor, the Augustan achievement of peace: he is also, I think, warning Augustus of the labor needed to preserve that peace. That is why he introduces the figure of Atlas in the passage quoted above. Atlas controls and sustains the whole world, as Augustus will, but Atlas's job is a painful one, a job demanding ceaseless strain, hard labor, and self-control, qualities that Augustus too will need.[2] Through Anchises Virgil describes the Roman character, and pinpoints both its defects and its strengths:

> Others, no doubt, will better mould the bronze
> To the semblance of soft breathing, draw, from marble,
> The living countenance; and others plead

2. Thomas Greene, *Descent from Heaven*, pp. 83–84, makes this point of another appearance of Atlas in 4.246–51; my whole discussion of Virgil's politics is indebted to his analysis of the criticism of Augustan values implicit in the Dido episode.

With greater eloquence, or learn to measure,
Better than we, the pathways of the heaven,
The risings of the stars: remember, Roman,
To rule the people under law, to establish
The way of peace, to battle down the haughty,
To spare the meek. Our fine arts, these, forever.

[6.847-53]

The admission of mediocrity in art—though it is true that
Virgil does not mention literature, only the fine arts—is a
terrible charge to issue from a man who prized his art above
all else, who, for example, could write pastoral poetry in the
midst of civil war. Furthermore, the paean to Roman power
is pacifistic, not military: "to establish the way of peace,"
"to spare the meek." Virgil's dream was not so much of
Roman power as of a universal peace, established, for lack of
a better way, through Roman power. And, once again, this
is more of a warning than a celebration—he is urging Augustus
to control himself, to keep the peace.

One more point about Roman politics. I have mentioned
Shakespeare's *Antony and Cleopatra* because its story is so
similar to the story of Aeneas and Dido. Antony must choose
between Cleopatra and Octavius, between Rome and Egypt,
public duty and private love. The issues are the same for
Virgil, except that Aeneas is both Octavius and Antony compressed into one man, and his battle is fought within: Rome
and duty, or Carthage and love. King Iarbas, Dido's rejected
suitor, makes clear how far Carthage has turned Aeneas from
the Roman ideal of *virtus* or manliness:

And now that second Paris, with his lackeys,
Half-men, I call them, his chin tied up with ribbons,
With millinery on his perfumed tresses,
Takes over what he stole, and we keep bringing
Gifts to your temples, we, devout believers
Forsooth, in idle legend.

[4.215-18]

Shakespeare speaks of the "ne'er-lust-wearied Antony" dressing effeminately in Cleopatra's "tires and mantles." One may also notice the parallel with Paris: Aeneas is indulging in one of the very Trojan sins he is supposed to be expiating. And yet in book 4 Virgil is not merely criticizing Aeneas for dallying; he is warning Augustus not to fall into the soft traps that peace holds out, the traps that caught Antony and started another civil war. He knows the real value of the beautiful artifact that Carthage is, and the value of the full, sensuous, and deeply personal life that Dido holds out for Aeneas; but he also knows their snares, and knows their relevance for the Rome he was part of.[3] Carthage is an attractive place, and Virgil makes us feel its worth, but he also wanted Augustus to see the danger that lurked beneath the surface of its opulence. Here he avoids the charge of chauvinism, of simple-mindedly exalting Aeneas for leaving Dido, in two ways: first, he grants what is non-Roman its full value; and second, he is aware that the very Roman virtues, and the peace they have brought about, are in danger of succumbing to what in Carthage is false, emptily materialistic.

Virgil does indeed celebrate Roman virtue and Roman control; but because he constantly insists on the self-control that political control ultimately derives from, and because he is so conscious of the dangers and the shortcomings of Roman virtues, it is clear that his epic is more than an advertisement for the Roman imperium. He was patriotic in the best sense: he had a reverent love for Italy, for Italian lakes and forests and mountains and the Italian people. But his final concerns went beyond the national: "to battle down the haughty, to spare the meek." He was, as I hope to demonstrate, in the fullest sense humane. In the *Aeneid* the note of warning always accompanies the note of praise; and there is another

3. In Greene's words, "Virgil was writing, not for an audience whose achievement of culture was precarious and thus uncritical, but for an audience whose traditions of austerity were threatened by power, luxury, and corruption" (p. 84).

note, too, that in the end utterly drowns out all others: the elegiac note, the Virgilian melancholy, the sense of loss and sorrow that pervades the poem from beginning to end. My purpose in what remains is to characterize that elegiac note; I have chosen to do so by exploring how it is evoked in the account of Palinurus's death in book 5.

Book 5 seems on the surface to add little to the *Aeneid*. It barely advances the plot at all, though at the end Aeneas is at last smoothly on his way to Italy. The funeral games for Anchises add to the sense of ritual piety toward the past that the whole poem is designed in part to foster, and of which Virgil's literary piety toward Homer is a part, so that the games are rightly modeled on the funeral games for Patroclus in book 23 of the *Iliad*. They also offer both emotional relief after the tense scene of Dido's self-immolation and a last refuge of thoughtless pleasure before we enter the graver subject of books 7 to 12. The death of the pilot Palinurus at the end returns us to the harsh real world, though its peculiar bloodlessness does not altogether dispel the blandly hopeful mood that the games have encouraged. Beyond these general uses, the book seems to have little relevance. Yet if we penetrate, as Putnam has so effectively done, beneath its surface at all, we can find in it a variety of meanings central to the total meaning of the poem.

Before Aeneas sets sail on the final leg of his journey to Italy, toward the end of book 5, he stands at the bow of his ship and offers a libation to the sea. Venus asks Neptune to grant him a safe journey, which Neptune does, stipulating only that "one be lost in the flood, one life alone / Be given for many." He calms the sea, "So that Aeneas, in his turn, was happy, / Less anxious at heart."

> The masts are raised, and sail
> Stretched from the halyards; right and left they bend
> The canvas to fair winds: at the head of the fleet
> Rides Palinurus, and the others follow,

As ordered, close behind him; dewy night
Has reached mid-heaven, while the sailors, sleeping,
Relax on the hard benches under the oars,
All calm, all quiet. And the god of Sleep
Parting the shadowy air, comes gently down,
Looking for Palinurus, bringing him,
A guiltless man, ill-omened dreams. He settles
On the high stern, a god disguised as a man,
Speaking in Phorbas' guise, "O Palinurus,
The fleet rides smoothly in the even weather,
The hour is given for rest. Lay down the head,
Rest the tired eyes from toil. I will take over
A little while." But Palinurus, barely
Lifting his eyes, made answer: "Trust the waves,
However quiet? trust a peaceful ocean?
Put faith in such a monster? Never! I
Have been too often fooled by the clear stars
To trust Aeneas to their faithless keeping."
And so he clung to the tiller, never loosed
His hand from the wood, his eyes from the fair heaven.
But lo, the god over his temples shook
A bough that dripped with dew from Lethe, steeped
With Stygian magic, so the swimming eyes,
Against his effort close, blink open, close
Again, and slumber takes the drowsy limbs.
Bending above him, leaning over, the god
Shoves him, still clinging to the tiller, calling
His comrades vainly, into the clear waves.
And the god is gone like a bird to the clear air,
And the fleet is going safely over its journey
As Neptune promised. But the rocks were near,
The Siren-cliffs, most perilous of old,
White with the bones of many mariners,
Loud with their hoarse eternal warning sound.
Aeneas starts from sleep, aware, somehow,
Of a lost pilot, and a vessel drifting,

Himself takes over guidance, with a sigh
And heartache for a friend's mishap, "Alas
Too trustful in the calm of sea and sky,
O Palinurus, on an unknown shore,
You will be lying, naked."

[6.827-71]

The moving, evocative beauty of this passage is apparent.
It moves us partly because Palinurus is, as we are told here,
guiltless. But he is more than guiltless. We have seen him to
be, and we see him here to be, absolutely faithful and absolutely reliable, a good pilot. His death off the very Italian
shores he has been steering toward for so long seems purely
gratuitous, altogether unjust. He takes part in the struggle but
misses the goal. Aeneas has earlier referred to the "forever
receding shores" of Italy; he finally gets to them, but for
Palinurus they continue to recede. Yet Virgil makes no direct
appeal to our emotions, does not stress the pathos; instead
the sudden violence is controlled by the gamelike atmosphere
that the book has not yet lost, that Virgil indeed sustains by
describing the fleet as if it were still engaged in a race. "They
sweep the waters in happy rivalry," we have been told as the
journey starts, and Palinurus at the head of the fleet, with the
other ships strung out behind him, is not altogether unlike
Cloanthus leading the others, who strain to catch him, in the
boat race that is part of the funeral games.[4] The god of
Sleep seems to be enjoying himself, tricking Palinurus off his
guard and then dumping him into the sea, tiller and all. And
Palinurus seems to slide into the water without a splash,
without disturbing "the clear waves" or the calmness of the
night. The fleet continues to "go safely over its journey":
Neptune and then Aeneas casually replace Palinurus, and
Aeneas dismisses him with a single sigh, heartfelt though it
may be. He seems altogether dispensable—we are not torn by

4. On the connection of the Palinurus passage with the games, see Michael
Putnam, *The Poetry of the Aeneid*, pp. 75-81, 93-95.

his death as the ship is, or as we are by the death of Dido.

I want to emphasize Virgil's intricate verbal texture here. Virgil was the most painstaking of literary craftsmen: he worked on the *Aeneid* for ten years, was still actively revising it when he died, and left instructions that it be burned, such was his dissatisfaction with what he had produced. To be sure, one may work fifty years on a poem without improving it, but Virgil in his ten years managed to incorporate into his poem a verbal resonance that is almost endless. An example from this passage is the use of the word *head*. Neptune has said that "one life" must be given for many. The Latin is "one head"—*unum caput*. A few lines later, when Palinurus first enters the scene, he is said to be "at the head" of the fleet—the Latin there is *princeps*, "leader," not connected etymologically with the word *caput*, but sharing, as Humphries's translation rightly suggests, in the general notion of primacy that *caput* invokes. *Princeps* means literally "the one taken first." We have no inkling at this point that Neptune had Palinurus in mind, but part of the later poignancy of Palinurus's death stems from the contrast with his splendid position as the leader of the fleet. And when we recall that position we may notice in retrospect that Virgil has given us from the start an inkling of his danger. Then Sleep urges him to "lay down the head"—*pone caput*—and here the irony has come rather pointedly to the surface.[5] Finally, when Sleep has shaken the dewy bough over his temples—a word chosen, I think, not without care—he falls headfirst (*praecipitem*) into the sea.

I think that the reader was intended to be jarred by Neptune's phrase "one head," and so to see the irony and danger of Palinurus's position from his first introduction, and through the agency of the word *head* to see the almost unbearable double entendres in Sleep's whole speech: "Lay down the

5. Cf. ibid., p. 97: "*Pone caput*, Lay down your head, Somnus commands, a phrase which ostensibly looks to sleep but in effect ironically reflects Neptune's decision that *unum caput*, one life, would be sacrificed for all the others."

head,/Rest the tired eyes from toil. I will take over/A little while." A little while is all Sleep needs to take over with a vengeance, to take Palinurus over, and lay those tired eyes to rest forever.

One may also note the ironic anticipation in the reference to Palinurus's "swimming eyes," and the fact that it is *dew*, water, from Sleep's bough that precipitates his drowning, which takes place in the "dewy night." These details gradually gather about Palinurus, so that when the climax comes and he actually falls headfirst into the water, though we are still shocked by it, we must also see it as inevitable. Palinurus of course does not actually drown, nor is this the scene of his actual death. When he meets Aeneas in Hades in the next book, he tells him that he swam for three days and nights, and was just reaching for the rocks of the Italian shore when "barbarous people,/Ignorant men, mistaking [him] for booty," slew him with swords, and left him in the waves by the shore. Aeneas's phrophecy comes true: Palinurus is "naked on an unknown shore." But at this point we do not know that, and even when the passage is reread with a knowledge of book 6 in mind, there is still an unmistakable finality about this event: it is here that Palinurus as a living man disappears from the poem forever, and, whether immediately or after a three-day swim and some barbarian swords, his fall into the sea is clearly the death of him.

This scene, then, is dense with warnings and resolutions, like many throughout the *Aeneid*. But a series of individual scenes, rich though they may be in themselves, does not make a poem, and the next step in interpretation is to relate this scene to a wider context: first to book 5 as a structural unit, and then to the larger concerns of the whole poem, particularly its first half.

The death of Palinurus is far more than a mere poignant scene to end book 5. It is rather the climax to that book, a climax that Virgil has clearly had in mind throughout the book—and in many ways it is also the climax of all Aeneas's voyaging. As book 5 opens, Aeneas, as is his way, is looking back to the walls of Carthage; Palinurus is looking up and ahead. (At the end of the book, when Aeneas no longer has Palinurus to rely on—in fact, no longer needs him—he replaces him as looker-forward.) Palinurus sees a storm coming on and asks, "What threat is Father Neptune preparing over our heads?" "Over our heads" is an addition by Humphries, but the irony is still obvious: Father Neptune has a nice little surprise in store for Palinurus. It continues when he says, "I'd have no hope of reaching Italy," for it is he, Palinurus, who alone will fail to reach Italy. The entire opening passage establishes not only Palinurus's importance in this book but also his respect for the sea, his intimate connection with the sea that at the end of the book will submerge him completely. Palinurus and the sea begin and end the book, and with the end of Palinurus, Aeneas will also end his voyaging. Furthermore, Palinurus is here connected with the violence of the natural world, a violence from which the funeral games provide a momentary escape, and the return to which will be marked by the return to prominence of Palinurus.

But the games are not wholly divorced from reality. They are rather a parody of reality, a means of observing reality—the real events of the poem—from a reverse perspective,[6] almost, perhaps, from the point of view of the gods. Thus the footrace in which Nisus and Euryalus take part is an innocent version of their fatal adventure on foot from the Trojan camp to seek Aeneas in book 9; in both instances Nisus sacrifices himself for Euryalus, here comically. The boxing match between ranting Dares and reluctant Entellus prefigures the single combat between Turnus and Aeneas that ends the poem. Here Entellus's deathblow is shunted off harmlessly on a bull; Turnus will not be so lucky. Ascanius and his all-boy cavalry, here engaged in an amusing March of the Little

6. This is the main point of Putnam's analysis of the games; my account of the relation of the boat race summarizes his analysis of it (Putnam, pp. 75–80).

Toy Soldiers, anticipate the more serious role, both for good and for ill, that Ascanius will play in the "greater mission" that constitutes the second half of the poem.

Similarly, the boat race that opens the games is a harmless anticipation of Palinurus's death. The pilot Menoetes is pitched headfirst into the sea (the word *praecipitem* is also used of his fall); the ships are in danger from the rocks, just as they are later from "the Siren-cliffs, most perilous of old,/ White with the bones of many mariners"; Sergestus's ship is damaged, as Aeneas's ship is when Palinurus pulls part of it with him into the sea; and the leader Cloanthus makes a sacrifice to the Nereids, the nymphs of the sea—a "slight and comic version," in Putnam's phrase, of the real sacrifice of the leader Palinurus to Neptune. The games constantly skirt death (Menoetes reaches the rocks, but finds no barbarous swordsmen there) or result in the deaths of animals—the sacrificed bulls, or the dove in the shooting match. The book ends in the sacrificial death of a man. The intimate connection of the games with Palinurus's death most profoundly underlies the details in the death scene itself that suggest the race is still going on, as if the characters themselves cannot wholly separate game from reality: "they sweep the waters in happy rivalry."

But before we reach the climax that the boat race has foreshadowed in such detail, the games are interrupted by another, more violent reminder of reality. Aeneas has begun the book by reflecting "with foreboding" on the flames and smoke of Dido's funeral pyre, on "the way of a woman with frenzy in her heart." What was foreboding now comes out: the Trojan women in a frenzy commence to burn the ships. A prayed-for cloudburst quenches the fire, and all but four of the ships are saved. This partial loss of ships anticipates the much greater loss of Palinurus the pilot, but it also has a symbolic meaning that goes beyond the immediate concerns of book 5, as indeed does Palinurus's death itself. I want now to turn to those larger meanings.

The burning of the ships, as Putnam notes, is one of several ordeals by fire that Aeneas must undergo to divorce himself wholly from Troy and his past.[7] I mentioned Aeneas's looking backward at the opening of book 5. One of the things Aeneas slowly learns in books 1 to 6 is to stop looking backward, to stop mourning for the past and look to the future. The first thing that fire destroys is Troy itself, and the first intimate possession connected with Troy that Aeneas loses in that fire is Creusa, his wife, whose appearance to him as a shade ends book 2. He makes a vain attempt to hold on to her: "Three times/I reached out toward her, and three times her image/Fled like the breath of a wind or a dream on wings." The past is elusive as a dream, but it is also a very real burden, and Aeneas leaves Troy with his father on his shoulders. He sheds that burden too—book 3 ends with Anchises' death, and the death by fire of Dido at the close of book 4 marks the end of Aeneas's attempt at Carthage to compromise between past and future. As book 5 draws to a close, Aeneas is almost in Italy, and it is right that he should leave behind him those physical emblems of his wandering, the ships. Thus the burning of the ships is a final symbolic destruction by fire of Aeneas's past. And the death of Palinurus complements that destruction. When ships are no longer needed, neither are pilots. Palinurus represents that part of Aeneas that is attached to the sea for its own sake, and can have no final part in the founding of Rome. Thus Palinurus's death plays a significant role in the whole movement of the first half of the poem; for all its self-contained poignancy, it reaches out beyond itself, and its symbolic role is the source of its fullest meaning. And this aspect of necessity, the rightness of the death, its positive sacrificial value in freeing Aeneas of the burden of the past, will also help to explain the bloodlessness I referred to earlier, the emotional clarity, the absence of tears with which the scene is described.

7. Putnam, p. 99.

There are other, smaller ways in which the scene is imaginatively connected with larger patterns within the poem. In
book 2, in a memorable and overtly symbolic scene, Laocoon is strangled by two monstrous snakes that arise from
the sea: the incident forecasts the destruction of Troy that
is soon to come from the agency of another monster that approaches Troy from the direction of the sea, the Trojan
horse. Early in book 5, as Aeneas opens the funeral games
with pious rites at Anchises' tomb, a huge snake appears and
glides around the tomb, "without a hint of menace." That
may be so, but one cannot altogether suppress either the objective connotations of snakes or the ominous qualities they
possess in book 2. Here the snake may predict some minor
recurrence, in the midst of the general festivity, of the theme
of the destruction by a fraudulent monster of Troy or of
Trojan associations. And when Palinurus replies to Sleep's
seductive urgings, "Trust the waves,/However quiet? trust a
peaceful ocean?/Put faith in such a monster? Never! I/Have
been too often fooled by the clear stars/To trust Aeneas to
their faithless keeping," he is placed in Laocoon's role, the
role of one man facing a destructive monster, fearing guile.
But since that very guile is the instrument of destiny in
furthering Aeneas's ultimate goal, the lone opposer must be
destroyed, and Palinurus like Laocoon finds death in the
embrace of the monster. The necessary and beneficial aspects
of his death match the benevolence of the snake by Anchises'
tomb—but that snake was still a snake, and this death is still
a death. The word *monster*, in short, serves both to anticipate Palinurus's death and to place that death in the broader
context of events.

There are other ripples moving outward. The dewy bough
and the other ominous underworld associations of Lethe and
Stygian magic prepare us for Aeneas's journey to the underworld, golden bough in hand, in book 6, the ultimate symbol
of his death to the old world of Troy. He finds in hell that
Palinurus has preceded him there—his pilot has led the way

to one last place. Aeneas's prediction that Palinurus will "be lying on an unknown shore, naked" has a striking imaginative connection within this passage itself with the picture, a few lines before it, of the Sirens' rocks, "white with the bones of many mariners." Though it is not logically stated, it is impossible to avoid the feeling that Palinurus has already become a heap of sun-parched bones, as if he had been allowed to bypass the normal stages of decomposition as one more way of removing all sense of ugliness from his death. But the prediction also ironically recalls Dido's curse on Aeneas in book 4: "let him lie unburied on the sand" (620). Aeneas had to leave her, and the curse will not fall on him; but Dido of course had a point or two in her favor, and her curse is fulfilled vicariously by Palinurus.[8]

One more small connection that goes beyond book 5: I have said, following Putnam, that the pitching of the pilot Menoetes into the sea in the boat race earlier in book 5 anticipates Palinurus's death. Actually it has been anticipated much earlier by a similar loss of a pilot in the first sea scene, the first scene in fact, of the poem. As the ships battle the storm in book 1, we are told, "over the stern of one, / Before Aeneas's eyes, a great sea falls, / Washing the helmsman overboard" (114–16). Virgil dramatizes the toll that the sea exacts from Aeneas by having him lose a pilot in the first and last sea scenes of the poem. And he specifically connects the two passages in two ways. One is his usual device of close verbal repetition. Humphries translates, "Washing the helmsman overboard"; but Virgil wrote "excutitur pronusque magister / volvitur in caput": "the pilot is knocked overboard,

8. Cf. ibid. Strictly speaking, the events of Aeneas's death, which Virgil does not relate, bear out the letter of Dido's curse. According to legend he fell at the Numicus River, and his corpse was not found for burial because he was translated to heaven ("You will bring to heaven lofty-souled Aeneas.") See Ovid's fanciful account in *Metamorphoses* 14.581–608. But that is hardly what Dido had in mind. Palinurus can be said to fulfill the curse both because his death takes place within the poem and because it fulfills the spirit of the curse whereas Aeneas's does not.

turned on his head as he leans over." The second way Virgil connects the two passages is ironic: here the pilot is lost "before Aeneas's eyes"; when Palinurus goes, Virgil makes it a point to tell us that Aeneas was fast asleep.

I have singled out this passage because I think it serves well to represent Virgil's poetic methods, to demonstrate the peculiar intensity and resonance with which he has woven his poem. I will close by examining what the passage suggests about Aeneas himself, and about the Virgilian elegiac mood. One thing that may strike us about Aeneas is the peculiar instinct he has to displace himself from the center of important action. In book 1 he thinks the rest of the fleet is lost, but we discover that it is they who have stayed together in a larger group and preceded him to Carthage. There Aeneas is like a strayed child who insists that his mother is lost, not he. In book 2, though he fights valiantly to beat off the Greeks, he never achieves anything like heroic stature in his fighting, and he stands by helplessly and watches Pyrrhus slaughter Priam. Later on, in book 8, when the Trojan fortress on the shore of Italy is besieged by Turnus, Aeneas is off celebrating his alliance with Evander in Pallanteum. He constantly misses the chance to be a hero. Of course he succeeds in the end; he grows in stature throughout the second half of the poem, and finally kills Turnus in single combat. But even there he fights only after great reluctance, and it is really Turnus, whose spirit "went indignant to the shadows," who expresses heroic resistance. Aeneas's role is consistently passive: the only occasion in the whole first half of the poem when he really takes charge is ceremonial—at the funeral games. He is "pious Aeneas" because he accepts destiny; on the few occasions where he seems to resist destiny, as in the love affair with Dido, he fails, and loses face. Virgil never allows us to forget that Rome was founded by a defeated people, led by a man who fled Troy while he could and was not altogether successful even in flight, for he lost his wife, rather carelessly.

But that is not the whole truth. Rather, it is Aeneas's particular heroic dilemma that he is forced by his destiny to suppress his personal human desires in favor of his larger historical role—a role for which he was chosen, not that he chose. It is true that he stands by and watches Pyrrhus murder Priam, but that is because he is not allowed to help, not because he does not want to. Again and again in book 2 he tries to be a hero, to organize a desperate resistance against all odds, and again and again he is foiled by forces larger than himself. "I call to witness Troy, her fires, her ashes,/And the last agonies of all our people/That in that hour I ran from no encounter/With any Greek, and if the fates had been/For me to fall in battle, there I earned it" (2.431–33). During the storm in book 1, he cries, "O happy men, thrice happy, four times happy/Who had the luck to die, with their fathers watching/Below the walls of Troy" (94–96). Here he is not merely wishing he could have avoided the trouble of the storm; he is cursing the fate that denied him the chance for personal glory. He loses Creusa because the mission thrust upon him forbids him to indulge in merely personal concerns. Her loss hurts him deeply, and it is behind his attempt to reassert his personal right to love when he meets Dido. He is meant to seem to jilt her: the point of the Dido episode is the loss of humanity that Aeneas's institutional role forces on him. His devotion, not willed by himself, to the impersonal force that is Rome causes him to lose not only Dido but also the human sensitivity that would make him understand what he is doing to her. He is not naturally insensitive: Roman destiny makes him insensitive, and Virgil intends us to see and to deplore that malevolent aspect of Roman power as well as praise its greatness.

In the Palinurus passage Aeneas exercises heroic responsibility and resourcefulness, and shows us his own human sensitivity as well. He senses that the ship is drifting because he is a responsible captain, but also because he loves Palinurus and is sensitive to his loss. He rises quickly and takes over guidance; his lament for Palinurus is sincere and touching. If it seems a bit brief, too easy a dismissal, that is not Aeneas's fault, but just one more instance of the damage that duty inflicts upon private feelings.

But there is more at issue here. Why is Aeneas sleeping in the first place, if he is so attentive to duty? And has he really taken over guidance? How can he guide the ship? Palinurus has taken the tiller with him. Aeneas seems to be in control, acts as if he is in control, but in fact he is not: Neptune is doing all the work.[9] Furthermore, Aeneas underestimates Palinurus. "Alas, too trustful in the calm of sea and sky," he says. But Palinurus was *not* too trustful, and his guardedness was in Aeneas's interest: "I have been too often fooled by the clear stars/to trust Aeneas to their faithless keeping." Aeneas's very lament is impugned by the injustice it does to Palinurus.

I have said that Aeneas's heroic dilemma is that he is forced to suppress his personal human desires in favor of his larger historical role. Here the fact that his seizure of control both precedes and foreshortens his lament for Palinurus, and the fact that his lament judges Palinurus imperfectly, exemplify that suppression. But his dilemma is really worse, for his personal efforts, even when directed toward fulfilling that larger historical role, are often misguided, unnecessary, or positively harmful. Thus he suffers personal loss not only to what might be called his domestic sensibilities, but even to those of his qualities that are more directly related to his public duty. He becomes more and more an impersonal functionary in events that are far larger than he is, trying to assert himself but ultimately failing.

The successive deaths of Creusa, Anchises, Dido, and Palinurus represent, as I have said, the necessary dismissal of Aeneas's past. But they also represent the loss, in some

---

9. "Nor can Aeneas very well plot the course of a ship bereft of its helm. He is sublimely, though unknowingly, in the hands of the gods" (Putnam, p. 76).

cases rather callous, of his most intimate human ties: wife, father, and beloved are the visible expressions of his own humanity, and Palinurus, as I have suggested, is part of himself. I have left untouched relations between the *Odyssey* and the *Aeneid*, though of course no one who reads both poems can fail to notice that not only the basic plot but also many of the incidents of the first half of the *Aeneid* imitate the *Odyssey*. One way to see the difference between the two poems is to compare the story of Elpenor, the man who falls off Circe's roof, to the story of Palinurus. Another difference may be put this way: Odysseus gradually regains his full identity, an important element in the process being his winning back his father, wife, and son.[10] Aeneas moves in the opposite direction: he gradually loses his personal identity, and he loses his father and his wife. If he does not lose his son, neither does that son gain a strong personal identity, as Telemachus does. The tragic fact about Aeneas is that he cannot make any advance toward fulfilling his destined goal without some attendant loss to his humanity. The loss of the tiller, like the loss of the pilot, symbolizes the end of seafaring, but it also symbolizes Aeneas's incompleteness as a man. The ship speeds on toward its destiny without a tiller, but surely a corollary is also true—that, in view of Neptune's condition that some sacrifice must be made, it cannot achieve that destiny and keep its tiller. Yet Aeneas "takes over guidance," nonetheless, and perhaps the most telling measure of the human loss that he has suffered is that he does not altogether realize that he has lost anything.

Here, then, is the final relevance of Palinurus to the entire poem. The *Aeneid* is not about the heroic deeds of Aeneas; it is not a paean to the glory of Rome; at its deepest level it is a very humane statement of the paradox that no human

10. On Odysseus's establishment of identity see the essay by George E. Dimock, Jr., "The Name of Odysseus," *Hudson Review* 9 (1956): 52–70, reprinted in *Homer: A Collection of Critical Essays*, ed. George Steiner and Robert Fagles (Englewood Cliffs, N.J.: Prentice-Hall, 1962), pp. 106–21.

achievement, however great, is unaccompanied by human loss. And the image of those ships sailing gaily and safely onward, with a confident Aeneas at a tillerless helm, while Palinurus hugs the tiller and calls in vain to his sleeping friends, then passes imperceptibly into one more pile of white bones on the shore, is a full and precise, imaginative, and altogether moving statement of that meaning.

BIBLIOGRAPHICAL NOTE

Publius Vergilius Maro was born near Mantua in 70 B.C. and died at Brindisi (on his way home to his farm near Naples) in 19 B.C. The *Aeneid* was composed between 29 and 19 B.C. and not yet completed to Virgil's satisfaction at the time of his death.

The verbal texture of the *Aeneid* is such that no translation can do it full justice. Any reader who knows some Latin will find the Loeb Classical Library edition, with its Latin text and facing literal translation by H. Rushton Fairclough, indispensable. But for coming to know the whole poem in English and sensing its narrative excitement, a verse translation is far superior to any prose translation. I have used the Rolfe Humphries translation (New York: Scribners, 1951).* I like it because of the easy movement of Humphries' lines: he makes the poem a pleasure to read (as it is in Latin) and yet stays true on the whole to the verbal texture. Allen Mandelbaum's translation (Berkeley: University of California Press, 1971)* is accurate and good English verse, although his very effort to translate fully makes the poem appear bulkier than it is in the original. Mandelbaum includes a useful annotated bibliography. Both Humphries and Mandelbaum seem preferable to C. Day Lewis's sometimes intolerably clichéd *Aeneid* (Oxford: Oxford University Press, 1952).* The classic modern prose translation is that by W. F. Jackson Knight (Harmondsworth: Penguin, 1956).* R. W. B. Lewis's perceptive essay "On Translating the *Aeneid:* 'Yif that I can'" (in the collection of essays edited by Steele Commager cited below) is one that I admire, although its assessment of certain translations differs from my own.

This essay owes special debts to many others on whom I have relied. I wish first of all (and most of all) to acknowledge the illuminating criticism of the *Aeneid* found in Michael C. J. Putnam's *The Poetry of the Aeneid* (Cambridge, Mass.: Harvard University Press, 1966). Putnam's study provided me with the idea that it would be possible to use the Palinurus episode as a focal point for a general interpretation of the poem. While his purposes sometimes differ from my own, I owe him many details of my account of book 5. Also important to the ideas in this essay are Thomas Greene, *The Descent from Heaven* (New Haven: Yale University Press, 1963);* Adam Parry, "The Two Voices of Virgil's *Aeneid*," in *Virgil: A Collection of Critical Essays*, ed. Steele Commager (Englewood Cliffs, N.J.: Prentice-Hall, 1966);* and Viktor Pöschl, *The Art of Vergil: Image and Symbol in the Aeneid* (Ann Arbor: University of Michigan Press, 1962).

A well-annotated edition of Virgil's poems is that of John Conington and Henry Nettleship, *P. Vergili Maronis Opera: The Works of Virgil with a Commentary*, Vol. 1 (*Eclogues* and *Georgics*), 5th ed. further revised by F. Haverfield (London: Bell, 1898); Vol. 2 (*Aeneid* 1-6), 4th ed. (London: Bell, 1884); Vol. 3 (*Aeneid* 7-12), 3d ed. (London: Bell, 1883). A classic nineteenth-century study of Virgil is Sainte-Beuve's *Étude sur Virgile* (Paris: Garnier, 1957). The work that fathered all twentieth-century understanding of Virgil's art is Richard Heinze, *Virgils epische Technik* (Leipzig: Teubner, 1903). Two collections will suggest the range of recent work: *Virgil*, ed. Donald R. Dudley (New York: Basic Books, 1969) and the Steele Commager collection of essays cited above. Also useful are W. F. Jackson Knight, *Roman Vergil* (London: Faber, 1944; rev. ed. Harmondsworth: Penguin, 1966);* Brooks Otis, *Virgil: A Study in Civilized Poetry* (Oxford: Oxford University Press, 1963); Kenneth Quinn, *Virgil's Aeneid: A Critical Description* (Ann Arbor: University of Michigan Press, 1968).

*Paperbound available.

THE *INFERNO*

James Nohrnberg

I

The subject of this essay is the *Inferno*, but it is useful to know from the outset that this canticle is the first of three, and that it anticipates a purgatorial and paradisal sequel. The *Inferno* is what Dante is saved *from*; the *Purgatorio* and *Paradiso* are what he is saved *for*. Dante tries to climb a hill at the opening of the *Inferno*, but only at the end of this part of the poem does the *Divine Comedy* as a whole begin to take on its proper form, namely, that of a romance quest. A few words about the whole are essential before we can approach the first part.

The quest in literature may be described as the allegory of purpose: it is the chief fiction for expressing determination, from its first motions in anticipation, initiative, and vocation to its consummation in accomplishment and self-fulfillment. In other words, the character of this fiction is teleological, like the character of the virtues in Aristotle which have as their goal, or end, the realization of happiness. The quest typically takes its protagonist through such ordeals and adventures as come between him and union with an object of desire. Dante's object is Christian beatitude, and his quest leads him through the valley of Hell—a valley of the shadow of death—and up the mountain of Purgatory to a rendezvous with the love of his life, a departed mistress named Beatrice. Their reunion takes place in the earthly paradise at the mountain's top.

Purgatory is conceived as a seven-story sacred mountain, roughly architectural in shape, something like a pagoda. On its terraces the souls of the penitent work out their salvation after death, to the music of the seven beatitudes. At the summit of their labors they will have recovered their generic innocence; they therefore find themselves in the forest of Eden. At this point the pilgrim has become a kind of second Adam; typologically, Beatrice occupies the place of a new Eve. Purgatory is a kind of wedding cake with the original bridal pair at the top.

Beatrice, as the mistress of a love poet, causes the poet to experience love; but she is also the poet's muse, since he is inspired to write love poetry. Dante's world and everything in it is moved by love, that is, by the love excited in it by God, the First Unmoved Mover, more or less as Aristotle taught. Beatrice herself, at the outset, is moved by love, like Venus in the *Aeneid*, who intercedes with Jupiter on the hero's behalf. Dante also has this "prologue in heaven"; his service to Beatrice does not belong to the mutual obligations of Roman family piety, however, but to the courtly love convention, in which the Provençal celebration of adultery and female beauty was treated as an ennobling species of devotion. This adoration developed an orthodox counterpart in the cult of the supremely courteous Mary, who in turn inspires Beatrice. The rationalization of the courtly love convention goes no further than it does in the *Divine Comedy*; Dante indicates as much when he makes the pilgrim pass a large number of lesser troubadours on his way up Purgatory. Rather pointedly, the one he passes last is purging himself of lechery in the ring of fire encircling the forest of Eden.

Since Beatrice offers the beatific vision of the *Paradiso*, she is not only a courtly love mistress: she is also Wisdom, the inviting bride of Solomon in the Song of Songs. Her invitation is to "see God." Saint Bonaventure describes the "mind's road to God" as a striving toward a speculative truth whereby we "mount step by step until we come to the high mountain where we shall see the God of gods in Zion"; comparably, the apex of Purgatory is diametrically opposite Jerusalem, on the "speculative" or "other" side of the earth.

> Since, then, we must mount Jacob's ladder . . . let us place the first rung of ascension in the depths . . . by which ladder we shall mount up to God, that we may be true Hebrews crossing from Egypt to the land promised to our fathers; let us also be lovers of wisdom, which calls to us says, "Come over to me, all ye that desire me, and be filled with my fruits."
>
> [Vulgate: Ecclesiasticus 24:26]

This passage illustrates the relation between Dante's quest myth and the one in the Bible; like the saint, Dante puts the first rung of ascension in the depths.

The design of Dante's poem fulfills the pattern of a major quest-romance fiction, that of the marvelous journey. If we look at the traveler as a pilgrim, we find two motives for his journey: the motive of exile or banishment and the motive of invitation. Dante was a political exile who knew "the bitterness of climbing another man's stair"; the purgatorial form of this ascent, however, leads to communion and initiation into the mystical body of the Church. The two motives develop formal equivalents in the narrative digressions that prevent the quester getting any nearer his goal, and the dream-vision that pre-joins the dreamer with a communing or wish-fulfilling world at the outset. From the point of view of salvation, the *Inferno* seems like a digression from the start, while the *Paradiso* is a dream-vision to the end.

The sense of exile from a noble or chivalric fellowship and the sense of initiation into a noble or chivalric vision provide two of the four cardinal points of the *Divine Comedy*. One is the place where ordinary experience begins to turn into a visionary experience of damnation; the other is the place where an initiation into or recovery of innocence begins to turn into a vision of Paradise. The other two points are the place where the nightmare of damnation is exhausted, at the bottom of Hell; and the point were the vision of Paradise is transfigured, and the visionary's eyes open upon a vision of God. These four points supply the termini for the three canticles of Dante's poem. They are found at the surface of the earth, the apex of Hell, the apex of the purgatorial mountain, and in the Primum Mobile. Each of the four realms has its proper focus: the saints are in orbit around God; the damned are in orbit around Satan; the progressively more innocent are in orbit around the Garden of Eden; and the fallen—you and I on the surface of the earth—are turned by Fortune.

Three of these four realms are "allegorical," or other than ours. Our modern training tends to make us think of literature as the recreation of ordinary experience according to canons of verisimilitude and likelihood; but little time in Dante's poem is spent in our world, and we must therefore look for *analogies* for ordinary experience rather than a persuasive duplication of it. The first place to look is in those episodes of the poem located closest to the earth's surface. Three similitudes for ordinary life present themselves at the opening of the poem: the dark and bewildering wood; the chaotic vestibule of Hell; and the noble castle in Limbo in which the virtuous pagans are domiciled. Dante finds himself in the first, "lost" in what he elsewhere calls a "wood of error." The natural point of departure for the medieval romance is the uninitiated knight setting forth on his first adventure, but Dante's opening images show the pilgrim in retreat from any dragon-slaying role. The three beasts from which he flees function to get him into the other world (like the White Rabbit at the opening of *Alice in Wonderland*); there we meet them again, but now in the guise of human society. So far Dante's is an inverted quest—Virgil tells him right away that it is the task of a savior figure to drive such beasts back to Hell, rather than letting them drive us there. Dante is lost, as Adam was when God asked ".Where art thou?" He has lost his sense of direction.

On the other hand, Dante has become aware of his condition, at which point he meets another exile, an exile of the afterlife, the dead poet Virgil. Virgil hails from Limbo, which is the marginal first circle of Hell. Limbo is not a totally evil lot, but we are warned by it that the life of conscientious moral virtue and humane rationality, lived for its own sake and without hope of better, is finally a heavy burden to the human spirit. Between the wood and the illuminated darkness of Limbo lies the vestibule of the pusillanimous, the uncommitted and selfish life which is really no life at all.

<h2 style="text-align:center">II</h2>

Virgil is allowed to journey from Limbo to Eden; his liminal status in both places represents him as a spirit caught between two different worlds, like his own Aeneas. Virgil's presence in Dante's poem in fact corresponds to the termini of the underworld in the sixth book of the *Aeneid*: it begins with the disappointed Palinurus in a kind of Limbo and ends with the dead Marcellus celebrated in the Elysian Fields. In turn, Marcellus is an elegiac version of the wonder child celebrated in Virgil's Fourth Eclogue. The opening of this quasi-messianic prophecy of a new golden age earned Virgil the epithet "prophet of the Gentiles" in the Christmas service in Rouen cathedral—and also Jerome's scornful repudiation of a tradition of a "Christian without Christ." And yet, in the *Paradiso*, the Emperor Trajan is almost exactly that.

As early as Tertullian, Christian thinkers began to think of the universal Roman state as an ally, as if the Pax Romana were an earthly counterpart for the Lukan evangelium of peace on earth. Dante believed the timing of the Incarnation sanctified the "idea of Rome" more or less for all of history. Christ began his life by being included in the ecumenical Roman census, and ended it when he was tried under Roman jurisdiction. Thus, if Virgil was an honorary or adoptive Christian, Christ was an honorary Roman: Heaven is that Rome where Christ is a Roman. These are the implications of Dante's pairing of Aeneas and Paul at the outset of the poem. Dante also mentions Peter here, anticipating the bottom of the *Inferno*, where we meet their satanic counterparts, Judas, Brutus, and Cassius.

It was Virgil's own lot to miss the revelation he prophesied. His misfortune inspired great compassion in the Latin Middle Ages: the liturgy at the Mantuan's birthplace included a passage on the Feast of Saint Paul that had Paul weeping at Virgil's tomb because the apostle did not have a chance to save the poet. Dante's own tears for Virgil, in the earthly paradise, belong to this tradition. "Vespers have rung already on the tomb of the body in which I used to cast a shadow: it was transported from Naples to Brundisium"; the sense of elegiac foreclosure in these words of Virgil clings to him throughout the poem. His slight reluctance to talk about what he has missed suggests a mystery for us, comparable to God's displeasure with Moses. Like Moses, Virgil can bring his charge to the Promised Land, but he disappears from the top of the high mountain at the advent of Beatrice, having seen the salvation which has been prepared, but unable to enter into it.

We are meant to take the comparison implying the parity of Virgil and Moses rather seriously. The Schoolmen understood both classical philosophy and the Jewish law to be a "preparation for the gospel." The offices of Virgil and Moses are also parallel because Dante understood both authors to have described an exodus: halfway up the mountain of Purgatory the two examples for sloth are the generation that died with Moses in the wilderness, and those who did not endure toil to the end with Aeneas. We may extend the theme by noting that both the Trojan and Jewish holy cities are relocated at the site of Rome. Christian legend also has a more strictly mythological exodus myth, that of the Harrowing of Hell. Christ leads the Hebrews out of their bondage in Limbo sometime between Good Friday and Easter Sunday, which thus becomes the time assigned to the action of the *Inferno*.

III

The *Inferno* itself is a kind of song of wrath, like many other epic productions, except that here the wrath—being God's and being absolute—is elaborated in what one could call eschatological space: the wrath's alleviation in time, for the majority of the poem's figures, is not an issue. The subject of the *Inferno*, to quote Dante's letter to Can Grande, is the way in which man, by bad deserts and in the exercise of his free choice, becomes liable to punishing justice. Zeus's first speech announces a similar theme for the *Odyssey*; but Dante's own story, going far beyond Homer in its educational intent, implies that Hell can be re-harrowed by the soul's cognition and repudiation of sin. Should we find ourselves unwilling to share in this process, we will never really get beyond the beginning of the poem, where the neutrals occupy the vestibule: Pilate-like, we too refuse to judge. The poet, in contrast, ultimately passes a judgment upon sin that might almost make the Last Judgment seem redundant.

There is very little moral suspense in the *Inferno* overall. The reader who cannot entertain Dante's judgments is in effect more deficient than Dante's sinners, who never express surprise at their final condition. They are shown charging into damnation at the spurring of Divine Justice, with which their will ultimately concurs. The sinner has virtually chosen Hell, and chosen the retribution he gets, according to a kind of poetic version of the law of retaliation, which is life for life. The sinner will die, Ezekiel says categorically, and it is no great difference to think of him as being as good as dead already. A related cautionary notion conceives of sin as preparing its own punishment, or acting as a nemesis unto itself. The impersonal operation of this law receives proverbial expression in the Bible: the schemer who digs a pit will fall into it; the instruments of sin will be made the instruments of punishment; the man making an idol will become like unto it. Where sin entails such exactments, it is easy to treat the incriminated state as the punishment itself. Like Plato before him, Dante allegorizes this basic tautology; in the Platonic parable, the souls coming before Minos after death exhibit the scars and wounds that they have acquired as a consequence of wrongdoing in life. Dante calls this principle of poetic justice the *contrapasso*: the reflexive action of sinning upon the sinner. "Vengeance is mine," the sin itself might well declare.

Besides being the spectrous persons of the dead, Dante's characters are "shadows" in the technical sense of being adumbrations of definitive realities, including their own ultimate selves. The damned have lived a life of prophecy for a death of fulfillment. They are now more or less frozen into the attitudes into which their habits were all along casting them; in a parody of what it means to have an identity, or sameness of self, they can only repeat—and never improve upon—the fixed ideas of their former lives. Here we have a travesty of the sacramental discipline of the *Purgatorio*, where the confessional life of contrition, repentance, and satisfaction is understood to continue beyond the grave.

As early as the *Odyssey* we find the insistence in fiction that objects of retribution condemn themselves out of their own mouths. When we listen closely, we will almost always find that Dante's characters are two-time losers: they keep betraying themselves, and betraying the fact that they would do it again. No one in the *Inferno* can make a "good confession." The sinners do characterize their vices, but so does an incurable smoker when he calls his cigarette a "coffin nail." He also accedes to his just deserts, assimilating them to an imagery both eschatological and poetic: the deed returns upon the doer in a final form which is also a similitude for the deed itself. An apt example here would be Dante's hypocrites. Hypocrisy, with its enforced decorum and rigid sardonic smiles, is a kind of rigor mortis of inhibition. The hypocrites wear magnificent copes lined with lead: their habits preserve them in the form proper to corpses.

IV

Hell is sin's product, but we must also understand Hell as a process. Stepping back from the whole, we may reconstruct the *Inferno* as a descent into damnation.

We begin by losing our sense of direction; we are unable to maintain a moral purposiveness. Like Jonah running away from his God, we retreat into the mouth of the monster. Our first desire, really, was to be left alone, to do what we wanted. This is the neutrality found in the vestibule, a kind of morally aimless tolerance or indifference. Such an abdication of responsibility is incompetent even to sin, and yet it is closely allied to sin, since it is easy prey for compliance in the evil will of another: tolerance subjects one to all kinds of impositions. We begin with the pleasurable compliance in a natural act, exhibited in Francesca in the second circle; the sins descending from Francesca's are all, in a way, "natural" sins. That is, they are sins entailed in the appetites of the natural man. The natural man wants sex; he wants food; he wants money and the things it buys, or the sense of power to be found in spending it. We are now in the fourth circle, and the images of drift, passivity, and soddenness that show us at the mercy of our drives are replaced by the image of the deadlocked circle. The unregulated pursuit of what we wanted has ended in the loss of our power to control our lives. Here the description of Fortune, as the angelic intelligence of the unmoving earth, properly makes its appearance. The ensuing sense of frustration is duly acknowledged in the next circle, where we meet the sin of anger. We also find the sin of sullenness, a kind of deeper and more frustrated form of the indifference found in the vestibule: an ingrown and embittered sloth, and a deeper image of the incapacitated will.

On the other side of anger is Hell proper, *nether* Hell. Dante, confronted by the rising Furies of an alienated conscience, again wants to retreat. The rising walls of the City of Dis present what Dante elsewhere calls a "threshold of assent." Transitions from one circle to another are not so prominent until this point, but hereafter the frontiers will be more vertically marked, until the whole poem emerges as a stairway, that is, a hierarchy of thresholds.

Dante rhymes the word *threshold* (*soglio*) with the word *will* (*voglio*) five times in his poem. The word *threshold* is used in connection with most of the major boundaries of the poem, such as Saint Peter's Gate, and therefore each threshold represents a state or stage of the will. A crucial passage here is Virgil's lecture on the nature of our inclinations. Our loves are innocent, we are told, and rightly directed toward pleasing objects. Nonetheless, one can go wrong in following them. In order to make every secondary desire conform to the innocence of the primal wish—for it is the form of the soul to love—"there is, innate in you, the virtue that counsels, and which must occupy the threshold of assent." The "counselor power" is added to inclination to make sure that we do not get attached to the wrong object. This power actually makes possible the freedom of the will, which is properly understood as *libero arbitrio*, or free choice. Hell-gate is "the threshold denied to none": although the Lord does not rejoice in the damnation of the sinner, neither does he deny him the choice of it.

The characters in the vestibule suffer a suspension or paralysis of the will; their abdication of free choice is the larger "great refusal" here. Unable to surrender to death, they are also spared this assent, in that they never were alive. Francesca, on the other hand, is the very type of passionate surrender—she is, in fact, rather forward. It is love that moves the whole creation, and, as a consenting adult, Francesca is no exception. All sin arises from a disorder in the affections and proceeds to a disorder in the will: Francesca's is the right character study with which to begin the "slide" over the threshold of assent into the infernal condition.

This slide is arrested at the City of Dis, for its "threshold of assent" is also presented as an impasse. The term *impasse* may be allowed to stand opposite our starting point for the quest, the adventuring or initiative that, at the other end of the quest, will become initiation. In between the knight may lose his way, and wander into error; this error deepens into trespass, and trespass leads to impasse. The knight, stymied or unable to proceed, eventually clears the impasse after a mysterious intermission or suspension of the quest (such as the arrested progress during the nights of the *Purgatorio*), and is then enabled to behold and comprehend symbols for the completion of the quest (such as the immense signs of the *Paradiso*). Given our hemispheres of exile and initiation, we can now see a cycle of four cardinal points for the quest:

POINT OF DEPARTURE—DETERMINATION OF THE QUEST

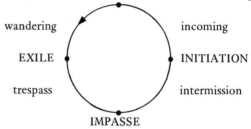

Clearing an impasse, of course, turns that impasse into a point of departure, and the bottom of Hell is a veritable revolving door in this respect.

The entry to the City of Dis represents the point where the sinner starts organizing his life consciously for sin. That is why, just on the other side of the walls, Virgil for the time unfolds Hell's plan: Hell has designs upon us. From here on, the sinners' confessions particularly insist upon our studying their motives, as opposed to their mere inclinations. We may also understand this threshold positively: it must represent the point where the sinner faces up to his own complicity in the damnable part of his life.

In our remorse for a history of intemperance, the moment is ripe for a second abandonment of our counselor power. Virgil, who symbolizes this power, begins to feel very lonely himself—he is unable to cope. Until this point, the sinner was merely passively willing; now he is in danger of taking matters into his own hands. He can become an actively wilful sinner, one who despairs of anything better than self-destruction. The demons at the gate threaten to bring the Gorgon, and Dante is implored not to look beyond the Mosaic veil of Virgil's hands. Thus the Gorgon must stand for whatever it is that hardens the sinner's heart and stiffens his neck. All of the sinners inside the walls must have looked upon the Gorgon, proceeding from anger to fury, and from a debilitating and paralyzing desperation to the pride in obstinacy exhibited by Farinata just within the walls.

Farinata is guilty of heresy, a wilful intellectual obduracy in the face of "the door of the future." Here the door of the future is the prospect of the afterlife. The heretics denied the immortality of the soul; and yet their punishment places them in a landscape out of paintings of the Last Judgment, when the lids on other graves will be opening, even as these are finally sealed shut. The future is an important theme here, because at every threshold of assent one settles a part of one's future.

If the Gorgon represents the sinner's despair of anything better than damnation, then the defense against it must be hope. Virgil encourages Dante with echoes of the biblical promise that God will not abandon the Psalmist's soul to Hell, nor allow his holy one to see corruption. And the stirrings of Dante's wrath, which Virgil a little before has hailed as messianic, indicate his power to reject a bad choice. Here we should recall that the demons blocking Dante's advance are a standard feature of Christ's Harrowing of Hell. Dante presumably alludes to this legend in the sudden and dramatic descent of an angel. The appearance of angels is itself a traditional hopeful sign. The righteous will does not go unsupported by grace, and the angel walks on water and opens Hell's gate. This messenger figure resembles the classical Hermes, but in Matthew such an angel descends like lightning, transfixes the opposing guards, and rolls back the stone of Christ's tomb to let the apostles enter in and see the defeat of the grave. The open graves of the heretics, who did not hope for the biblical "resurrection of the just," lie immediately beyond the analogous infernal threshold.

We should pause here to note Dante's other allusions to the Harrowing of Hell. In the *Purgatorio*, at a place in the narrative that seems to correspond to this level of the *Inferno*, the poet Statius is sprung from his penitentiary on the cornices of sloth and greed; this is accompanied by an earthquake, one of the Harrowing's traditional effects. The earthquake occurred at the time of the Crucifixion; the crack it left in Hell's structure remains to memorialize Christ's victory over death. Our attention is drawn to this testimony twice. First, there is an exposed and ragged escarpment leading down from the circle of the heretics to that of the violent, who are murders. This fault represents the passage from a denial of God's power to raise the dead to the attempt to put God's Son to death. Secondly, much deeper down, the earthquake has broken the bridge over one of the ten ditches of fraud, that of hyprocrisy. Caiaphas, the high priest who preached that it was expedient that one man die for the people, is punished there. There is always hypocrisy in the decision to execute an innocent scapegoat. Since its bridge is broken, the only way to cross this ditch is by descending into it. Other than that, one can pass directly from the circle of violence to the final rings of treachery— where Judas is punished. One can pass directly from violence to treachery with only a little dip into hypocrisy.

V

Once inside the City, the sinner has made a kind of decision for Satan, leaguing himself with the fallen angels. A principal evidence of his newfound allegiance is pride, which is closely linked to rebellion from God's omnipotence. Dante has already passed Fillipo Argenti, whom he condemns for arrogance, the kind of contempt that makes a man insolent. But we arrive at something like pride proper with Farinata: "Who are your ancestors?," he demands of Dante: this is caste pride, the hauteur and scorn of the "elect." Farinata's high disdain succeeds in communicating his sense of injured merit, but at the same time we know that he is an inveterate and contumacious *grand seigneur.*

More important here, Farinata is proud of his inveteracy. Thus Virgil expounds Hell's plan just after the sinner expresses his contempt for an alternative. The vehemence and ferocity of this expression are allowed to emerge in the circle below, which treats various forms of violence and violation: extroverted violence, against our fellows; introverted violence, against our own person; and violence against *being* in general—the creator, his creation, and the second creation which is art. The whole level is surrendered over to destructive impulses.

For the collusion of the destructive impulse with pride, a fair example is the suicide Piero della Vigna. He is a type of eternally discredited soul—his is the story of the unjustly disgraced steward. His thorny and reflexive language shows he cannot face the things he talks about. In fact, his broken branch does the talking—he went to pieces. Because the suicide has abused his motor power, he is only able to synthesize a stationary vegetable in Hell: Piero is a crippled and knotted thornbush. It seems cruel to accuse such a broken man of pride, and yet we cannot miss it. He commits suicide partly from an inability to live with an irreparably damaged ego; his vanity is unmistakable in his exaltation of his office. It is ironic that Piero is still trying to rehabilitate his slandered reputation, for in the general resurrection the suicide will not be able to resume even his body; it will be draped on his inglorious bush. Piero is the injured innocent, with his bitter thorns and poison and eloquent wounds. His whole circle, a ring or garland of thorns, presumptuously awards him a martyr's crown.

A deeper rebellion from God's will is found in the violent

against God. The rebellious will inhabit parched places, according to Scripture, and Capaneus, who defied the gods, lies here on a burning desert. The desert amplifies the sterility of his defiant vaunt. Lower still, among the fraudulent, we meet the thief Vanni Fucci; his obscene gesture toward God, according to John Ruskin, is found in illustrations of the Psalter where it says, "The fool in his heart hath said there is no God." Almost alone in this respect, Fucci mentions God directly, and yet there is certainly a sense in which he has said in his heart that there is no God.

At the bottom of the pit we behold the ambitious giants. Ambition is a part of pride, along with vainglory, and the giants are traditional types of presumption—a presumption, implicit in what has gone before, to rival God. Ephialtes tried to build a stairway to Heaven; Nimrod, to make a name for himself, built the Tower of Babel. Nimrod is reduced to the idiocy of a private language; Ephialtes is a mere anarchic convulsion, the last stages of the anger of Fillipo Argenti. Antaeus, a third in this company, is simpleminded and foolishly vain. In any case, the giants are not very smart. Their bulk naturally suggests the tyranny of grandiose self-conceptions. The poet, however, explains it as the dangers of power allied with intelligence—too little intelligence, we must assume, like children playing with matches or unthinkable nuclear devices. The Book of Baruch says the proud giants perished from want of wisdom.

In terms of the description of the will in the *Inferno*, the giants seem to resemble our passions: they are earth-born, brutalized, primordial, preconscious. We would call them the remains of the "old brain," with its territorial imperatives and unconditioned aggressive instinct. They stand around the inner pit in the form of a monumental Stonehenge, and they tell us that pride is senseless. Their degradation opens upon the greater one of Satan, for which the authority is scriptural: "Hell from below was in an uproar to meet thee at thy coming, it stirred up giants for thee. . . . Thy pride is brought down to hell. . . . How thou art fallen from heaven, O Lucifer. . . . And thou said in thy heart, I will ascend into heaven, I will exalt my throne above the stars . . . I will be like the most high."

VI

Let us now go down to the sides of the pit. I wish to address myself to the organization of the most complicated zone in the *Inferno*, the *malbolgia*. The "evil pouches" are ten ditches in which fraud is punished according to its kinds. Here the destructive impulses of the upper level of nether Hell are rationalized. The sins of the leopard are appetitive sins; they are sin's self-indulgent youth, as it were. The sins of the lion are those which abuse power; they are sin's arrogant and brutal manhood. The sins of the wolf are secretive and entrenched sins, in which force is replaced by cunning; they are sin's crafty old age.

The ditches form a spider-web structure: fraud shares its complexity with art. The image of ten circles meets us elsewhere in the poem, in the ten circles of the *Paradiso*. The motion of the heavenly spheres is communicated to them from the penultimate Primum Mobile, the sphere of the loving and ardent seraphim, inside the Empyrean. Next comes the sphere of the contemplative cherubim, which moves slowly in the opposite direction. Inside of these are the seven planets. Where the planets are energized by love and contemplation, the motor power of the malbolgia seems to be cupidity and malice: these are the ardor and intellectual capacity of Hell. There is an analogy with the first of the malbolgia, which holds the seducer and the pandar; they move in opposite directions around their circle. We may think of them as types of lust and greed, an extroverted and introverted cupidity. The two crimes, seduction and pandaring, set up an alternating series, like a pattern of ripples, that extends through most of the rest of the *bolgia*:

(1) Seducers	Pandars	1
2 Flatterers	Simonists	3
4 Sorcerers	Barrators	5
6 Hypocrites	Thieves	7
8 False Counselors	Schismatics	9
10 Falsifiers		

Odd-numbered bolgia mainly treat sins of cupidity (greed) but, more largely, sins against the public interest. Even-numbered bolgia treat sins against the truth: sins against *ratio*, human reason, and *oratio*, human speech.

All of the criminals in the righthand column subvert human institutions. One can see the analogy among the first three. The pandar sells the institution of marriage. The simonist sells the Church, the Bride of Christ—or Beatrice. The barrator sells the state—or threatens Virgil. The thief subverts the institution of property, which Dante understands as a part of man's legal body. The schismatic divides truth in two parts, especially the truth taught by the Church. More widely, he divides the unity of men. This is an institution too, at least ideally, for Dante believed in one world government. To the schismatics we could add the giants, who divide themselves from divine as well as human society.

Some support for this analysis comes from the alternating moods of the circles; they are mournful and outrageous by turns. Even-numbered bolgia, from two through eight, are depressive; odd-numbered bolgia are manic, being equipped with tormentors, as well as torments: horns and whips among the seducers, Dante's sermon at the simonists. The episode of the barrators becomes a menacing and dangerous satyr-play. One is caught in a trap with a predatory phalanx of hooks, gaffs, talons, claws, torn frogs, and trapped mice. The thieves are tormented by former colleagues in the shapes of reptiles—Satan himself stole the form of a snake. The schismatics are sundered by the angel with the terrible, swift sword; they travel a round of opening and reopening wounds that represents the history of schism. My system for the intestines of Hell breaks down about here, just at the point where Mahomet comes into view spilling his innards. In the final two bolgia the imagery portrays society collapsing into mere heaps of discordant bodies: the schismatics are a battle-field, the falsifiers a malarial swamp.

In the left-hand side of my list are the crimes against other minds, crimes which abuse and finally outrage reason. The seducer, who accomplishes an evil persuasion, corrupts an-other will by way of a dark understanding: he tells plausible lies. The flatterer, with his malicious suggestions, corrupts— or prostitutes, according to the imagery—the language of ap-praisal, smothers it in vanity: he tells pleasing lies. The magi-cian, or diviner, corrupts the truth by deforming it into intelligence about the future. Divination is the attempt to exert compulsion on the divine counsel. The diviner also falsifies prophecy, and in the Bible false prophecy is usually flattering: the divine tells fantastic lies. The hypocrite cor-rupts intelligence by saying one thing and harboring another. He is pharisaical, a canting dissembler of virtue, pretentious in the deeper sense: he tells sly or insidious lies. The false counselor corrupts intelligence by means of intelligence. His lies ambush the mind of another, but they also deprave the conduct and purposes of their victim, as well as disarm him. His counsel corrupts judgment—he tells collusive and sub-versive lies. The falsifiers corrupt the very identity of truth: perjury, counterfeiting, faking of precious metals, and im-posture all belong here. Especially apt is the corruption of the medium of exchange. Lying, which is an intellectual act, requires an operation by the reason: we remember what a good liar the intelligent Odysseus was. But the telling of nothing but lies ends in a kind of abdication of reason, where there is nothing reliable left to corrupt, and no standard left by which to judge. We cannot miss the images of madness here, along with characters who have falsified their very bap-tism. A culminating figure is Sinon, the fantastic con artist of the second book of the *Aeneid*: the very master of plausible, pleasing, future-twisting, insidious, and ruinous falsifications.

Now there is yet a further refinement to be made upon this scheme, which is surely a model of duplicity already. As it stands, the model shows that every fraud against the public interest is only one remove from a crime against the use of reason. And that is a very Dantesque lesson. But the crimes also seem to group themselves into triplets. Seduction, pandaring, and flattery are linked in the first triad; then simony (which comes by its name through Simon the Magician), magic, and barratry. As seduction and flattery are linked in the first triad, so simony and barratry are linked in the second. In the third, hypocrisy and false counsel are similarly linked, with the thieves as the antithetical interpolant. Aquinas says that the hyprocrite steals a reputation among men. False counsel qualifies as a kind of theft too; Dante punishes it in the "thievish fire," because false counsel steals a man's reason. To be a triplet, our last grouping must include the falsifiers between the schismatics and the giants— the giants are a second, primeval kind of schismatic. The scheme may then be represented as here:

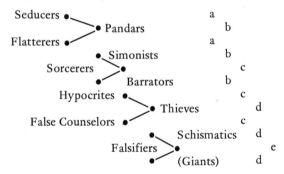

The sombre movement common to the ditches of the sorcerers, hypocrites, and false counselors ranks them together, on one side, just as the merchandising of communal institutions ranks pandar, simonist, and barrator together on the other.

The general pattern of including a new sin between two varieties of a sin already introduced belongs to the poem's whole mystery of advance and retardation. The pattern con-

forms to the requirements of the *terza rima*, the rhyme
scheme of the poem, which may be described as two steps
forward (a, b), then one step back (a), and so forth: aba,
bcb. . . . This is the larger pattern of Dante's quest: one step
back into the pit of Hell, two steps forward into the lower
and upper Paradises.

An analysis of a selected episode from either side of the
diagram will show the satiric tendency in Dante's treatment
of crimes against the public interest, and the ironic tendency
in his treatment of crimes against the rational faculties.
Among the simonists we find the popes, where the governing
conceit is the institution of Peter, turned upside down. Peter
is the rock upon whom the apostolic succession is founded,
the first to take up Christ's injunction "Follow me." Here,
with each pope crammed into the rock, and into the funda-
ment of his predecessor, we are treated to a perfect image for
the founding of the Church's hellish counterpart: Simon
Magus is traditionally a rival for Simon Peter. In his first
Epistle in the Bible, Peter describes the Church as being made
up of "living stones"; here Dante describes the rock as *pietra
livida*, "livid stones." In the *Paradiso* Peter himself will turn
red with shame at the present state of the papacy; here the
pope's feet turn red, whether with conscience or anger Dante
does not know. The apostolic mission was confirmed by the
Pentecostal tongues of flame; here tongues of flame batten
on the sacramental oil of the pope's feet. Peter's first Epistle
reports that Christ "preached to the spirits who were in
prison," traditionally in Limbo; here Dante confesses a priest
and preaches to a pope. Things are upside down when the
laity must assume the priestly office. When Dante gets to
Heaven, Peter commissions him to write down what he has
heard: his appointment to preach is apostolic. Finally, Pope
Nicholas is planted in the ground like a post or a pile; traditionally, Peter was crucified on a stake upside down.

Of perpetrators of crimes against other minds, the natural
choice is Ulysses. On the whole, Dante does not let the

rogues predominate over the gallery. Nonetheless, certain characters in the *Inferno* are allowed to make quite an impression, Ulysses among them. Hell, after all, is the home of the great individualists, the strikers of poses, or cultivators of a cult of personality. Ulysses makes a speech a little like that of the tragic protagonist near the end of a Shakespearean play—that is, from a perspective normally obtainable only after the hero's fall. Out of the deep moral chiaroscuro of such passages there vainly shines, however fitfully, the former splendor of a noble nature. Virgil tells us that Ulysses is damned for finding Achilles and persuading him to join the Trojan War, and for the trick of the Trojan horse. But Ulysses tells us about something apparently quite different; he tells the tale of his last voyage.

Since all sin entails the sinner's self-destruction, the way in which he has damned himself might be analogically connected with his mode of death. Such a connection makes for a poetic density of theme. Thus Ulysses' last voyage could be expected to manifest covertly those impulses that have elsewhere issued in his crimes. And if the state of soul at the moment of death determines its final lot, Ulysses' soul must also shipwreck on his unrepentance. That is why he dies in view of the mountain of Purgatory, without ever reaching it.

Ulysses' torment in his flame is based on a passage in the Epistle of James about the evil tongue being set on fire by Hell; this tongue in turn sets the cycle of nature on fire. The imagery of the voyager following the sun's track owes something to this image: Ulysses fires his men to follow him into their own sunset. Ulysses has the gift of tongues. He is punished with his old henchman Diomedes, and hence their tongue is a forked one. Virgil is the interpreter for the Greek-speaking shade, just as he interpreted Homer's Odysseus for Latin culture in the *Aeneid*. It is this evil Odysseus that Dante knows.

Ulysses is a type of subversive intelligence, especially as we use the word to mean intelligence about an enemy or victim.

He regards life as a "brief vigil of the senses"—he is a spy. He helped steal the Palladium, the image of the goddess of reason; he takes away a man's better judgment. His speech to his men, a typically Odyssean speech within a speech, is a temptation to acquire a knowledge bordering on omniscience. It may be that he was just controlling his bag of wind, but he also becomes a kind of Siren to himself, self-enchanted by his promise of an intelligence of all things done on earth.

Dante's Ulysses did not go home; he sailed from Circe's isle to the land of the dead. By the time he arrives at the western end of the Mediterranean he is old; he almost seems to have aged before our eyes. For him, knowledge is an endless voyage in horizontal space, and only in his last moment, when the tower of Purgatory looms before him, does he have any intimation of a vertical dimension in human intellectual experience. Ulysses passes the marks of the Pillars of Hercules to enter upon an unpopulated realm somehow beyond human limits: the word for landmarks here is *segna*. It turns up in this sense once again in the poem, in the *Paradiso*, where a redeemed Adam explains to Dante that man's original sin consisted in disobedience—in exceeding a *segna*, or limit. Ulysses tells his last crew that they are on the track of virtue and knowledge; he wants to become expert in men's vices and worth. Thus he builds up a classical counterpart for that biblical temptation to a virtual knowledge of good and evil, which we are promised will open our eyes and make us like gods.

Ulysses' speech twice echoes the first book of the *Aeneid*, the tempest and shipwreck passages. "O socci," O comrades, says Aeneas to his men, and his message moves them from their conquest of Charybdis to their destiny to found a new home. "O frati," O brothers, says Ulysses, but his message leads his crew away from home to the unpeopled world of the sea and maelstrom. And the maelstrom closes, fourth time down—"as Another wished"—over the ears of those who listened to Ulysses.

For a moment we cannot believe that this man sinned. Columbus and Faustus seem like natural partners; studiousness is twin-born with curiosity. Yet the Devil was the first false counselor, and there is an evil curiosity that is tempted to try anything. We have felt something in Ulysses that looks right through us, a fixation on the horizons where the polestars are lost, and we have sensed in him something that has never heeded another's wish. His is a glassy-eyed autohypnosis that carries the voyager out like a lemming to his death.

VII

The last images of Hell are those of ruined towers and sinister giants. One feels human consciousness contracting here, and the unconscious and irrational looming incomprehensibly larger. The giants themselves seem to sum up a vast range of body imagery found throughout the *Inferno*. The lustful are borne on the winds that are the sighs with which they ventilated their passions. The gluttons lie under a sodden deluge representing the flow of matter they guzzled and released in life. Out of such observations emerges the image of Hell as a gigantic, shadowy creature suffering the interior life of the fallen man. It breathes with the lovers; it is nourished with the gluttons; it is irrigated with the polluted river of tears; it is steeped in the blood of our violence. It ruminates upon the sinners immersed in its fluids and canals, and it is half-poisoned on the wastes that clog its visceral foul pouches. Finally, though locked by an icy waste that is all impasse, it is voided by a cathartic vision of evil.

The last circle is a nightmarish prison world of devouring ogres, cruel hunters, treacherous and paralyzing attachments, and checkmated victims. The teeth that chatter here present Homer's gibbering shades in a new form—here "the seas of pity lie,/Locked and frozen in each eye." As at the beginning of the poem, only now more damningly, we find ourselves in that pass that no one before has ever left alive. It is the pass where Roland died, ambushed and betrayed.

The great story here belongs to Ugolino. Like Francesca, he designs it as a tear-jerker, but in fact the story terrifies us as almost nothing else in literature can: Dante does not weep. We need to know that Ugolino once betrayed a grandson into the hands of his enemies and then refused his victim's appeal for aid; Ugolino, in turn, dies a victim of the very party to whom he once betrayed the grandson, with his own sons at his side, asking why he does not help them. We almost hear the forsaken cry from the Cross here, as Dante himself confirms. One can also show that a parody of the same Psalmic cry has been put into the mouth of the unintelligible Nimrod. Ugolino's story, like Nimrod's, includes the destructive tower and the cruel manhunter, but worse follows. Starving inside the nailed-up tower, Ugolino's dying children suggest to their father that he eat them. "Then fasting had more power than grief." Did fasting have the power to kill Ugolino, as grief had not? Or did fasting—hunger—overcome his scruples, and did he sink to this last degradation? The concluding line of the story refuses to tell us which, and Ugolino says no more. Then he turns to cannibalize the head of his killer, and we dare to think the worst.

Nothing could really follow Ugolino's harrowing tale in its kind. As John Freccero has remarked, it contains the fundamental mystery of iniquity, that the innocent are allowed to suffer with the guilty. And yet it is precisely this that has made Christian redemption possible. At the bottom of the mystery is the traumatized father-son relationship not only of this "new Thebes," but of the Bible itself: the pitying father who nonetheless suffers the death of son, like Abraham; or the father who will not give his son a stone when he is asked for bread, in the example of fatherly love offered by Jesus.

Ugolino's story is as deep as the tragedy of Hell can take us, and something violently satirical now begins to take shape in its place. We are told, for example, the story of a treacherous host whose soul has descended "quick" into Hell, while his body continues its animate life upon the face of the earth, because its motions have been taken over by a demon. Such a story is sardonic, and it takes us one step past the human dimension into pure demonism. Indeed, this "invasion of the body snatchers" balances the parody of immortality in the first circle. There we found those who could not die, because they were never alive; here we meet one who continues to be alive, even though already dead. Hell has both a Waiting List and a procedure for Early Admissions.

Finally, Satan. He is immobilized in ice, a parody of the Unmoved Mover. His batlike wings move on the face of the deep, like the brooding Holy Spirit in Genesis; he churns out the wind that makes Hell freeze over. His canto begins with an infernal variation on the hymn sung in honor of the Cross. There is a patristic tradition that makes Christ on the Cross a giant *in extremis*, and Satan is a chagrined giant too. He sheds tears and foams blood, Hell's version of the sacramental blood and water flowing from Christ's side. He is eating Judas, the first of Satan's Christian apostolate, and Judas kicks his feet in the air like the pope in the ditch of simony. The Gospel says that Satan entered Judas; now Judas enters Satan. Here then is Hell's creation, a sterile waste; Hell's communion, a cannibal feast; and Hell's Trinity, a Geryon-like monstrosity. "The banners of the Prince of hell go forth," the poem intones. Nothing really does go forth, of course: Satan is here to stay. That wavering banner of the first circle comes to mind: Hell begins with a dithering confusion of inconstant standards and squandered motion; it ends in a complete loss of capacity—an appalling devastation at the center of which three godforsaken criminals are caught in the jaws of an eternal Golgotha.

The poem's vision of repudiation is now thoroughly exhausted, and Dante crosses a great divide. It has taken him thirty-three cantos to get to the dead center of the earth, but it takes only a few lines to return him to the earth's surface. At its utmost extremity, the pilgrim's regress reverts to progress—the retreating hero is suddenly treading the three-headed monster underfoot. In canto 1 Dante confessed himself unable to recover the precise "point" at which he lost his way, but now, coming out of Hell, he draws attention to the earth's central point, as if he were making good his earlier loss, and showing where he refound the way. The pilgrim's almost parenthetical regaining of the upper world corresponds to that intermission, or null space in the quest, which we said intervened between its phases of impasse and initiation, and which divides the *Inferno* from its sequel. The center constitutes an almost speculative reversal of direction and perspective, but it is clearly here, at his literal rotation, that we must mark the pilgrim's figurative conversion—the turning of his sinful soul around toward God, with the consequent righting of his fallen will and affections.

By crossing what is the International Date Line, Dante also regains twelve lapsed hours, and can thus rise with the sun on Easter, forty-eight hours after he entered Hell. Like his prototype, the Christ who harrowed Hell, Dante has kept the Jewish Sabbath in the tomb. The Church accordingly advances the Lord's Day—the day of the Resurrection—from the end of the week to the beginning of the next. A curious twelve-hour gap still remains between the Jewish and Christian calendars, since the Jewish holy day begins Friday evening. Thus the whole mystery of the renovation of time is contained in this nexus of Dante's journey: from the point of view of Purgatory, where it is twelve hours earlier than in Jerusalem, it might seem that we are still beginning our days at the wrong time. The length of Christ's burial is itself problematic. The Vulgate version of Matthew is particularly uncertain, for it says that Christ rose in the evening *and* the morning of the Sabbath. Commenting on this text, Bede explains that night follows day in ordinary experience; for the redeemed man, day follows night. At any rate, Dante has reconciled the contradiction, for he rises at both times.

God's power to turn back the clock on the life of the sinner is secretly alluded to in the poem's very first line. King Hezekiah fell sick "in the midst of life": "I said, in the midst of my days I shall go to the gates of hell." But God promised to restore the king, saying that Hezekiah would be able to go up to Zion in three days. Hezekiah asked for a sign, and God made the sun's shadow retreat ten steps on the royal sundial. "Thou hast delivered my soul," the king rejoices, "that it should not perish: thou hast cast all my sins behind thy back."

The final movement of the *Inferno* also recalls another Old Testament song of salvation, the one Moses sang at the Red Sea: "And with the blast of thy anger the waters were gathered together: the flowing water stood, the depths were congealed in the midst of the sea." There are Jewish and Christian legends that say that God *froze* these waters. Furthermore, typology makes the Red Sea passage protobaptismal, and hence a deliverance from bondage to sin. The Church Fathers readily allegorized the scuttled Egyptians as our perishing sins, and Pharoah—Ezekiel's dragon in the midst of his rivers —became a type of Satan. Satan's aboriginal precipitation from Heaven, as a memorable simile in book 1 of *Paradise Lost* reminds us, occupies the same typological space as Pharoah's overthrow at the Red Sea.

Behind us lies the land of bondage, with its rivers turned to blood, its palpable darkness, its stench and plagues and disease and frogs. Before us waits an imagery belonging to the Moses cycle also: Dante and his leader emerge on a reborn landscape, one featuring moving water, springing reeds, a freshening dawn breeze, and the safe landing of an ark filled with redeemed souls. The boat is powered by an angel called the Bird of God, and the souls are singing a psalm about the exodus from Egypt. The *Comedy* proper has at last begun.

In his famous letter to Can Grande, where the exodus is given the traditional fourfold interpretation, Dante also talks about the natures of tragedy and comedy. He says that tragedy is something fetid, like a goat. Satan is rather like that, for he has the hairy flanks and shanks of a satyr. But satyrs are not strictly tragic, and there are Latin traditions that connect them with the origins of comedy. Satyrs, at any rate, are slightly ribald, and prone to being caught in ridiculous or obscene poses. We have already seen the satiric way in which Dante regards Pope Nicholas, and Satan—Old Nick—is the pope of Hell. God will hold his enemies in derision, according to the psalmist. On the far side of the *Inferno* we are finally in a position to take God's point of view.

BIBLIOGRAPHICAL NOTE

Dante Alighieri was born in Florence in 1265 and died in Ravenna in 1321. He began his *Commedia* around 1307 while in political exile from his native city.

I have used J. D. Sinclair's prose translation of *The Divine Comedy*, 3 vols. (London: John Lane, 1940–46),* which is especially useful for its facing Italian text and its generous commentary. The most important recent translation is Charles Singleton's work, in six volumes of text, facing prose translation, and careful annotation (Princeton: Princeton University Press, 1970–). Available verse translations include Laurence Binyon's, reprinted in *The Portable Dante*, ed. Paolo Milano (New York: Viking, 1947);* Dorothy Sayers's and Barbara Reynolds's (Harmondsworth: Penguin, 1949–62);* and John Ciardi's (New York: New American Library, 1954–70).* All verse translations, to some degree or other, come to grief on the shores on Dante's *terza rima*: Ciardi's solution to the problems of the form results in the least affected English. H. R. Huse's line-by-line prose translation, with interpolated explanatory matter, is useful for beginners, and looks like verse (New York: Rinehart, 1954).*

I am conscious of some very specific debts in this essay: to Dorothy Sayers on the sin of pride, in *Introductory Papers on Dante* (London: Methuen, 1955), and, on the giants, in her notes to her translation of the *Inferno*, mentioned above; on Piero della Vigna to both Irma Brandeis, *The Ladder of Vision* (London: Chatto and Windus, 1960),* and Leo Spitzer, "Speech and Language in Inferno XIII," in *Dante: A Collection of Critical Essays*, ed. John Freccero (Englewood Cliffs, N.J.: Prentice-Hall, 1965);* to Charles H. Grandgent, for remarks in his introduction to canto 23, in his edition of *La Divina Commedia* (1933), revised by Charles S. Singleton, (Cambridge, Mass.: Harvard University Press, 1972); to Northrop Frye, for my strategy for dealing with the end of the *Inferno*, in the "Third Essay" of his *Anatomy of Criticism* (Princeton: Princeton University Press, 1957);* and to John Freccero, for observations on Ugolino, from a lecture.

Essential works for the student of Dante are: Paget J. Toynbee, *Dictionary of Proper Names and Notable Matters in the Works of Dante*, 2d ed., revised by Charles S. Singleton (Oxford: Clarendon Press, 1968); Umberto Cosmo, *A Handbook to Dante Studies* (Oxford: Blackwell, 1950); and William John Vernon, *Readings on the Inferno of Dante*, 2d ed. (London: Methuen, 1906). Vernon's *Readings* extend to the *Purgatorio* and *Paradiso* (London: Macmillan, 1897–1900).

Useful introductory studies are: Erich Auerbach, *Dante: Poet of the Secular World* (Chicago: University of Chicago Press, 1961);* Allan H. Gilbert, *Dante and His Comedy* (New York: New York University Press, 1963); Thomas Bergin, *From Time to Eternity* (New Haven: Yale University Press, 1967); Francis Fergusson, *Dante* (New York: Macmillan, 1966);* and *Discussions of the Divine Comedy*, ed. Irma Brandeis (Boston: Heath, 1961).*

More technical matters may be found in: Charles Singleton, *Dante Studies I* and *II* (Cambridge, Mass.: Harvard University Press, 1954–58); Erich Auerbach, "Figura," in his *Scenes from the Drama of European Literature* (New York: Meridian, 1959);* A. C. Charity, *Events and Their Afterlife* (Cambridge: Cambridge University Press, 1966); Robert Hollander, *Allegory in Dante's Commedia* (Princeton: Princeton University Press, 1969); and John G. Demaray, *The Invention of Dante's Comedy* (New Haven: Yale University Press, 1974). Two important older works are W. H. V. Reade, *The Moral System of Dante's Inferno* (Oxford: Clarendon Press, 1909); and Etienne Gilson, *Dante and the Philosopher* (New York: Sheed and Ward, 1949).*

*Paperbound available.

DON QUIXOTE

Maria DiBattista

The *Odyssey*, the *Aeneid*, and the *Divine Comedy* all share a common theme—the definition of the heroic personality. Odysseus, Aeneas, and Dante, of course, are dissimilar heroes. Each fills the heroic mold in his own way. Yet the mold itself has a formal integrity that ultimately minimizes their differences and emphasizes their similarities. Each hero is a representative man, an Everyman, and in that mutual identity their heroic careers coalesce. "Sing in me, Muse," begins Homer, "that man skilled in contending, the wanderer." The Odyssean hero is first defined characteristically—the man skilled in contending—then generically—man the wanderer. So, too Aeneas, whose piety does not exempt him from his fated odyssey. So, too, Dante, whose gentle heart and stern moralism are subsumed into the figure of Dante the Pilgrim. We are accustomed to defining man as *homo sapiens*, man knowing, but the epic poet concentrates on *homo viator*, man *traveling*. In *Don Quixote* we meet a comic avatar of the wanderer, the vagabond in the guise of knight-errant. Much of the comedy of *Don Quixote* depends on the generic and etymological link between the epic wanderer and the knight-errant. Errant—wandering—gives us our modern word *erring*—going off the right track. Andres, a victim of Quixote's generous illusions, who receives a whipping rather than deliverance from his cruel master, makes precisely this point. "God be with you, sir, and with all knights-errant, and may they be as erring to themselves as they have been to me.''

Don Quixote is perhaps the world's richest comedy of errors. The central idea of its comedy is a parody of chivalric romances, but the implications of the parody affect the epic form as well. The romance hero, like the epic Odyssean hero, must earn his identity through a series of encounters with military, moral, and metaphysical enemies. But whereas Odysseus must define himself against the infinite and enchanting world of the sea, the knight-errant is usually land-locked. For the knight-errant, as for Dante, all erring is in the Dark Wood. The enchanted wood in romance, like the sea in the *Odyssey*, is the environment of giants, enchanters, and enchantresses, of death-defying adventures. The geographies of epic and romance, then, are predisposed to the hero's quest. They provide him with a world in which heroism is possible. Cervantes, seizing upon this formula with a genius's instinct for comic possibilities, comes up with an interesting variation. He places an aspiring hero in a thoroughly demythologized landscape. What becomes of the hero when he is deprived of a heroic environment is one of the essential problems in *Don Quixote.*

Don Quixote's epithet, the Knight of La Mancha, is a clue to his ambiguous heroic status. ''La Mancha'' is a modified form of an Arabic word meaning dry earth, land that can neither retain the abundant waters of the epic nor support the lush vegetation of romance. This barren land forms part of the larger region of Spain called New Castile, the new land of Castles. The comic paradoxes of the novel are embedded in the physical landscape of Spain itself, a land where fabulous structures rise up from a devastated landscape. Unamuno has written beautifully about the desolate birthplace of Cervantes and his alter-ego, Don Quixote:

> It is a landscape that awakens no voluptuous sensations of joie de vivre. . . . Here are no lush green meadows inviting indolent repose. . . . Nature does not here recreate

the spirit. Rather it detaches us from the low earth and enfolds us in the pure naked unvarying sky. Here is no communion with nature, no absorption in her exuberant splendours. . . . Man is not lost in it so much as diminished by it, and in its immense drought he is made aware of the aridity of his own soul.

Out of this drought-plagued earth emerges the gaunt figure of Don Quixote, a man as wizened as the land over which he travels. Born into a land that, as Unamuno says, fails to re-create the spirit, Alonso Quijano, aged fifty, refreshes his arid soul by immersing himself in the tropical forests of romance. Where life is deficient, art is abundant. Quijano's madness begins to surface when he sells his arable land for books, exchanging nature's dubious fertility for the guaranteed bounties of art. This remedy of course proves temporary. Books end, and life goes on. So Quijano, finishing a book that concludes with the promise of endless adventures, feels inclined to take up his pen and finish it off himself. But he is diverted "by other plans and purposes of greater moment." He will not write the book of endless adventures; he will *live* that book.

Art, we may more or less agree, pretends to imitate life. But should life try to imitate art? That literature influences life is not new to us. In the *Divine Comedy*, Paolo and Francesca consummate their love as the sequel to Lancelot and Guinevere's kiss. Quixote, too, lives by the book, or, more precisely, lives the book itself. That a staid fifty-year-old man should believe it is necessary to become a knight-errant is, the narrator tells us, the oddest fancy that ever entered a madman's brain. It is an extraordinary conception, but a fertile one in its own way. Most mythic quest figures, pagan and Christian, are credited with miraculous origins; Oedipus's birth on Cithaeron, Christ's Immaculate Conception are familiar enough examples. Quixote puts them all to shame. He gives birth to himself, to the self he wants to be. He christens that ideal self "Don Quixote" and on that note of spontaneous self-generation Quijano justifies his name as "our imaginative hero." Cervantes ironically insists on Quixote's heroic nature. In a discussion of his literary ancestors—Ulysses, Aeneas, Amadis of Gaul—Quixote observes that these heroes are never described as they were, but as they should have been. They are not real, but ideal, figures. Quixote, by analogy, is also an exemplary hero, at once a celebration and a critique of the idealizing imagination. There is no higher form of imagination, as Unamuno suggests, than that which recreates the spirit; there is no higher form of madness than that which believes the self-created to be real.

Having created that ideal self, Quixote sallies out to live the book of endless adventures. That it is endless adventures he seeks is important. The concept of the unending story is central to the novel. Sancho at one point narrates one about goats ferried across the river. Such unending stories are ancient ones, their appeal answering to a desire both primitive and profound. Unending stories, by protracting, then finally eliminating, the conclusive end, suspend their subjects—be they goats or knight-errants—in the literary limbo of ceaseless life. To have endless adventures is to exist, like the Neutrals in Dante's Hell, neither in the world of the living nor the world of the dead. At one point Quixote, meeting up with the gypsy-rogue Gines Pasamonte, is informed that Gines is writing his autobiography. "Is it finished yet?" Quixote asks. "How can it be finished," answers Gines, "when my life isn't finished yet" (p. 215). What strikes us as comically obvious is actually at the heart of Quixote's quest. He wants the book of his life to take the ideal form of the unending story. This explains why Quixote is a hero who voluntarily goes into exile. His literary ancestor, Odysseus, feigned madness to escape conscription in the Achaean cause, and his subsequent odyssey is motivated by the sheer longing for return. Aeneas reluctantly leaves the ruins of Troy in search of the promised land. Dante is exiled from Florence, the City of Man, but is rewarded when he enters his true home, the City of God. They *want* to come home, the place of their marriage, their reign, their redemption. Don Quixote's final homecoming, the end of his career as an erring knight, coincides with his death. La Mancha is not the Promised Land—it is the Wasteland. Quixote is assured endless life as long as he is on the road. He is always complaining about the reversals of Fortune. "Our misfortunes can't last forever," he keeps reassuring the beleaguered Sancho. But Quixote's real hope lies not in the reversibility, but in the inexhaustibility of fortune. As long as he has adventures, fortunate or unfortunate, he is safe from serious mortal harm. So he sets across the arid plains of Castile, seeing in those dusty landscapes the mirage of his own deliverance into the "immortal" annals of romance.

It is the first sally that confirms Quixote's destiny. His mad escapades begin, appropriately enough, with Quixote conversing with himself, a monologue that parodies the traditional invocation to a Muse: "O thou wise enchanter, whosoever thou mayest be, whose duty is to chronicle this strange history" (p. 63). His opening soliloquy, like his adventures, is addressed to a nonexisting reality, a Muse that does not exist—yet. In chapter 9, Cervantes is compelled to create a fictional biographer—Cide Benengeli, one of the many instances in the novel in which illusion generates an answering reality. We as readers are obliged to accept Benengeli as the "true father" of Cervantes's imaginative offspring. "I am," says Cervantes in the prologue, "in reality his stepfather." Having insured that his deeds will be faithfully recorded by the proper Muse, Quixote then proceeds to an inn, which he calls the "palace of his redemption," to seek initiation into knighthood that culminates at the inn's horse-trough.

Quixote's vigil over the horse trough is in many ways the most serious test in his mad career. Previously, his mad fictions are subject to debate, not verification. Here, for the first time, they collide with a reality that actively resists them, and the impact releases the first in a series of farcical events. This scene, like many of Quixote's adventures—the

tryst with Maritornes, the killing of the giant wine skins—
takes place at night, again suggesting that the madman's
illusions are rooted in the dream world of idealized desire.
In Quixote's midsummer knight's dream, the horse trough
becomes an altar, his pasteboard armor, holy arms. We readily
appreciate the burlesque. The prosaic reality Quixote encounters undercuts his idealizing imagination. But, oddly
enough, Quixote succeeds in rescuing his vision of the sacred
from the profane. When muleteers threaten to desecrate his
altar by watering their mules at the trough, Quixote defends
his poetic appropriation of objects. He attacks those infidels
and he triumphs. The function of art, Malraux once noted,
is to *change* the nature of objects. Quixote succeeds in that
metamorphosis, transforming prosaic things into poetic objects. So complete is his victory over the muleteers that the
innkeeper, impressed with the madman's prowess, agrees to
officiate the dubbing ceremony. Using his straw and barley
account books as a sacred text, this ad hoc priest dubs
Quixote "with a hearty blow on the neck and a mighty
thwack on the shoulders" (p. 73). Quixote's madness is both
ridiculous and sublime, for it allows him to enlist the commonplace in the service—and search for—a sacred mission.

Inspired by his sense of a now divinely ordained quest,
Quixote sallies out from the inn (a temporary home) where
another adventure awaits him, the test of the crossroads. We
know from Oedipus and Dante the momentousness of such
threshold crossings. From Quixote we learn their arbitrari-
ness. Halting before a road that branches in four directions,
Quixote, following chivalric precedent, lets his mighty steed
Rozinante, whose name means the greatest hack horse in the
world, lead the way. And Rozinante does—right back to his
own stable. An animal's homing instinct, not divine Fate, sets
Quixote on his destined course. Rozinante reminds us of the
inevitability of homecoming, reminds us that the quest for
endless adventures is doomed to failure. "It is not my fault,
but the fault of my horse that I am stretched here," wails a

stricken Quixote to the group of traders who beat and desert him (p. 79). Injured, Quixote must return home. Rozinante leads the way.

But our imaginative hero is as yet undaunted. When he is finally rescued by a neighbor who insists Quixote is not a knight but the staid gentleman Master Quixana (or Quijano), Quixote firmly replies, "I know who I am." The Quixotic personality, a product of Quijano's militant faith in his illusion about himself, survives its rough contact with reality. Now a confirmed believer in his sacred destiny, the recuperating Quixote remains unbothered by "the pleasant and mighty inquisition held by the curate and barber on his library" (p. 80). Their literary witch-hunt, designed to cure Quixote's madness by removing its cause, proves to be too little and too late. Quixote has already been initiated into his faith. He accepts the confiscation of his library as the work of his mortal enemy, the enchanter Freston, he of the Malignant Eye. It is characteristic of Quixote to attribute his misfortunes to evil magicians. He thinks he is pursued by enchanters who want to deprive him of his glory. In fact, he is hounded by disenchanters who want to restore him to his senses. Here the barber, in his role as bleeder, and the curate, as spiritual adviser, are called in to consult on his case. It is they who have the malignant eye of disenchantment, misperceiving the nature and the necessity of Quixote's quest. They will appear again to bring Quixote home from his second excursion, still failing to see that curing may mean killing their mad patient.

It is the barber and the curate, then, not Sancho Panza, who are the stubborn realists, the anti-questers in *Don Quixote.* Sancho appears on the scene when their opposition to Quixote's quest is foiled. Sancho is a type of the heroic helper, a faithful guide or friendly magician who usually possesses a knowledge crucial to the successful completion of the hero's quest. The helper is a persistent figure in quest romances, from Dante's Virgil and Arthur's Merlin to the Lone Ranger's Tonto. Sancho, however, is not distinguished

by his special intelligence but by his little wit. It is tempting
to see Sancho as the exponent of reality in the knight's mad
equations. But the temptation ought to be resisted. Sancho
enlists in Quixote's cause in return for an island. What island?
Quixote's island, of course, an island only to be found in the
never-never lands of chivalric romances. Sancho is not a
skeptical realist. He is an illiterate peasant whose great expectations are founded in a literature he cannot even read.
"Sancho awake," the narrator reminds us, "was worse than
his master asleep, so greatly had the latter's promises turned
his brain" (p. 365). Quixote, on the other hand, is fully
aware of the "unreal" nature of Dulcinea's existence:

> For what I want of Dulcinea of El Toboso she is as good
> as the greatest princess in the land. . . . Do you think that
> the Amaryllises, the Phyllises, the Sylvias, the Dianas, the
> Galateas, and all the rest of which the books, the ballads,
> the barber shops, the comic theaters are full, were genu-
> inely ladies of flesh and blood and the mistresses of those
> who celebrated their charms? Certainly not. Most of
> them were invented to serve as subjects for verses and to
> enable poets to prove themselves lovers or capable of
> being such. [p. 249]

Quixote is content, as he says, to imagine and then believe in
the mistress who inspires his quest. He knows it is neither
necessary nor likely that Dulcinea be really flesh and blood.
Sancho, on the other hand, believes Quixote's world of
ideality to be real. Quixote's fertile imagination finds a breed-
ing ground in Sancho's empty head. "That was an unlucky
hour when you became impregnated with his promises, and
worse still when that island you crave entered your brain,"
cries the exasperated barber. "I'm not in child by anyone,"
retorts the offended Sancho (p. 476).

Sancho's perpetual confusion of the conceptual with the
literal is a clue to his function. Sancho does not represent the
real to Quixote's ideal. He is, rather, the thoroughly natural

man; his wisdom, to know what it means to have a body: "I come from my vineyards, I know nothing; what's more, Naked I was born, and naked am I now, I neither lose nor win" (p. 240). Sancho introduces the spiritualized Quixote to the world of the flesh. Sancho responds to all the calls of nature, thus giving Quixote a crash course in human physiology. In one such session, Sancho tries to coax Quixote to try some food. "How little you understand!" cries the frustrated knight:

> "In all the books I have delved into I have never found that knights-errant ate, unless by mere chance or at some costly banquets prepared in their honor . . . and although we know that they could not live without eating or without performing all the other functions of nature, because they were men like ourselves, yet it is clear that roaming as they did most of their lives through forests and uninhabited wastes without anybody to cook for them, their daily fare must have been coarse country food such as you offer me. Therefore, friend Sancho, do not be troubled about what pleases me, and do not try to make a new world or lift knight-errantry off its hinges."
>
> "Pardon me," [responds] Sancho, "seeing that I can neither read nor write . . . I've not yet understood the laws of the knight's profession." [p. 115]

The unwritten law of epic and romance is, of course, that heroes, although men, are never described in the ordinary situations of men. Even Homer, so faithful in describing the normative human world, sees all natural functions—eating, sleeping, making love—transfigured by their ritualistic, divine, or heroic context. Sancho, in insisting on the performance of natural functions purely as natural functions, threatens to lift the heroic world off its idealized hinges. In doing so, he does create a new world, the world of the novel, that innovative form rooted in a sense for the *facts* of life. Cervantes often interrupts Benengeli's narrative to praise the historian

for his exactness in details, however trivial. He holds up
Benengeli as an example to those "grave historians who give
us such brief accounts that we hardly get a taste of them, and
of carelessness, malice or ignorance leave in their inkhorns
the most substantial part of their work" (p. 156). *Substantial*
is the key word here, and it is Sancho, he of the mighty belly
and the keen eye for detail, who provides the novel with
much of its substance. "Eat Sancho, my friend," says Quixote.
"Sustain life, for you have more need of it than I, and let
me die a martyr to my thoughts and a victim of my misfortunes. I Sancho, was born to live dying, and you to die
eating . . ." (p. 946). Despite his good intentions, however,
Quixote, the aspiring martyr, must follow Sancho's example.
Sancho forces Quixote to amend his imaginative constructs
to allow for the body's contingencies. He must and does
accept the food Sancho offers. Quixote's acceptance of
Sancho's sustenance points to what Salvador de Madariaga
has termed the Sanchification of Don Quixote. Quixote's
ideal world—the world of romance—digests and assimilates
Santho's naturalistic world—the world of the novel.

As in all good mergers, however, the partnership works
both ways. The Sanchification of Don Quixote is counterbalanced by the Quixotification of Sancho Panza. The world
of daily life cannot coexist with the world of romance without eventually becoming itself transmuted. As the novel progresses, Sancho, initially contradicting Quixote's perceptions,
comes to accept his master's interpretations or misinterpre-
tations of reality until he becomes the only character to
believe that his master's words are Gospel truth. Like Shakespeare's Bottom, Sancho easily adjusts to the dream world
into which he is seduced. Sancho begins to flirt with Quixote's
idealism, often distrusting the evidence of his own senses. If
reality betrays illusion, the betrayer is neither the illusion nor
the reality, but the traitor Freston. Sancho, like Quixote,
becomes convinced of the necessity of enchantment when
reality is impoverished or inadequate. Thus only Sancho ex-

periences and comprehends the richness of Quixote's madness. It is a crazy alliance, but no more mismatched than the novel, that fictional form designed to incorporate the existential and the exemplary, the prosaic and the poetic, the real and the ideal. The knight and his squire do inhabit different worlds, but these worlds commingle rather than collide. Without Sancho, *Don Quixote* would be pure burlesque. The comic formula that determines the adventures of the first sally is relatively naive and straightforward. In each instance Quixote's illusions are pitted against a reality that contradicts them. The joke is always on Quixote, the laughter usually at his expense. With the addition of Sancho Panza, Cervantes complicates the comic equations by introducing a go-between between illusion and its antithetical reality. Sancho mediates between the world of sacred objects and the desacramentalized world of everyday life. He is a kind of referee, now deciding in favor of reality, now in favor of illusion. He sees windmills where Quixote sees giants. But he never doubts the reality of the island he has never seen. No man is without his illusions. The presence of Sancho turns Quixote's soliloquies addressed to an unsympathetic reality into real dialogues. The most important consequence of this dialogue is in creating the possibility that master and squire can laugh not only at, but with, each other.

The second sally relates the attempts of Quixote and Sancho together to revive the profession of knight-errantry in the modern world. Epics like the *Aeneid* or chivalric romances like *Amadis of Gaul* treat the dual theme of arms and the man, love and war. Love determines the knight's private destiny, war defines his worldly mission. The first leg of Quixote's and Sancho's journey is an extended exploration of the theme of love. Quixote's first important set speech is a disquisition on the Golden Age, that time before the "amorous pestilence" corrupted maidens, left widows unprotected and orphans undefended (p. 117 ff.). Quixote's subsequent adventures provide a condensed allegory of how the Golden

Age degenerated into the Age of Iron. The allegory is compressed into five key episodes: the army of sheep, the incident
with the corpse, the adventures of the mills, the transformation of the barber's basin into Mambrino's helmet, and the
freeing of the galley slaves.

The conversion of the two flocks of sheep into armies
parodies the medieval concept of the Holy War, the glorious
battle between Christian and Infidel. Quixote launches into a
mock-epic catalogue of the sheepish knights and, in the name
of Christian righteousness, charges into the flocks, spearing
the sheep as if they were his mortal enemies. This illusory
epic battle is followed by another adventure of ghosts, as
Sancho calls them, in Quixote's rescue of a corpse. The incident is suggestive of the death of knight-errantry: that the
corpse is no knight, as Quixote believes, but a holy man,
suggests that the Holy War between good and evil has always
been fought over spiritual, not earthly, ground. It is at this
point in his career, the moment when the Golden Age of
chivalry is pronounced dead beyond revival, that Sancho
christens Quixote with his new, this time fairly permanent,
epithet, the Knight of the Rueful Figure, "El Caballero de
la Triste Figura" (p. 183). Quixote's melancholia is rooted in
the demise of the medieval epic world. His next three adventures carry him further away from the objective theater of
the epic into the subjectivism of modern times. The adventures of the mills and the barber's basin are purely sensory
experiences, one in sound, the other in sight, and the encounter with the galley slaves is almost exclusively a verbal
rather than a military exchange. Quixote has moved from the
Golden Age to the Iron Age where men are "strung together
like beads on a great iron chain" (p. 209). The modern man
is not a knight, but a *picaro*, a Spanish word meaning gypsy-
rogue. The picaro is also a man of error, but his roving career
is motivated, not by a golden ideal, but by the iron shackles
of economic necessity. If the Golden Age is to be revived and
recovered, it is to be revived and recovered within. It is

finally love, the subjective power, not war, the power of arms, that can usher man into the ideal state; Eros, not Mars, that can reclaim the lost territory of innocence and social justice.

There are two ways that lead back to the Golden Age, one the avenue of romance—Quixote's route—the other the avenue of the pastoral—the route of the novel's distracted lovers. The pastoral represents an ancient and complicated tradition, but its central feature involves the retreat of unrequited lovers into the supportive world of nature. Quixote evokes and parodies this tradition during his penance in the Sierra Morena when he begins calling upon the "fauns and satyrs of the woods, on the nymphs of the streams, and on the damp and doleful echo to respond, console and listen" (p. 257). The diverse routes of the knight-errant and the shepherd converge in their mutual search for an environment that will respond, console, and listen to the needs of the human spirit.

All the lovers Quixote and Sancho meet—Marcela, Cardenio, Dorotea, Luscinda—are, like Quixote, disillusioned by their world. Their response to life's disappointments, like his, is to abandon life and assume a fictional identity. Where Quixote becomes a knight, the lover becomes a shepherd. Both transformations are equally ridiculous. Cardenio in rags is as absurd a figure as Quixote in pasteboard armor. Cervantes pointedly calls attention to their similarities when Cardenio, the Ragged One of the Sorrowful Figure, embraces Quixote, he of the Rueful Figure, "as though he had known him for a long time" (p. 229). It is one of the great recognition scenes in all of comedy, this embrace of melancholy madmen. The knight and the shepherd are both cases of literary self-stylization and both compete for dominion over the rocky wastes of the Sierra Morena. Theirs is properly a battle of madmen over literary domain. In part 2 of the novel, Cervantes will apologize that the pastoral interpolations of part 1 digress from rather than support the main plot of the story. We

should take his apology under advisement. The pastoral episodes are meant to compete with, not complement, the
novel's central parody of romance. They provide an alternate
parody of the psychology of idealization, this time as it
works its way into the pastoral mode. The ideal beauty of
Dulcinea, for example, is only equalled by the ideal beauty
attributed to the mistresses of the fanatical lovers. Each
lover believes his mistress to be unique in her beauty. The
love theme finally erupts in a sly parody of the Judgment of
Paris. When the beautiful Moor appears on the scene, the
question of the fairest of them all becomes quite comically
pressing. Taking off her veil, the lovely Moor reveals a face
"so lovely that Dorotea thought her more beautiful than
Luscinda, and Luscinda judged her lovelier than Dorotea,
while the others were of the opinion that if any woman was
the equal of those two in looks, it was the Moorish lady, and
some of them even considered that in certain ways she was
the loveliest of the three" (p. 386). In *Don Quixote*, of
course, all beauty contests end happily and everyone receives
a prize.

Quixote, however, perhaps sensing throughout these proceedings a possible usurpation of his imaginative powers of
idealization, unconsciously keeps interrupting the lovers'
narratives. He insists that of the two modes of imitation, the
romance form is the superior. It is only in part 2 of the novel,
when Quixote is forced to retire from the profession of
knight-errantry, that he seriously considers becoming a shepherd. The final irony of his career will be that the Arcadian
world he moves in throughout the greater portion of his adventures will become inaccessible the moment he has need
of it.

Quixote's defense of romance rests on its epic scope. Romance, that is, treats not only love but war. It is concerned
not only with individual lives but with the regulation of
human society. There is no doubt, Quixote argues, that as an
art the profession of arms surpasses all that men have in-

vented, for by arms, he explains, "states are defended, kingdoms are preserved, cities are protected, roads are made safe,
and seas cleared of pirates." "Indeed," he continues, "without arms, kingdoms, monarchies, cities, seaways, and land-
ways would be subject to the ruin and confusion that war
brings with it as long as it lasts and has license to use its
privileges and powers" (p. 390). Quixote's praise of the
superior profession of arms is immediately followed by the
Captive's story. This adventure in war, like the adventures
in love, seems, on first reading, one more improbable adventure in a book filled with improbable hapenings. Yet this is
the one story based on events in Cervantes's own life, the
period of his seven-year imprisonment in a Moorish prison.
Here truth does indeed seem stranger than fiction—or at least
on a par with it. As part 1 moves to its conclusion, the divid-
ing line between illusion and reality becomes increasingly
hard to locate. At the moment the captive is telling of his
"real" deliverance of the lovely Moor, Quixote is dreaming of
the deliverance of the "unreal" Princess Micomicona from a
wicked giant. Both miraculous deliverances take place at the
inn, the junction of all the novel's literary societies. Here the
picaresque world of rascally innkeepers, lusty wenches, and
muleteers, the pastoral society of lovers (Cardenio, Dorotea,
Luscinda, Don Fernando, Dona Clara, and Miguel), the profession of letters, represented by the Judge, and the profession of arms, Don Quixote and Sancho Panza, are unified in a
single literary community. It is the generous Quixote who
presides over this comic reunion. "There are no quarters so
cramped or so uncomfortable," he says to the Judge, "that
they cannot make room for arms and letters. Enter therefore, I pray, into this paradise, wherein you will discover
stars and suns to accompany the heaven your worship brings
with him. Here shall he find arms at their zenith and beauty
at its prime" (pp. 432-33). The Golden Age has been revived in the only place in which it existed—the spacious
quarters of a mythic mind.

The first act of this newly formed comic society is to decide on the question of Mambrino's helmet. To the outrage
of the barber, the unanimous vote is to award the basin-
helmet to Quixote. By this vote, the novel's society legislates
into the novel the law of illusion, and appoints Quixote the
executor of that law. Now illusion becomes the special
privilege, the unique authority, of the enchanted knight.
Their social contract becomes a form of the narrative contract in which we as readers willingly suspend our disbelief
in order to enter the enchanted worlds of fiction. That a man
of letters, the rogue-scholar Sanson Carrasco, will ultimately
be the one to disenchant Don Quixote, is one of the most
disturbing ironies of the novel. But it is after all perfectly apt
that a man of letters must put him to death since a man of
letters gave him life. Despite Quixote's wishes, no illusion,
however fruitful, lasts forever. However, *Don Quixote* never
courts the tragedy of disenchantment, not should we, its
delighted readers. Don Quixote's quest does succeed on the
only level possible for it to succeed, in bringing to the dry
earth of La Mancha and to the arid soul of Alonso Quijano
the life-giving waters of illusion. The last episode in part 1
describes Quixote's encounter with a group of penitents who
wander, like himself, throughout La Mancha "beseeching
Heaven to open the flood gates of its mercy and send them
rain" (p. 509). Quixote attacks the caravan, unaware of their
common quest: the replenishment of the exhausted, drought-
plagued earth, the refreshment of a barren life.

In part 2 of *Don Quixote* the barber, trying to dissuade
Quixote from his third and final sally, tells him a story of a
madman, believed cured and sane, saying farewell to his mad
inmate. The inmate, who believes himself to be Jupiter, the
god of Thunder, rises up and threatens to punish the ignorant city that lets his friend loose by refusing to rain on it for
three years. The cured madman remains unperturbed. "Take
no notice of what this lunatic says," he responds, "for if he
is Jupiter and will not rain, I am Neptune, the father and
god of waters, and I will rain as often as I please and when-

ever it is necessary" (p. 534). Quixote, though embarrassed by the anecdote, fails to see its central relevance to his situation. "I, Master Barber," he says, "am not Neptune, the god of the waters" (p. 535). Quixote, as always, is both right and wrong, off and on the right track. He sets out for, but only just reaches, the sea. Nor are the floodgates of heaven ever opened for him. But waters metaphorically abound in the bounteous inscapes of Quixote's imagination. He is not the liberal father of waters, but the prodigal son of the dry earth. *Don Quixote* is Cervantes's loving but ambiguous testament to a fertile, generous, and greatly erring spirit.

BIBLIOGRAPHICAL NOTE

Miguel de Cervantes was born in Alcalá de Henares in 1547 and died in Madrid in 1616. He published the first part of his *El Ingenioso Hidalgo Don Quixote de la Mancha* in 1605 and the second part in 1615.

I have used for this essay Walter Starkie's translation of *Don Quixote* (New York: Signet, 1964),* a fine, readable, and easily available version. J. M. Cohen's *Don Quixote* (Harmondsworth: Penguin, 1950)* is also worthy. Older standard translations are Peter Motteux's eighteenth-century version, *The Ingenious Gentleman, Don Quixote de la Mancha* (New York: Modern Library, 1930);* John Ormsby's *Don Quixote* (New York: Macmillan, 1885; frequently reprinted); and Samuel Putnam's *Don Quixote* (New York: Viking, 1949).

This essay, while drawing on the established critical canon on *Don Quixote*, is primarily indebted to the following works: Erich Auerbach's analysis of Cervantes's modes of representation in *Mimesis* (Princeton: Princeton University Press, 1953);* Jorge Luis Borges's suggestive readings and parables in *Labyrinths* (New York: New Directions, 1964)*; René Girard's view of fiction and mediated desire in *Deceit, Desire, and the Novel* (Baltimore: Johns Hopkins University Press, 1965); Miguel de Unamuno's writings on the Castilian ambiance of the novel in *Our Lord Don Quixote* (Princeton: Princeton University Press, 1967)*; and Dorothy Van Ghent's introductory essay in *The English Novel: Form and Function* (New York: Rinehart, 1953).*

Other important and useful works are Aubrey F. Bell, *Cervantes* (Norman, Oklahoma: Oklahoma University Press, 1947); Alban K. Forcione, *Cervantes and the Persiles* (Princeton: Princeton University

Press, 1970); *Cervantes: A Collection of Critical Essays*, ed. Lowry Nelson, Jr. (Englewood Cliffs, N.J.: Prentice-Hall, 1969);* Salvador de Madariaga, *Don Quixote: An Introductory Essay in Psychology* (London: Oxford: Clarendon Press, 1935); Jose Ortega y Gasset, *Meditations on Quixote* (New York: Norton, 1961);* Richard Predmore, *The World of Don Quixote* (Cambridge, Mass.: Harvard University Press, 1967).

For a general background to the later Renaissance period, I suggest a fine essay by Thomas Greene, "The Flexibility of the Self in Renaissance Literature," in *The Disciplines of Criticism*, ed. Peter Demetz, Thomas Greene, and Lowry Nelson, Jr. (New Haven: Yale University Press, 1968), pp. 241–64. Also helpful is Wylie Sypher's *Four Stages of Renaissance Style* (Garden City, N.Y.: Doubleday, 1955).* For an excellent essay on modes of picaresque fiction, I suggest Claudio Guillén's "Towards a Definition of the Picaresque," in his *Literature as System: Essays Towards the Theory of Literary History* (Princeton: Princeton University Press, 1971).

*Paperbound available.

ULYSSES

Michael Seidel

In October 1921 a famous Irishman responded by letter to a request from Sylvia Beach, Joyce's publisher, that he purchase a subscription to *Ulysses* upon its release on February 2, 1922, Joyce's fortieth birthday:

Dear Madam,

I have read several fragments of *Ulysses* in its serial form. It is a revolting record of a disgusting phase of civilisation; but it is a truthful one; and I should like to put a cordon round Dublin; round up every male person in it between the ages of 15 and 30; force them to read it; and ask them whether on reflection they could see anything amusing in all that foul mouthed, foul minded derision and obscenity. To you, possibly, it may appeal as art: you are probably (you see I don't know you) a young barbarian beglamoured by the excitements and enthusiasms that art stirs up in passionate material; but to me it is all hideously real; I have walked those streets and known those shops and taken part in those conversations. I escaped from them to England at the age of twenty; and forty years later have learnt from the books of Mr. Joyce that Dublin is still what it was, and young men are still drivelling in slackjawed blackguardism just as they were in 1870. It is, however, some consolation to find that at

least somebody has felt deeply enough about it to face
the horror of writing it all down and using his literary
genius to force people to face it. In Ireland they try to
make a cat cleanly by rubbing its nose in its own filth.
Mr. Joyce has tried the same treatment on the human
subject. I hope it may prove successful. . . .

G. Bernard Shaw

Ulysses, for George Bernard Shaw, is comic narrative gone
sour—little but an exercise in naturalistic putrefaction. This
was the early reaction to his novel that Joyce most feared.
But another tack was taken against *Ulysses* even before its
publication. Joyce's Irish narrative was less "a revolting
record of a disgusting phase of civilisation" than an elaborate parody of literature's culture epics, a "poached epic,"
as Ezra Pound called it, a maze of correspondences, puns,
puzzles, and buried allusions. *Ulysses* was bizarre, difficult,
perhaps even subversive—the British censorship office sus-
pected several episodes were written in code when Joyce
mailed manuscript copies from Zurich during World War I.
Much later, Oliver St. John Gogarty, the stage-Irish Buck
Mulligan of *Ulysses*, wrote that "only in America could Joyce
be taken seriously, the country *par excellence* of the detective story, the crossword puzzle, and the smoke signal."

The opening words of *Ulysses*, "Stately plump," in reference
to Mulligan as pseudo-priest, provide an initial compressed
clue to the double structure of the novel. A stately form, an
epic, suffers its mockingly plump deformation to share
parodic space. *Ulysses* keeps its epic memories and liberates
its mocking antitypes. Double worlds and double spaces
continue to measure the day. The epic hero is a parodied
urbanite, the spinner of marvelous yarns is a modern ad man,
the kingly husband is a pathetic cuckold, the epic queen is an
overweight lethargic Dublin soprano, the princely son is a
puling Jesuit aesthete. Joyce's comic genius encourages his
readers to circulate in both the greater and smaller day of

Dublin's limits, and to see Dubliners both for what they resemble and what they are in his novel's expanding narrative.
Ulysses always sustains its double vision. At one point in
the "Circe" episode of the novel, we hear the refrain of a
moth, Bloom's paternal grandfather metamorphosed and
reduced:

> I'm a tiny tiny thing
> Ever flying in the spring
> Round and round a ringaring.
> Long ago I was a king,
> Now I do this kind of thing.

[p. 517]

The refrain is emblematic of Joyce's novel, in which kings
of long ago are imaged in down-at-heel European Jews.
Bloom is like his grandfather. Long ago he was a Homeric
king, now he only sees himself as the citizen Mr. Leopold
Bloom, who does the "kind of thing" he can—he recalls a
few entropic anagrams when asked to expand his name in
"Ithaca":

> Leopold Bloom
> Ellpodbomool
> Molldopeloob
> Boolopedoom
> Old Ollebo M.P.

[p. 678]

For Joyce, however, Bloom is always, potentially, the
wandering or returned ghost, the hero of migratory quest
epics. Elements of his day touch upon important patterns
in previous literary documents from the Old and New Testa-
ments to the *Odyssey* to the *Divine Comedy* to *Don Quixote*.
Bloom repeats the trials of exile and the joys of homecoming,
the agony of betrayal and the subtle pleasure of revenge.
Bloom is an allroundman, a watered-down Odysseus, Hamlet *père*, and Parnell. For expanded measure Joyce also sees

him as Everyman, the Wandering Jew, Sinbad the Sailor, Robinson Crusoe, Rip Van Winkle, and even the Apollonian god of the rising sun, "Darkinbad the Brightdayler." This is more than a sequence of literary allusions for Joyce; it is a way of embedding the long progress of the Western culture epic into local territory for local extraction on June 16, 1904. Narrative is partially movement for Joyce, and movement is a form of translation, a figurative carrying across to new places and new times. Joyce merely changes the radical mode of epic presentation for his Dublin odyssey.

One learns a good deal about the fictional strategies of *Ulysses* by plotting the transitions from the confirming and repetitive structures of past narratives to the novel's represented Dublin world. Joyce refines a set of literary techniques for fictional translation, and he names these techniques. The best clues for how to read Joyce are found *in* Joyce. For *Finnegans Wake* he even included in the text its own authorized commentary, but in earlier works Joyce simply focuses on key words, words like *epiphany*, *metempsychosis*, and *parallax*, all of which mean something in one context and define a narrative process in another. In *Stephen Hero*, for instance, Joyce uses the word *epiphany*, a Twelfth Night revelation, a showing forth, to name a process in which the artist arrests time and connects space. The large-scale epiphanies of *Ulysses* occur when Joyce's naturalistic Dublin plot connects with incidents from the Mediterranean *Odyssey*. Smaller-scale epiphanies can even take the form of a pun. Puns are, after all, miniature signals of connected meaning; and for that reason are important for Joyce from the early pages of *Portrait* to the polyglot spaces of *Finnegans Wake*. To take an example from *Ulysses*: Bloom recalls how Molly refers to a particularly heavyset Dublin singer, a bass-baritone named Dollard, as a "bass barreltone." Even Bloom sees the aptness of the pun, the connection, the linguistic epiphany linking register and girth: "it all works out in the end," he says. What is true for the pun is true for the novel. It, too, all works out in the end—Bloom huddled at Molly's posterior as the day rounds to a conclusion in "Penelope," the final homecoming narrative movement.

Not only do connected events give *Ulysses* its expanding shape, but so do accretive events. Early in the day, Molly Bloom gets confused about the meaning of the word *metempsychosis*. "Met-him-pike-hoses," is Molly's best effort— "Who's he when he's at home?" Bloom patiently explains: "It's Greek: from the Greek. That means the transmigration of souls" (p. 64). He goes on: "Some people believe . . . that we go on living in another body after death, that we lived before. They call it reincarnation" (p. 65). For the reader responsive to epic form, *Ulysses* must, in part, be read as a reincarnated and reincarnating narrative—its texture is the literary metempsychosis of personality through time.

For Joyce's novel, history keeps repeating itself like the Platonic year. Bloom, however, points out an important qualification: "History repeats itself, but with a difference" (p. 382). Earlier in the day he came upon another Greek word, *parallax*, and recalled his musings on metempsychosis: "Par it's Greek: parallel, parallax. Met him pikehoses she called it till I told her about the transmigration" (p. 154). In optics, parallax is a measure of apparent displacement when the same object is viewed from more than one fixed point. Parallax hints at another epiphanic structure in *Ulysses*. Bloom is a Greek hero by displacement, a reincarnated Odysseus with a measurable difference. Metempsychosis is repetition; parallax is differentiation. Joyce generates an expansive plot for his novel by allowing repetition and differentiation to occur at the same time. And it is this expansion that allows us to speak of the formal order that *Ulysses* can bring to its one epic and naturalistic day.

Whatever happens in the restricted narrative time of *Ulysses* can be reduced and magnified, debased and revalued. But because Joyce encourages temporal, spatial, and modal adjustments there remains something confirming about the deeper structure of *Ulysses*. As a narrative it revolves around its own axis and around the axis of an entire narrative tradition; it records and rerecords its own time and time through the ages; it remembers itself as it progresses through versions of itself. The eighteen-hour, day-night vision of a city and its citizens is a reduced epic schema: wandering and homecoming. And the day is capped by Molly Bloom's monologue, a feminine ending that mimics the turns and returns of the earth's motion.

The cyclic structure of *Ulysses* is itself part of a special kind of fable. In many of the epics discussed in this volume it is possible to see a plot, a narrative movement, resolving with the fulfillment of a specific goal or with the achievement of a cultural objective. Epic narrative usually moves in linear fashion toward an ameliorative or, in the case of the *Aeneid* and the *Divine Comedy*, a teleological end. The *Iliad* provides a perspective on its own ending when Priam and Achilles measure the tone of events that will lead to the inevitable Greek victory. The *Aeneid* lays the necessary groundwork for the Roman *imperium* that will become manifest in time. In the circular movement through the rings of Dante's *Inferno* there is an implied linear movement toward Purgatory and Paradise. Even in the comic variety of romance-epic fiction, we see in the widening circles of Don Quixote's wanderings a progress out of lunacy and into psychic peace. For Joyce, however, the straight line always bends and curves, beginnings and ends touch at the same point. Joyce was interested in progression as the potential for continuation, and it is not mere coincidence that he chose the *Odyssey* as a narrative model. Joyce is drawn to the *Odyssey* partly because of its cyclic, potentially renewable structure. Movement toward resolution in that Homeric poem is not as direct a line as it might seem. We know from Dante what Homer only hinted—Odysseus sails west again toward the rim of the world in trying to extend the world. Inevitably, Odysseus repeats himself; he marks the path of the sun (*di retro al sol*) past the Pillars of Hercules, past the Straits of Gibraltar. Joyce repeats Odysseus in Dublin by extending the epic line as it circles the earth—extending the line which follows the cyclic track of the sun northwest to Ireland. Molly Bloom, of course, has spent half her life on Gibraltar near the legendary isle of the *Odyssey*'s Calypso. Joyce, in effect, takes up where Homer and Dante leave off. Molly's move to Dublin provides a Mediterranean substance for Joyce's larger translation. And in the "Calypso" episode of *Ulysses*, Joyce has Leopold Bloom give voice to the idiom of the novel's revolving axis: "Somewhere in the east: early morning: set off at dawn, travel round in front of the sun, steal a day's march on him. Keep it up for ever never grow a day older technically" (p. 57). Technically, then, Bloom is a solar hero—he is the Darkinbad Brightdayler whose end is his beginning. Bloom includes in his limited library at 7 Eccles street a volume bound in yellow cloth with running heads at the top of the page repeating the title, *In the Track of the Sun.*

To follow (or precede) the sun west is, ultimately, to seek its origins in the east. Bloom, the easterner, the Dublin Semite, observes in that chapter of renewals, "Nausicaa," that "the longest way round is the shortest way home" (p. 377). The process repeats daily for the sun and elliptically in time for the hero, epic or comic. Bloom's limits are his extensions. The questioner of "Ithaca" asks of Bloom:

> Would the departed never nowhere nohow reappear?
> Ever he would wander, selfcompelled, to the extreme limit of his cometary orbit, beyond the fixed stars and variable suns and telescopic planets, astronomical waifs and strays, to the extreme boundary of space, passing from land to land, among peoples, amid events. Somewhere imperceptible he would hear and somehow reluctantly, suncompelled, obey the summons of recall. [pp. 727–28]

This is obviously comic, comic in that Bloom imagines Molly placing a missing person's ad for him in the newspaper;

but also in that it is meant to be comically hyperbolic. Bloom, finally, prefers the comforts of bed to the uncertainties of a cometary elliptical journey. Motion in cyclic literary form is the prelude to rest before *re*newed motion. The last we see of Bloom, the parodic traveler, he is in his own bed, at motion and at rest at the same time, in the fetal position lying next to Molly, the earth goddess Gaea-Tellus, Joyce's ever-turning, ever-renewing body divinity. Molly, from Gibraltar, and Bloom, native Irish Semite, continue the path of epic narrative beyond Homer's Mediterranean. It serves Joyce well that Molly Bloom is the fictional matrix from which the day and the novel can be born again in Ireland:

> In what directions did listener and narrator lie?
> Listener, S.E. by E.: Narrator, N.W. by W.: on the 53rd parallel of latitude, N. and 6th meridian of longitude, W. at an angle of 45° to the terrestrial equator.
> In what state of rest or motion?
> At rest relatively to themselves and to each other. In motion being each and both carried westward, forward and rereward respectively, by the proper perpetual motion of the earth through everchanging tracks of neverchanging space. [pp. 736–37]

The recurring sense of rest and daily renewal, the earth's gift of infinite chances, is perhaps the most affirmative sense in which *Ulysses* can be read. Molly's proof of the existence of God is simply that the sun comes up every morning. Cyclic form encourages both continuity and hope. Joyce's fiction always turns in and then around on itself. The very title of his last book, *Finnegans Wake*, is as much a pun on repeated structures as is *Ulysses*. In fact, the title is a multiple pun on revivified forms: Finnegan's wake, that is, Finnegan's death, Finnegan at ultimate rest; and Finn, a mythical reincarnated Irish hero, is again awake. We have an epiphanized version of death and rebirth, resolution and renewal.

Joyce never deserted this basic structure. The note of all

poets, as Mulligan puts it, is "the white death and the ruddy birth" (p. 267). In *Ulysses*, two events of natural import occur during the day: a funeral and a birth. Paddy Dignam is buried and a son is born to Mina Purefoy. As Bloom says, confusing the line from the Burial Service but inadvertently describing the paradigmatic form of *Ulysses*, "In the midst of death we are in life. Both ends meet." (p. 108). In one of Joyce's significant little fictional gestures, Bloom also points out that the medical student, Dixon, who had treated him a few days before for a bee sting at the *Mater Misericordiae* near his home on Eccles street has transferred to the lying-in hospital on Holles street. The *Mater* is the ward for incurables, the death ward; in Holles street hospital, the obstetric ward, new life. Bloom says of Dixon, "He's gone over to the lying-in hospital they tell me, from one extreme to the other" (p. 97). This miniature fable even works out geographically in Dublin. Renewal replicates the path of the sun: the Holles street hospital, the matrix, is in the east of the city, the orient or origin; and the *Mater* in the northwest, the land of the setting sun.

The movement of the day, the reinvigoration of a westward dying sun by an eastern rising one, explains a good deal in *Ulysses*. It hints at the potential in the relationship between Bloom and Stephen (even if that potential is unrealized in a single day's action), but in addition it helps explain Joyce's obsession with cycles, solar cycles, female cycles, defecatory cycles. Joyce begins his novel at the point the human body is sundered from the womb—the first chapter therefore has its *omphalos* or navel, in the form of the Martello Tower ("ours is the *omphalos*," says Mulligan). And the progress of the day ends ready to begin the bodily cycle (and narrative cycle) again—with Bloom returned and reconciled in "Ithaca" as the "childman weary, the manchild in the womb" (p. 737). *Ulysses* is a day and a life; a novel with "embodied" form. For every wandering there is a cyclic return; for every sundering at the navel chord, as Stephen Dedalus puts it, there is a reconciliation. In "Lestrygonians" Bloom thought about the process of digestion, the interior journey, the cyclic "tour round the body." Naturally, the chapter ends with Bloom darting into the National Museum where he would, among other things, examine the mesial groove of the statue of Aphrodite for a posterior rectal orifice. Of course, at the end of *Ulysses*, Bloom rests next to Molly's posterior. For Bloom, as for Joyce, even the ideal in human form ought to be fitted with an end so that it might begin again. Vitality demands as much, and renewed vitality is part of the subject of Joyce's novel. In the final chapters of *Ulysses*, Dublin, the city of the dead and the dying, can have the sun shine for it, a city infused with the epic light of an orient and Mediterranean sun. In "Ithaca" Bloom at home in his yard stands and contemplates the apparition of a new solar disk in the eastern skies. Another of the novel's ghosts returns for a space of time as the day readies to repeat.

At the very simplest level, the plot of *Ulysses* might be summed up by the two words ending the overture section of the "Sirens" episode: "Done, Begin" (p. 257). Narrative, like the music of this episode and like life itself, aspires to formulaic repetition. Another of the novel's musical interludes allows Stephen Dedalus a say on the matter of rest and resolution in life and art. Epiphanic forms are again working in miniature to substantiate the larger narrative forms of the novel. In "Circe," Stephen sits at the pianola in the brothel banging out a series of "empty fifths" on the keyboard. A fifth is the fifth note in an octave progression, as far as one's ear is musically willing to move from the tonic note before the resolving voyage back to the octave. Fifths are, by their nature, irresolute if isolated. When Stephen begins to talk, as he will, about the resolution of the octave, he dwells on another instance of rest-renewal, parallax history repeating itself with a difference. As he will later put it in the voice of Phillip Sober in "Circe": "If I could only find out about octaves, reduplication of personality" (p. 518). The eighth note of an octave replicates the initial tone with exactly twice (or half) as many vibrations per second—the muse-mathematics is Stephen's version of metempsychosis. Earlier, at the pianola, Stephen contemplates what he is doing and finds himself on the subject of artistic resolution. He addresses himself to a talking hat, not odd in "Circe," an episode of transformations. "The rite is the poet's rest," says Stephen in reference to musical modes. The cap sees only paradox in cyclic aesthetics, and, in fact, mocks the very paradox upon which so much of *Ulysses* is constructed, the reincarnation of the Greek Odysseus in the Jew Bloom:

> *The Cap* (*with saturnine spleen*). Bah! It is because it is. Woman's reason. Jewgreek is greekjew. Extremes meet. Death is the highest form of life. Bah!
>
> *Stephen.* You remember fairly accurately all my errors, boasts, mistakes. How long shall I continue to close my eyes to disloyalty? Whetstone!
>
> *The Cap.* Bah!
>
> *Stephen.* Here's another for you. (*He frowns.*) The reason is because the fundamental and the dominant are separated by the greatest possible interval which . . .
>
> *The Cap.* Which? Finish. You can't.
>
> *Stephen* (*with an effort*). Interval which. Is the greatest possible ellipse. Consistent with. The ultimate return. The octave. Which.
>
> *The Cap.* Which?
>
> (*Outside the gramophone begins to blare* The Holy City.)
>
> *Stephen* (*abruptly*). What went forth to the ends of the world to traverse not itself. God, the sun, Shakespeare, a commercial traveller, having itself traversed in reality itself, becomes that self. Wait a moment. Wait a second. Damn that fellow's noise in the street. Self which it it-

self was ineluctably preconditioned to become. *Ecco*!
[pp. 504–05]

Stephen, of course, is talking about the expansive structure
of *Ulysses* whether he knows it or not. Expanded personality,
metempsychosis, is analogous to musical space and, finally,
to epic and mythic space. God, the sun, Shakespeare, and the
commercial traveler, Bloom, all follow an elliptical path, an
interval consistent with an "ultimate return": homecoming.
The naturalistic wanderings of the day are unresolved pro-
gressions, noises in the street that we first heard in the
"Nestor" episode. Noise in an urban novel is equivalent to
the dominant note in a musical chord. In "Circe" the noise in
the street is followed by Stephen's Italian expression, *Ecco*,
meaning "here it is," but *ecco* gives us homonymous pause:
an echo is a repeat, perhaps at the octave. Cyclic structure,
musical or narrative, sounds to sound again, returns to begin
again. In *Ulysses*, Bloom returns in "Penelope" to where he
began in "Calypso." "Penelope" and "Calypso" are, in a
sense, an octave apart, as Stuart Gilbert recognized long ago.
Molly's final, eight-sentence monologue reproduces the
structure yet again, and her "melonous" rump is a fundamental of sorts for the wandering hero. When Bloom returns
to Molly's musical spaces he brings the day back from an
urban ocean of troubles to a body of land: dominant to fundamental.

We can carry the musical model a bit further. *Ulysses* is
constructed so that the main characters, Stephen, Bloom,
and Molly, control the narrative voices in the beginning, the
middle, and the end of the novel, respectively. The movement of the novel, however, is mostly through Dublin city.
Dublin's voice is the dominant note; resolution can only be
a family matter. The day's action and the novel's voices rest
to renew near home. It is no coincidence, then, that Joyce
reserves his most elaborate and funniest sequence of verbal
"noises" for the episodes in his novel most closely associated
with the city. Parody is when the epic is furthest from home.

The degenerating newspaper headlines in "Aeolus" signal the beginning of the interval, the change of narrative voice. And the full-blown newspaper parodies in "Cyclops" continue the ellipse. "Circe," of course, is all noise. Parody, after all, is the middle of two extremes; it mediates between remembered and potential conditions, and it resolves neither.

The bulk of the day in *Ulysses*—and here is where we can return to Shaw's reaction to the novel cited at the beginning of this essay—is naturalistic and city-oriented. Joyce represents a world of material stuff and forms without a sense of fulfilled or fulfilling movement. There are few values and little plot in the ennui of a land's or a culture's urban metempsychosis. Bloom considers his errant "space" in the "Lestrygonians" episode:

> Cityful passing away, other cityful coming, passing away too: other coming on, passing on. Houses, lines of houses, streets, miles of pavements, piledup bricks, stones. Changing hands. This owner, that. Landlord never dies they say. Other steps into his shoes when he gets his notice to quit. They buy the place up with gold and still they have all the gold. Swindle in it somewhere. Piled up in cities, worn away age after age. Pyramids in sand. Built on bread and onions. Slaves. Chinese wall. Babylon. Big stones left. Round towers. Rest rubble, sprawling suburbs, jerrybuilt, Kerwan's mushroom houses, built of breeze. Shelter for the night.
> No one is anything. [p. 164]

Dublin is here potential without actualization, wandering without homecoming, dominant without fundamental. "No one is anything" counters the principle of metempyschosis. No Dublin home is complete without "Plumtree's potted meat"—that is, without a corpse. The city can be the negative embodiment of a civilized ideal, a paradox, a bloodless "Heart of the Hibernian Metropolis." During much of the day in *Ulysses* Dublin is a city of blowhards and gutter slang, a city of no men. Any city, modern or otherwise, ought to suggest a battle well fought and well won with the limiting factors of environment. In *Ulysses*, urban biology thrives apart from the needs of any of the citizens who live in the city, or it caters to those needs with pubs and brothels. The city is labyrinthine, as Joyce called it in the schema for his "Wandering Rocks" episode, and movement in it is frustrating: "a fatiguing day," says Bloom in late evening, "a chapter of accidents."

It is Dublin itself that most resists Joyce's literary sense of affirming epic structure, and the migratory epic risks stymied motion amidst the many none-too-silent partners in the urban corporation: drunkenness, poverty, chauvinism, sentimentality. Figures like Cashel Boyle O'Connor Fitzmaurice Tisdall Farrell parody epic movement by walking all day long in circles; figures like Mr. Breen appear directionally and sexually confused (U.P.: up); and figures like Paddy Dignam, the Citizen, Gerty MacDowell's father, and Simon Dedalus turn what substance they have to drink. To Simon Dedalus, for instance, Dublin life is death. He says to his daughter: "Wouldn't care if I was stretched out stiff. He's dead. The man upstairs is dead" (p. 238). Dead fathers are the bane of the *Odyssey*, but *Ulysses* is filled with them. Master Dignam remembers his "pa":

> A big coffin it was, and high and heavylooking. How was that? The last night pa was boosed he was standing on the landing there bawling out for his boots to go out to Tunney's for to boose more and he looked butty and short in his shirt. Never see him again. Death, that is. Pa is dead. My father is dead. [p. 251]

Ireland sober is Ireland stiff, and, as Bloom says, a Dubliner's home is his coffin. The day voice of urban Dublin is at best quaintly paralytic, at worst destructive of the novel's sense of renewal. And the city's night voice is no better. In "Circe," the Nighttown chapter, all the petty humiliations that Bloom, the citizen, has experienced for years in Dublin erupt from an underworld of fantasies, fears, and projections. The setting in "Circe" is unsteady, unsure—the chapter suffers, as the whore Zoe says, from locomotor ataxy. Early in the episode, an unseemly night wanderer, a deaf-mute with Saint Vitus's dance, moves past mocked by a gaggle of children. Later, Bloom is almost run down by a monster sand strewer on the tram tracks. Regardless of fault, Bloom is subjected to the indignity of insult at a moment's notice in Dublin: "Hey shitbreeches," the driver shouts, "are you doing the hatrick?" In correspondence with the "Circe" parallel in the *Odyssey*, movement becomes difficult in Nighttown, events transfigurative, hallucinatory, and bestial. In the hallucinations of the episode, old ladies squat to micturate, maimed armless men playfight outside a pub. Strange rituals of masochism and sadomasochism occur in the Black Mass that is part of the chapter's debased structure. Joyce had described the Catholic Mass to his brother Stanislaus as another returned-ghost story, a latter-day return, having the .same structure as the perilous mission of epic romance. The debasement of the Mass, whether by Mulligan in "Telemachus" or by the narrative voice of "Circe," subverts the very idea of mission—the very idea of quest or movement. This is deadly in a migratory epic where movement itself implies mythic reinvigoration.

It becomes clear in "Circe," *Ulysses'* city of dreadful night, that if the dominant urban world of the interior episodes of *Ulysses*, those Joyce called the wanderings, does not find its fundamental resolution, the question of homecoming in the novel will be a moot one. But it is in Nighttown that Bloom stops and considers what his efforts at mission are gaining him—whether one city victim (himself) is wasting his time trying to assist another victim (the lapwing Dedalus). "Wild goose chase this," mumbles Bloom in "Circe," "What am I following him for?" In this literal dump, Bloom puts into words what he is going to do for the first time in regard to Stephen, and then he acts upon it. He renews movement: "Still," says Bloom, "he's the best of the lot." The task is to get the drunken Dedalus out of Nighttown and home. After "Circe," and after a sobering session at the shelter in "Eumaeus," the burden of resolution is taken off the novel's urban world. Whatever finally happens at Eccles street, Bloom's home, the attempt says more than the result, the potential more than the realization. The three characters of prime importance in *Ulysses* are under one roof for a time. When Molly finally takes over the narrative, she rounds out the day and the novel. As Joyce observed in a famous letter to Budgen, her eight sentences turn like "the huge earthball slowly surely and evenly round and round spinning." Molly leaves her bed during the episode only to use the chamber pot—micturition and menstruation occur, the waters of the body and the cycles of the moon (Molly's mother, a Spanish Jewess, is appropriately named Lunita). Bloom rests at Molly's feet after he completes his elliptical orbit, a wanderer like the stars.

With full recognition of the human comedy and the cyclic comedy, Joyce tries in the final chapter of *Ulysses* to make his lone commercial traveler and his Dublin soprano meaningful in all their orbits. Molly takes us where she has been before, from Gibraltar to Howth Hill, from one bloom to another. On Gibraltar she had invented a lover to stay the advances of another lover. That invented lover, Don Miguel de la Flora, returns from her past and becomes her future: Don Poldo de la Flora of Howth Hill, Dublin. Life's and love's sweet song returns. The novel closes from the Mediterranean to Ireland, from "Gibraltar as a girl where I was a Flower of the mountain yes." The path is that of personal memory and epic renewal. It substantiates Joyce's narrative translation.

BIBLIOGRAPHICAL NOTE

James Joyce was born in Dublin in 1882 and died in Zurich in 1941. *Ulysses* was published in 1922 by Sylvia Beach's Shakespeare & Co. in

Paris. The first thirteen chapters of the novel appeared in serial form beginning in 1918 in the magazine *Little Review*. Installment publication broke off in 1920.

The essay is in debt to many critics of *Ulysses* and to a good deal of information about the book that seems to have been absorbed almost anonymously into the critical canon. I can only cite those works that I find most immediately useful: Robert Martin Adams, *James Joyce: Common Sense and Beyond* (New York: Random House, 1966);* Frank Budgen, *James Joyce and the Making of Ulysses* (Bloomington: Indiana University Press, rev. ed., 1961);* Richard Ellmann, *Ulysses on the Liffey* (New York: Oxford University Press, 1972);* Stuart Gilbert, *James Joyce's Ulysses* (New York: Knopf, 1930; rev. ed., London: Faber, 1952);* S. L. Goldberg, *The Classical Temper: A Study of James Joyce's Ulysses* (London: Chatto and Windus, 1961);* *James Joyce's Ulysses: Critical Essays*, ed. Clive Hart and David Hayman (Berkeley: University of California Press, 1974); Richard M. Kain, *Fabulous Voyager, James Joyce's Ulysses* (Chicago: University of Chicago Press, 1947); Hugh Kenner, *Dublin's Joyce* (Bloomington: Indiana University Press, 1956);* Harry Levin, *James Joyce, A Critical Introduction* (Norfolk, Conn.: New Directions, 1941).*

Richard Ellmann's biography, *James Joyce* (New York: Oxford University Press, 1959),* is indispensable for students of Joyce, as is the complete collection, *Letters of James Joyce*, Vol. 1, ed. Stuart Gilbert (New York: Viking, 1957), Vols. 2 and 3, ed. Richard Ellmann (New York: Viking, 1966). For Joyce's methods of composition, I recommend Phillip F. Herring's *Joyce's Ulysses Notesheets in the British Museum* (Charlottesville: University of Virginia Press, 1972) and A. Walton Litz's *The Art of James Joyce* (London: Oxford University Press, 1961).* For reference, I suggest Harry Blamires, *The Bloomsday Book: A Guide Through Joyce's Ulysses* (London: Methuen, 1966);* Don Gifford with Robert J. Seidman, *Notes for Joyce: An Annotation of James Joyce's Ulysses* (New York: Dutton, 1974);* Weldon Thornton, *Allusions in Ulysses* (Chapel Hill: University of North Carolina Press, 1969);* and William York Tindall, *A Reader's Guide to James Joyce* (New York: Noonday Press, 1959).* For an expansion of some of the ideas presented in this essay 'and for a much more detailed analysis of Joyce's use of Homeric material, I refer readers to my own study, *Epic Geography: James Joyce's Ulysses* (Princeton: Princeton University Press, 1976).

*Paperbound available.

THE DRAMATIC TRADITION

THE *ORESTEIA*

Michael Holahan

Greek drama, we should remember, is Athenian drama. All
the extant plays are by Athenians. More important, they exhibit a sense of public life that continually refers beyond the
theater of Dionysus to the surrounding city-state. Because
of this concern for a civic world, we should also remember
the circumstances of their composition. They were written
to compete in city festivals that marked days of religious
worship; the very structure of these plays developed from
earlier rituals of choral dance and song. In addition, they
were publicly financed, produced, viewed, and judged. The
actors and the chorus were for the most part citizens, not
professionals, and when not themselves performing they
joined a large, alert, and demanding audience. In short,
Athenian drama constituted a public event uniting religious
observance, different performing arts, communal organization, festivity, and even (in the votes selecting prize-winning
plays) an emblem of civic decision. For these reasons, and
because of a remarkable impulse to discern the universal in
the particular, Athenian drama is also essentially Greek. And
with good reason. After a breathtaking series of triumphs
against the Persian Empire, a fifth-century Athenian could
justly regard his city as the shield and flower of Greece.

For Aeschylus, the epithet *Athenian* held a special value.
It is the title of honor he bears in his epitaph, which records

rather than his dramatic triumphs his participation in the military triumph at Marathon (490 B.C.). The playwright is to be remembered as an actual defender of Athens and Greece. Yet what is omitted should not imply any devaluation of his plays. On the contrary, Aeschylus the Athenian took part in that historic action which secured both the city and her people, and left him free to contribute another kind of action to the emerging Athenian sense of identity in place and time. The dramatic victory which is the *Oresteia* (458 B.C.) is not opposed to but complementary to the historical victory. Both are civic feats. Athens in fact and Athens in imagination are symbiotic, as the *Oresteia*, the only extant classical trilogy, so brilliantly demonstrates. The city in history triumphs with the city on the stage.

I

Before triumph, however, lies disaster. In 480 B.C., while the Athenian fleet gathered for victory at Salamis, Xerxes' host burned Athens. This lesson from recent Greek history echoes throughout the first choral song of the *Agamemnon* —"Sing sorrow, sorrow; but good win out in the end" (121)— and becomes a divine law that governs both the general nature of human experience and the particular form of Aeschylean tragedy. "Zeus, who guided men to think,/... has laid it down that wisdom/comes alone through suffering" (176-78). To reach a wisdom that is good, the *Oresteia* begins with suffering and undertakes a long progress across space and through time. A beacon races the distance from Troy to Argos, signaling a transfer from one doomed city to another; the action of the trilogy reaches from Argos in the Peloponnesus to Athens in the east. And if Aeschylus evokes large spaces, he also evokes lengthy durations. One thinks immediately of the ten-year war in Asia Minor and of the blood curse twisting violently through the generations of the House of Atreus. We learn again of a brother plotting horribly against a brother and his children, of a mother nursing revenge for a daughter ten years dead, of children murdering one parent to avenge the other, of a ghost prodding underworld demons into furious pursuit of her son. In the *Oresteia*'s space and time, nothing cruel disappears; history lives on in savage memories and intentions; blood and fire can cross seas; the dead haunt the living. Most terrible of all, the family life which ought to create and sustain a human world torments and destroys it.

As it progresses, however, the *Oresteia* converts the choral refrain from the *Agamemnon* into the trilogy's plot. "Sing sorrow, sorrow; but good win out in the end." The enormous burden of crime and suffering from the past turns gradually from crisis to resolution. An Aeschylean emphasis upon length of time and various forms of waiting counteracts the repeating cycles of guilt and retribution. A good finally does emerge from the song of sorrow. But the large spatial and temporal perspectives of the *Oresteia* have a specifically historical and literary purpose. They encompass the space and time of Greece itself, the development of Hellenic culture through disaster and triumph from the Homeric kingdoms of the past to the Athenian city-state of the present and future. Defeating the Persians allowed a new confidence in assessing the past, for in the hands of Aeschylus this trilogy is not simply an assortment of plays; it is a complete work, a dramatic equivalent to Homeric epic, a new way of seeing and judging the city's emergence from the past.

The *Oresteia* requires, then, the context of Homeric epic—the stories of heroic glory and return. Aeschylus selects what he wants of this context by the title, subject, and opening of his first play—Agamemnon's return from victory at Troy to assassination at home. In the *Odyssey*, the king's fate and his son's revenge stand as warning and inspiration to Odysseus and Telemachus. Here the story appears in its own right as a disaster rather than a caution. It is released from the large romance which Homer presents as a healing of the tragedy of war. And lest we miss his revisionary purpose, Aeschylus

begins by contradicting Homer: the first character to appear,
the weary, troubled watchman who waits on the palace roof
for the signal of Troy's fall, is no paid creature of Aegisthus
(*Odyssey* 4.524–28) but a loyal subject of the king. The first
ominous suggestion of a rot in Agamemnon's kingdom comes
from a humble figure who is specifically not what Homer
says he is. A larger Homeric context is emphasized in the
parados, the play's first choral song (40–257), the longest
Greek lyric known, and a brilliant recreation of the first
sailing for Troy over ten years ago. The allusion is to Iliadic
material rather than to the *Iliad* itself, and the thrust of the
choral song is hardly the heroic glory gained in war. It presents the terrible cost of the war: the anger of Zeus taking in
the Greeks no less than the Trojans; the sacrifice of the innocent child Iphigenia; the cruel hardening in the king. The
Agamemnon starts *in medias res* with a linked ending and beginning—with a fiery sign of Troy's fall and a choral song of
the war's onset. Aeschylus brackets the entire war, draws that
legendary history from the *Iliad* and the *Odyssey* into the
concentrated action of his drama, and, while altering Homer,
gives to his work that sense of time and space that we associ-
ate with epic expansiveness. He does this, I would suggest,
not from a pious wish to continue Homer but from a desire
to compete with him. At stake, the *Oresteia* insists, is a true
account of the Homeric world as well as the claims of drama
against epic.

Here it is worth recalling the cultural value of the Homeric
epics. In the Greek world, they formed a bible, providing to
later generations a source of entertainment and education.
Their massiveness, impersonality, and range of materials gave
them a special authority as an encyclopedia of knowledge
and values. Their formulaic words were taken, one might say,
as the last word. It is with this received evaluation of Homeric
narrative that Aeschylus takes issue. In contrast to oral narrative, which is entirely a matter of words, a world of privileged words in fact, his drama mingles words and deeds, song

and dance, expression and action. Above all, it sets words and deeds, what is said or heard and what is done or seen, in creative competition. And rather than affirm the worth of heroic deeds through the inherited power of a formulaic language, Aeschylus subjects both words and deeds to the skeptical scrutiny of a public stage and an alert audience of citizens. The proper home of Homeric narrative is the court of a king; that of Aeschylean drama is the theater of a great city. Aeschylus presents Athens with a new *paideia*—visual, dynamic, public—with a civic education that locates the Greek past in specific relation to a present time and place. The cause of drama is the cause of fifth-century modernism. The attack upon Homer and poetic narrative as a means of wisdom, culminating later in Plato's *Republic*, begins ironically enough with a poetic dramatist.

How, one might now ask, does all this emerge dramatically? How and where would an audience recognize that the drama of guilt and justice in the *Oresteia* involves a profound revision of Homer? I have already mentioned two of Aeschylus's early signals—the treatment of the watchman and the presentation of Iliadic materials. But the crucial act of revision appears in the central moment of the play: the encounter between the warrior-king and his male-hearted queen. This meeting has been anticipated from the very start as watchman, chorus, queen, and herald contribute their various memories and forebodings to the experience of waiting for the king's return. We contribute our memory and foreboding too, for the story is a twice-told tale with its basic plot sketched in the *Odyssey* and fulfilled here. We become acutely aware of enormous ironies converging, of a situation so intensely charged that it dwarfs the stature of any one man, even "the man who has wrecked Ilium with the spade of Zeus/vindictive" (525–26). Then, as the chorus ends a lyric meditation on the disastrous evils of hubris—the glorylust of the Homeric warrior viewed morally—the king finally does enter. It is one of those scenes of impressive spectacle which distinguish Aeschylus. Agamemnon comes on stage armed, mounted in the chariot of war, and followed by what remains of his army and the booty from Troy. He appears as the embodiment of the Trojan War, of the heroic and aristocratic code of battle tested in the *Iliad* and resolved (if modified) in the very different return of Odysseus to his kingdom. Yet if Agamemnon's visible presence evokes Homer, the dramatic context belongs entirely to Aeschylus. In ways the chorus cannot understand their powerful lyric on pride and righteousness enmeshes the leader of the Greek forces no less than will the traps his queen has ready within the palace. There are indeed truths behind surfaces: within the queen and the palace, within the character of the king. We recognize that a man has come before us, and not one of the emblematic eagles of Zeus's will (49 ff.). "I am a mortal," he insists with an irony not his own, "a man" (923). Aeschylus has summoned the Homeric warrior onstage and called this "man" to account by setting his visible presence against the different languages of epic imagery and moral judgment. Before losing his life, Agamemnon loses the aura of heroic legend.

There is another antagonist present, and she is one of the great creations of dramatic rather than epic literature. Although her field of struggle has been the home front at Argos instead of the front lines at Troy, Clytemnestra is in her own way fully heroic. Aeschylus associates her with heroic matters by having her describe the passage of fire from Troy to Argos and then imagine the final assault on the great city. Through this remarkable figure the playwright displaces epic into drama and then inverts Homer by studying those who remained behind and the experience of desperate waiting. His concern lies with the fate of the city even and especially when the king is gone, and watching Clytemnestra we gradually understand how the destruction of Troy entails destruction in Argos. Because of that heroic war, she has suffered the loss of child and mate, suffered the dilemmas of loneliness and rule, suffered the half-death of failed suicides to which years of rumor have condemned her (866–76). She emerges from this experience male-hearted, at once betrayed and betraying, a champion of maternity and a destroyer of marriage. She is simultaneously a hyperbolist and an ironist: she can welcome the epic race of fire from Troy and also scheme catastrophe as the conclusion of Agamemnon's return. She has accepted the lover Penelope evaded; the treachery her sister Helen began she heightens, with an energy that mingles both cunning and hysteria. And most to the point, like her creator but unlike her husband, she is a superb dramatist, a contriver of acts, a disguiser of words, one who works her will and way by means of an impressive spectacle.

My argument is that the meeting between king and queen becomes a play within the larger play and, as an ironic rite of homecoming, further underscores the translation of epic into drama. The encounter assumes for itself an essentially dramatic shape, beginning with a conflict of characters, tracing a sequence of persuasion and choice, and finally achieving resolution in a single act that can be seen and judged. Although the conflict and the act seem slight—a domestic argument over walking into the palace on a precious fabric—behind them stands a duel of mighty opposites: proud Agamemnon, the warrior-king, leader of all Greece against Asia, the sacker of Troy, whose greatness rests in epic tradition; against him his male-hearted lion-queen, whose remarkable force of character—a deep appetite for rule and revenge—is largely the creation of the *Agamemnon.* Yet the precise point of this situation lies (against a background of massive ironies) in the theatrical foreground, in its elaborate slightness, its patent rhetoric, its diminishment of battlefield action into a problematic act of ritual and social indecorum. The traditional code of heroic pride and glory suddenly confronts another scale of values which Clytemnestra dramatizes impressively. The physical object at the center of the argument now stretches vividly across the stage. This richly woven, richly dyed fabric is conspicuously slight and delicate (such that the tread of an armed man will tear it), and though its apparent use is one of welcome we quickly see in it all those slight, delicate things (especially small birds, animals, and children) whose violent destruction the play continually records in imagery and allusion. Scholars will remind us that the mere act of walking on the rich fabric is not in itself a crime. Assuredly not. But the act is, as all drama aims to be, symbolic; and in this case it is a symbolic act summarizing and representing a whole manner of existence that has become criminally prodigal in its waste of finer things. Agamemnon's hubris is disclosed in the drama of the symbol. The fabric is not a legal but a dramatic reason for his death: so slight a gesture of tearing reveals so much of his character, his vanity, his arrogance, his weakness. We do not need to recall Zeus's condemnation of Paris (369–72) or the saffron mantle of Iphigenia, poured upon the ground of sacrifice (239), to recognize that in the slight act Clytemnestra stages she catches fast the conscience of the king. The tearer, it is clear, will be torn.

The crucial exchange between husband and wife fills with references to conflict, will, power, victory, and Priam of Troy:

> *Agamemnon.* I tell you, as a man, not god, to reverence
>   me.
>   Discordant is the murmur at such treading down
>   of lovely things; while God's most lordly gift to man
>   is decency of mind. Call that man only blest
>   who has in sweet tranquillity brought his life to close.
>   If I could only act as such, my hope is good.
> *Clytaemestra.* Yet tell me this one thing, and do not cross
>   my will.
> *Agamemnon.* My will is mine. I shall not make it soft for
>   you.

Clytaemestra. It was in fear surely that you vowed this course to God [i.e., not to walk on the fabric].

Agamemnon. No man has spoken knowing better what he said.

Clytaemestra. If Priam had won as you have, what would he have done?

Agamemnon. I well believe he might have walked on tapestries.

Clytaemestra. Be not ashamed before the bitterness of men.

Agamemnon. The people murmur, and their voice is great in strength.

Clytaemestra. Yet he who goes unenvied shall not be admired.

Agamemnon. Surely this lust for conflict is not woman-like?

Clytaemestra. Yet for the mighty even to give way is grace.

Agamemnon. Does such a victory as this mean so much to you?

Clytaemestra. Oh yield! The power is yours. Give way of your free will.

Agamemnon. Since you must have it—here, let someone with all speed
take off these sandals, slaves for my feet to tread upon.
And as I crush these garments stained from the rich sea
let no god's eyes of hatred strike me from afar.
Great the extravagance, and great the shame I feel
to spoil such treasure and such silver's worth of webs.

[925–49]

We witness a miniature version of the Trojan War with the returning king seduced by Clytemnestra into playing the role of Priam. We also recognize that the language is elevated and heroic, that one figure is armed, mounted, and masculine,

but that the victor is feminine, on foot, and fighting savagely
with considerable cunning. Quite literally she shames him
into yielding his scruples in order to demonstrate his power,
his free will, his equality with the great king he has conquered. And as Agamemnon gives way to his wife, he steps
down from the Homeric warrior's chariot onto the Aeschylean
stage, already falling in a battle whose methods are dramatic
and psychological rather than epic and military. The victor
of Troy is no match for the queen who has ruled Argos in
his absence; she can crack his will here and later with an
actual stroke will take both life and kingdom away. The play
within a play presents a vivid spectacle of the fate of the
Homeric warrior as he steps into the alien space and imagination of a civic tragedy. None of the nostalgia so richly and
powerfully developed in the *nostos* of the *Odyssey* is here.
Instead there is an ironic demonstration of the failure of
Homer's regal man to act with any kind of power or greatness.

The purple fabric which leads Agamemnon from the chariot
to the palace is associated with the sea. What is slight is
linked with what is mighty. Yet delicate as it is, it traces an
even more perilous journey than the disastrous sea voyage
from Troy recounted by the herald (636–80). The fabric
belongs, of course, to the realm of art not nature; it is in
every sense a part of Clytemnestra's craft, an important element in the menace of her various disguisings and acts. In
the civic world of drama, this crafted object becomes as
dangerous an obstacle as is the wine-dark sea in the narrative
of Odyssean wanderings. We might say that the sea-fabric
condenses the journey into a vivid symbol whose literal
properties of extension suggest a *from-to* relationship—specifically, a progression from the war chariot to the House of
Atreus, from Homeric battlegrounds to the treacherous
palace of the *Agamemnon*. The stained fabric, no less than
the robe of entanglement (the visible embodiment of the
yoke of necessity which Agamemnon put on at Aulis), takes
its place in an Aeschylean pattern ranging across space and

time to bind all in the concentrated symbolic design that is tragedy. It is a pattern of great power and implication, virtually the play itself conceived (in Lattimore's description) as a network of words, acts, and meanings, and it continually alerts the spectators to apply their own knowledge of the legend to a system of tightening links and correspondences. The effect is to diminish severely the figure of the man who crushes "these garments stained from the rich sea." How could Agamemnon know that his palace would become his slaughterhouse? that his return home would become his final departure from life? The purple fabric from the sea leads directly to the bloody bath and robe, to a monstrous sacrifice of family life that echoes across time and space both the banquet of Thyestes and the offering of Iphigenia. The spectacle of the doomed king standing in shame upon "such silver's worth of webs" (949) suggests that slight, fine things can acquire their own peculiar power within the ironic patterns of drama.

A major irony of the *Agamemnon* is, then, that the traditional figure of authority can know and do very little. Hardened by necessity into "the beast of Argos" (824), Agamemnon can speak only of destruction, even when his attention turns from ruining Troy to governing again in his own city (811–54). He is suspicious but in a blind way, and he clearly has no comprehension of the home to which he has returned—that knowledge died at Aulis long ago. The irony of his situation is only emphasized by the silent presence of his slave and mistress Cassandra, Priam's daughter, and one more reminder that Argos replays Troy. She remains on stage after her master's departure; she will share his fate within the palace; yet she knows everything about the past and future of his family and city. Not only can this Trojan barbarian or linguistic outsider (Clytemnestra's jibe, 1050–61) speak Greek, she can also articulate the doom that rests upon the House of Atreus. She acts as a precipitant upon the mood of the play. What we have intuited in the ominous hints of watchman and chorus, in the half-revealed motives of the queen, emerges suddenly and violently in the inspired truths of Apollo's lover-priestess-victim, truths which the chorus can understand less as they become clearer. The audience suddenly finds its own privileged knowledge upstaged by Cassandra's, for she seems literally to see the slaughtered children from the past and the doomed king of the present, to hear their cries and his groans mingle and the furious chant of hate "hanging above the hall" (1191). As this visionary perception of the palace and its secrets mounts in intensity, past, present, and future flow together. History at once repeats itself and acquires a fresh act of criminal blood: the divine curse upon the royal family fulfills and extends itself once again. As we behold this impressive and unexpected sequel to the appearance and departure of the king, we should recognize in it one of the technical triumphs of Aeschylean drama. Aeschylus shows us the simultaneity of all time acting through the curse upon the house. He also shows us the novelty of time, the particularity and suspense of this one event, the trapping and slaughtering of Agamemnon. Myth and history, pattern and event fuse together in the dramatic moment on stage in which character confronts scene (rather than chorus) and enacts a visionary perception of times past and future. There is a freedom here to embrace both repetition and novelty that Homeric narrative with its commitment to linear series can never quite achieve (despite the attempt in the *Odyssey* to create some sense of simultaneity by means of spatial shifts and temporal flashbacks or previews). The use of Cassandra, first as silent onlooker, then as articulate visionary investing the palace scene with its own significance, constitutes a brilliant dramatic experiment: the positioning of a single character to vary, intensify, and deepen the quality of tragic experience as a special knowledge of time and space.

Nonetheless, anyone approaching Aeschylus by way of Sophoclean tragedy will be uncomfortable with the structure of the *Agamemnon*. Bearing *Oedipus the King* (or even

Hamlet) in mind, we may be puzzled by the dramatist's refusal to integrate his tragic materials in a central character, especially after the promise of the title. Who precisely is the hero? Agamemnon, cold and anxious in a triumph he may suspect is near disaster, does not confirm the heroic ring of the play's title and his own name. Clytemnestra is a figure of surprising energy and power; yet to argue for her as an un-qualified heroic figure seems of a kind with such arguments for Milton's Satan or Lady Macbeth. And important as Cas-sandra's experience is, can we find in her visions the full dimension of tragic heroism? Instead of a single dominating character, there is a set of characters, each qualifying and qualified by the others, each trapped in a common situation, and it is the dramatic use of this tragic set or situation that Aeschylus asks us to understand.

A brief comparison with Sophocles' *Oedipus* with an eye to differences rather than similarities might be helpful here. Francis Fergusson in discussing tragedy and *Oedipus the King* has described an action or rhythm of purpose, passion, and perception.[1] The brilliant economy of Sophocles' play involves the integration of these different stages and kinds of action in Oedipus himself. His purpose is to find the slayer of Laius, his passion is the suffering quest, and his perception is not only the knowledge of the crime but also the discovery of himself. The distinct stages of the action become one at the end: his purpose is fulfilled which creates his true passion which is his knowledge of his true identity and parentage. Aeschylus, in contrast, does not chose to work with so in-tense an economy. One might borrow Fergusson's terms and say of the *Agamemnon* that purpose belongs to Clytemnestra, passion to Agamemnon, and perception to Cassandra. The play is not, of course, so impossibly neat. Clytemnestra's purpose arises from her suffering and carries with it a kind of knowledge that moves ironically over the first half of the

1. *The Idea of a Theater* (Princeton: Princeton University Press, 1968), p. 31.

play, although by the end she has blinded herself in blood.
Cassandra's perception is hardly a knowledge free from suffering; indeed her knowing all is precisely the ground of a
suffering that can never issue in action, her own or others'.
Agamemnon has the necessary stature for a tragic hero, and
he surely suffers; but he is surrounded dramatically by two
women and diminished by the greater purpose of one and the
greater knowledge of the other. He is the Homeric hero set
in the tragic lead and found wanting. If he comes to a moment
of perception in the palace, he has neither the time nor the
language to express that knowledge except in outcry. Drama
is too severe a form for this epic hero to stand by himself.
The tragedy belongs to the set of characters as a whole and to
the situation that binds them together. The dramatist's concern is not with Agamemnon but with the *Agamemnon.*

Yet even here there is a problem of part and whole. Although the *Agamemnon* is often produced or read alone, to
do either is to uproot it from its proper home. It belongs in
the trilogy for which it was composed, and certain of its
crucial effects depend upon that larger context. The play
closes in a rush with the revelation of the murder, with
Clytemnestra's justifications, and with the appearance onstage of her lover Aegisthus. The palace doors are swept
open, disclosing the bodies of king and concubine and, standing over them as if a priestess in some mad sacrificial rite, the
blood-spattered queen. We have heard about blood and
death, and now we see those words become facts, things,
visible presences, stained flesh and robes. Clytemnestra believes that what she has done, far from being a crime, is in
fact a "sacrament" (1396, 1431), a rite of cleansing, a conclusion to the murder, sin, and fury that have stained the
royal house (1574–76). Yet we are made powerfully aware
that her conclusion is no conclusion at all. We see gouts of
blood, nothing cleansed; and one more crime added to a
history of crimes. Her boasts of justification reveal her entangled in ironies she cannot or will not see: she does not

stand in a garden of God's springtime glory (1391–92), but
in the House of Atreus. That the play remains *in medias res*
and does not offer a real ending becomes most obvious in the
brilliantly delayed entrance of Aegisthus, who plays womanish
man to this male-hearted lady. By withholding him from the
stage until after the murder, Aeschylus underscores this element in his character and also accomplishes much more. So
late an entrance makes it difficult to entertain any sense of
final resolution. And the bitter arguing with the elders of the
chorus transforms the atmosphere of the play, dissolving the
earlier sense of ominous catastrophe into a melange of lamentation, boasts, and taunting. After the king's wife has described his murder as if it were a sacred duty, the angry
exchanges between chorus and tyrant project us into a dis-
tinctly unheroic world: "Crow and strut, brave cockerel by
your hen" (1671). The Homeric world seems quite distant
now, and we are presented, as John Finley suggests,[2] with
the mood of late sixth-century politics. Aeschylus shifts toward a dramatic technique of satiric disharmonies, reminding
his audience of the return of Orestes (1667) and letting us
see the utter wishfulness in Clytemnestra's last lines on bringing "good order to our house at least" (1673). The *Agamemnon* concludes with a strong motion toward *The Libation
Bearers*, where this tearer too will be torn.

II

The Libation Bearers continues the problem of defining a
just form of punishment, repeating certain elements of the
Agamemnon in a new context. The contest now lies not between the sexes but between parent and child; brother and
sister unite to make just this point. The play's situation and
point of view also change. Although the plot of revenge remains, we are not left in the bewildering, ominous uncertain-

2. *Pindar and Aeschylus* (Cambridge, Mass.: Harvard University Press, 1955),
pp. 264–65.

ties of the first play. We return to Argos with Orestes, see the
reunion with Electra, and then form an audience to the
funeral rites which summon the spirit of Agamemnon to vengeance. Orestes never is the mystery that Clytemnestra was.
We are privy to his plans, watch the plot to kill the queen
take shape and spirit, and witness that he acts largely from an
intense awareness of duty. The *Agamemnon* gave us a version
of the tangled drives and desires of the queen; in *The Libation Bearers*, while we recognize Orestes' conflicts, we understand that the invocation of the father forms an objectifying
ritual that justifies as it inspires the son. Even the revelation
of his identity to Electra is enacted in ritual fashion; and horrible as the murder of Clytemnestra is and is felt to be by
Orestes, it occurs nonetheless (as the play's title indicates)
in the context of ritual necessity rather than hidden personal
drives. *The Libation Bearers* dramatizes a shift from character to ritual action, a purgatorial movement that may in part
account for a modern tendency to favor the *Agamemnon* as
an Aeschylean *Inferno*.

The dramatist has turned, then, from a tragedy of will to
one of duty. The rites over the tomb of the dead king determine an external authority for Orestes' act. In contrast to
Clytemnestra, he is never simply the agent of his own desires.
He longs to avenge his father, but he does not act out a free
choice. God-sent, he must act to a standard set by Apollo,
and in lines 269–96 he describes the terrifying powers of "the
god's urgency" (300). It is significant that his purpose is
joined by a chorus of "slaves" (78), and that his sister sees
herself as "what a slave is" (135). Surrounded by slaves,
Orestes is driven to his duty—a duty that will become a new
crime—and in this sense, although he is an agent with a purpose rather than a passive seer, he is trapped by Apollo no
less than Cassandra was. To understand the horror of his experience at the end of the play, we must understand the
necessity trapping and driving him. And the best way to appreciate this force of necessity is to see the dramatist's
manner of expressing it onstage.

We come to the murder of Clytemnestra from the murder of Aegisthus. Last to enter in the first play, he is first to die here. This sequence keeps the sexual crime of the mother before us, and that crime is given added emphasis through Cilissa, Orestes' nurse and second mother (750), who is quickly persuaded by the chorus to fetch Aegisthus unarmed and without his tyrant's bodyguard. We note that the metaphorical mother assists in the killing of the sexual and political usurper. We have also noted by now the number of Orestes' accomplices, the extent to which they gather around him onstage, and their intimate relationship with the different stages of his life (nurse-mother, sister, and male friend). They seem to be extensions of his being, all coming together to fulfill this one duty. Orestes has reached the critical moment and act of his life, yet because of the characters set around him that life suddenly seems larger than, even separate from, the visible figure onstage. This impression—of a character dwarfed by his situation—is most powerfully sustained in the dramatist's use of Pylades. As Orestes and his friend confront Clytemnestra with swords drawn, it is clear that the blood of Aegisthus has slaked Orestes' vengeance. His mother's appeals cause hesitation and doubt. He turns to Pylades, who has been completely silent throughout the play, and who speaks only once, now. The sequence of speeches offers a fascinating example of competing appeals and bonds:

> *Clytaemestra.* Hold, my son. Oh take pity, child, before this breast
> where many a time, a drowsing baby, you would feed
> and with soft gums sucked in the milk that made you strong.
>
> *Orestes.* What shall I do, Pylades? Be shamed to kill my mother?
>
> *Pylades.* What then becomes thereafter of the oracles declared by Loxias at Pytho? What of sworn oaths? Count all men hateful to you rather than the gods.
>
> [896–902]

Orestes is literally the figure in the middle, as his act is at the moral center of the trilogy. He is torn between breast and oracle, maternity and divinity, the familial and the transcendent, the most intimate and the most distinct of relationships. Caught in this dilemma, he cannot bring himself to act. He turns to the silent friend who represents both an externalized conscience and a surrogate for Apollo—a visual sign and now a verbal sign that Orestes' act is not simply his own business. From the play's start, this figure has always been beside or behind him, creating the eerie sensation of a silent presence who overlooks the action of revenge. When Pylades does speak, he has nothing to say about the human dilemma of executing justice on one's own parent, and the economy of his one speech vividly expresses the economy of Apollo's will. The friend talks only of oracles, oaths, and the deity whom he represents onstage. His voice belongs to the god, as do the person and fate of Orestes. Dilemma vanishes before absolute commitment. Since the act must be his own, the justicer formally accepts his friend's counsel, hardens himself against his mother, and then with Pylades beside him leads Clytemnestra into the House of Atreus. If Apollo's justice has trapped the queen at last, it has simultaneously driven and trapped the son: her punishment is his duty and crime, and the single speech of the god-friend all but completes the terrible equation.

The palace doors open at the close of *The Libation Bearers* to reveal again the blood guilt of the royal family. The stained robe, held in witness above the bodies, makes this ending parallel the end of the *Agamemnon* and image the power of the past to twist time into horrible repetitions. Yet Orestes understands this as Clytemnestra did not. There is no trace of celebration here: "I grieve for the thing done, the death, and all our race./I have won; but my victory is soiled, and has no pride" (1016–17). Orestes can see himself as both justicer and murderer, son and serpent, victor and defiler. He knows that he must set out directly to cleanse himself at the shrine of Apollo. Having completed his own orphaning, he will repeat his condition on arriving and go "an outcast wanderer from this land" (1042). The story of his death in exile, by which he gained entrance to the palace (674–90), now carries at least a metaphoric truth. We recall that the play begins with his address to "Hermes, lord of the dead," and it is this same god—the traditional guide of shades to the underworld—who will later direct the exile to Athens. In the *Odyssey*, we could regard such tales of guilty wandering as inset stories (usually lies) and as ballast to the epic's romance conclusion. At the end of *The Libation Bearers*, however, guilty wandering seems the only possible world, and Aeschylus drives home the point with the sudden and startling entrance, before Orestes' eyes only, of the chorus of Furies. Again, as at the close of the *Agamemnon*, we are made aware of the structure of the trilogy rather than that of the play: neither play is complete in itself. A late entrance is used to transform the issues of each play and to suggest an ongoing action. The true form of justice is still missing.

Stories have come down of the *Oresteia*'s first performance in 458 B.C., of mass hysteria upon the sudden appearance of the Furies, of the premature labor induced in one woman by the terrifying sight. Whatever the literal truth of such stories, they remind us of the survival of older beliefs into a later time as well as of the primitive powers accorded to dramatic enactment and spectacle. Aeschylus could shock his Athenian audience into a moment of panic belief by summoning on-stage the dark goddesses of archaic Greek religion. The episode in the *Oresteia* to which the stories refer occurs in *The Eumenides* where the Furies are revealed within the shrine of Apollo, but I have run before myself to create a context for this play in which the Furies are apparent only to Orestes. *The Libation Bearers* opens and closes with Orestes' seeing the approach of a chorus of women, and the difference between them measures the nature of his act and fate. The middle sections of the play present a ritual address to an underworld figure—the spirit of Agamemnon—and then the consequent act—the murder of his treacherous queen. We notice in the complete sequence a progression from word to deed, from the underworld summoned in speech to the underworld appearing onstage. There is also a progression from dream to reality to nightmare world, for the viper Clytemnestra first dreams of the serpent-child who bites the nourishing breast (523–39), and then encounters the dream's truth in her actual son, who has already heard of the queen's "floating terrors" (525) and identified himself with "this hideous thing/of prophecy" (548–49). He in turn must face the horror he has both done and become as the Gorgon-like women, wreathed in a tangle of snakes, dance toward him across a sacred stage that has been violated once more by a member of the House of Atreus. This chorus remains unseen by the servingwomen; only Orestes can see "the blood drops of their dripping eyes" (1058), and this guilty nightmare vision magnifies the sudden isolation of the hero, joining him momentarily to the orphan seer of the previous play. Electra, who performed the ritual identification of Orestes, and Pylades, who confirmed his resolve, have disappeared. The only set of characters to surround him now represent the fury of his mother's revenge. The world of the play turns upside down. The trapper is now trapped; the victor, now victim. This part of the trilogy closes with no attempt at a definitive moral but with a series of anguished questions: "Where/is the end? Where shall the fury of fate/ be stilled to sleep, be done with?" (1074–76).

III

After the tangling actions of the *Agamemnon* and *The Libation Bearers*, *The Eumenides* works gradually toward a marvelous sense of expansion and release. This achievement is a matter of technique as well as theme. *The Eumenides* is one of the few Greek plays to employ and emphasize a change of scene, and the practice seems of a piece with an

Aeschylean interest in a dramatic version of epic expansiveness: the blurring of chronological time during the first choral song in the *Agamemnon*, the gap of time between that play and *The Libation Bearers*, the priority of the trilogy's structure over those of the individual plays. *The Eumenides* begins with Orestes at bay within the sanctuary of Apollo at Delphi and then moves to Athens where the civic goddess herself and a jury of citizens try the dispute. I will return later to the striking number and kinds of deities upon the stage. Here I wish to follow up the implications in the dramatist's division of place. To move from one place to another, in so economical a form as Greek tragedy, is to establish a significant contrast between them. The contrast lies in this case between the wilderness shrine of Apollo and the city of Athena, between the divine place that exists in and for itself and the divine place that is also the city of man. To go from the first to the second is to move toward a divine place and worship that is integrated with the social and political life of the community. But before such triumph lies terror and near-disaster. Apollo's priestess, the Pythia, looks back in her prologue to the powers of the various deities resident at Delphi, but this backward look cannot prepare us for the blasphemous, defiling spectacle of the Furies, asleep in horrible tangles around the man who clings to Apollo for sanctuary. It was at this moment, stories report, that Aeschylus infused his audience with the same terror which fills the priestess. The shrine is obviously no real sanctuary, but it will provide a way station for crucial instruction. Onstage at last, Apollo pledges himself to Orestes and tells him to flee for aid to Athens's "ancient idol" (64–84). There in the city of man which bears the name and presence of the goddess, resolution and release will be possible. In short, Aeschylus uses a technical element of drama, the division of place, to create a means-end relationship between shrine and city. The structure of the play enacts a historical progression toward community and freedom in the dealings between men and the gods.

The Pythia provides another way of looking through *The Eumenides* to the larger design of the *Oresteia*. By making her prologue a prayer, Aeschylus emphasizes the presence of a formal religion, complete with its own history and with hints of the play's conclusion ("But Pallas-before-the-temple has her right in all / I say," 21–22). We have come by stages to this formal religion, having seen the growth of ritual from the tragic prophecies of Cassandra through the different sacrificial rites performed by Clytemnestra and Orestes to the latter's desperate search for cleansing. Early in *The Eumenides* it becomes clear that the isolated shrine is not able to resolve his guilt; its ministry is partisan rather than definitive. The thrust of the action is now toward Athens. With Hermes, Orestes is sent on to the city; the ghost of Clytemnestra rouses her chorus to pursuit, seeming to disappear into them as they wake. Then, for the first time, the stage is cleared of mortals; formal religion becomes theological drama; the ancient powers and the new god confront one another in a manner that recollects but goes beyond the bitter quarreling between Aegisthus and the chorus of Argive elders. The quarrel still concerns a polluted house, this time the shrine of Apollo, but the issues have been expanded from the domestic and political realm of the House of Atreus to the cosmic realm where earth goddesses are pitted against a sky god. The basic problem, however, remains. What rite or ritual can be found to bring an end to generational repetitions of blood for blood? What measure of just control can man exercise on or in his own history?

The rite Aeschylus has in view is a legal rite, and the *Oresteia* ends with an etiological myth, or story of causes, about the founding of the legal system enshrined on the Areopagus. The legal debate, although occasioned by Orestes, set in a city, and tried by Athenian citizens, is essentially a debate among the gods. Aeschylus has gradually shifted our viewpoint so that the intensely human conflicts of the *Agamemnon* are now seen in the largest and most general

terms: immortal terms. And here the problem of the generations involves basic and ultimate questions about the powers
of old and new deities. Are old powers to be ignored when
new powers emerge? Can one in fact choose between them?
If jurisdictions overlap and conflict, how does one reconcile
them? Aeschylus settles these questions by considering the
case of Orestes and then by considering the case of the
Furies. He creates two endings in effect and shows them both
to be compatible within the civic context of Athens. The city
itself becomes the place of resolution and new possibility.

Orestes is and has been in complete dilemma. Denied both
parents in their lives, haunted by their deaths, he has been
commanded by Apollo to transgress primal bonds in order to
avenge his father. As a result, he is simultaneously innocent
and guilty. That is, under the new Olympian dispensation, he
has through various rites cleansed himself of his mother's
blood. The Furies, of course, recognize nothing of the sort
and continue to demand their ancient satisfaction. They
have no concern for the murder of Agamemnon since his
relationship to Clytemnestra involved marriage not congenital
blood. From their point of view, marriage is an artificial not
a natural bond, and they are asserting the priority of nature
over art. Apollo counters with a different argument from
nature: that between mother and child there is no true parental relationship because the mother merely serves as vessel
for the father's seed. He goes further, denying the mother
any real biological participation and pointing to Athena as
evidence of the father's absolute power. "There can/be a
father without any mother. There she stands,/the living witness, daughter of Olympian Zeus,/she who was never fos-
tered in the dark of the womb/yet such a child as no goddess
could bring to birth" (662–66). This argument may sound
completely nonsensical to us. Yet it blends the myth of
Athena's birth from the forehead of Zeus and fifth-century
scientific speculation concerning the processes of generation,
and behind it, indeed behind the entire trial and trilogy, rests

the very difficult issue of biology as a special authority in matters of social organization and action. As if to indicate precisely that difficulty, the victory for Orestes is extremely narrow. The male jury divides, and the margin is provided by the very figure who stood as Apollo's proof case. This outcome should suggest that the argument and decision make sense only in terms of certain cultural and religious myths that are themselves under scrutiny. The discord, for example, involves a conflict not only of male and female wills but also of their political extensions into patriarchy and matriarchy. There is, in addition, an opposition between old and new gods which invokes both historical and cosmological dimensions to the dispute. We recognize that the contest, although beginning with Orestes, goes far beyond his dilemma. His victory in court is not the end of the trilogy which bears his name. He leaves the world of the play, pledging the loyalty of Argos to Athens (a forecast of fifth-century Athenian empire), and the audience finally reaches a clear vision of issues. Quite simply, we see the chorus of Furies faced by Athena, the tribe of underworld women turning against the single male-hearted goddess, each in radically different ways, and with a sublime irony, transfigurations of Clytemnestra. In particular, we see "the living witness" who represents, far beyond Apollo's use of her, the vital complementarity of the sexes—the strangely born goddess, armed like any heroic warrior and devoted to the protection of her namesake city.

The Eumenides ends with the intermingling of ancient and modern as a way of defining the wisdom of justice and progress. The power of this ending rests in a brilliant integration of theme and structure; that is, the dramatic structure enacts the very process it describes. The play presents the assimilation of the ancient Furies into the civic home of Athens. It reveals them as exiles, wanderers, outlanders no less than Orestes, and by means of persuasion, the dramatic power of the word to determine a course of action, they are offered an end to wandering within the legal order that will literally form the foundation rock of the city. The Furies, after a change of name and purpose, will be escorted to caves underneath the rock of Ares, transforming the underworld from threat to support. But before this can occur Athena must face the Furies with a verdict at once her own and the city's and persuade them to accept this new way of law and life. Orestes is no longer of concern to them; their wrath is now directed against Athens, the city and land whose decision has upset ancient custom, disinherited their rights, and humiliated them before all men. To express that rage, Aeschylus makes effective use of choral repetitions (778–880). With duplicated dances and songs, he dramatizes the rigidity of these archaic deities, while against them he sets the single voice and figure of Athena. We see in and behind this situation the very beginnings of Greek drama, for the *Oresteia* assimilates into its vision of progress the old confrontation between the chorus and the single actor. Athena employs persuasion, transformed from ironic flattery into gracious appeal, to invite the Furies into a new home, law, and honor, all of which will not diminish their stern powers but place them in a new context of creativity—the good life of the city, its institutions, its people. The Furies become the Eumenides or "Kindly Ones," a euphemism perhaps, but also a sign that what is archaic and dark can be generous toward what is new and enlightened. The close of the trilogy fulfills a hope that the disastrous past need not be the shape of the future. If Agamemnon is a name of sorrow that cannot change, Eumenides is a name that embodies the change of sorrow into a good.

Any audience to the *Oresteia* can sense the fullness of this achievement in the manner of the work's conclusion. So much of the trilogy has involved intense opposition and conflict. We recall the encounters between king and queen, mother and son, even the inner conflicts of Orestes. We have just witnessed a trial not far removed from the battlefield—at least the violent threats against the jury remind us of the savagery that legal process sublimates. And finally there is the opposition between archaic and Olympian deities. Here verbal conflict—speech against speech, argument against argument—slowly yields to harmony. The two parties gradually complement one another in bestowing both warnings and blessings upon the city, land, and people. Atonement or at–onement is achieved, and Athena then summons other companies of women onstage to escort the Eumenides to their new homes:

> Flower of all the land
> of Theseus, let them issue now, grave companies,
> maidens, wives, elder women, in processional.
> In the investiture of purple stained robes
> dignify them, and let the torchlight go before
> so that the kindly company of these within
> our ground may shine in the future of strong men to come.
> [1025–31]

There are no single actors now in the theater of Dionysus; all belong to the great choral procession. We see recreated before us the earliest form of Greek spectacle which was inseparable then from religious worship. After the day-long performance, as night comes to the theater of the god, the chorus escorts the "daughters of Night" (1034) from the stage in robes of dignity rather than horror. A purple stained robe stretching across the stage no longer means blasphemy and death; the end is not the same as the beginning. At the start of this trilogy, a watchman in Argos searched for a light in darkness as a sign of saving grace. He could not, of course, see these processional lights, but the dramatist enables his audience to see both and to measure the space and time traversed as a saving progress toward civility. His original audience, moreover, could view the torchlight procession as it wound from the stage toward their own city, as the world of the play and the world of the audience joined harmoniously together, as dramatic plot and scene became civic history. Under Aeschylus, tragedy metamorphoses into an Athenian divine comedy, a *komos* or procession embracing both festive and civic associations. We applaud not the fall of Troy but the rise of Athens; not the tragedy of the Homeric warrior but the celebration of Athenian citizenship. At the end of the *Iliad*, the city stands only for heroic destruction; at the end of the *Oresteia*, the city stands for just ways of fulfilling life by reconciling the darkness of the past with the enlightenment of the future. The shield and flower of the city is now the glory of the goddess. On that remote island-kingdom at the end of the *Odyssey*, she had only begun to preside over men. Here she presides fully, and with a spacious view of her city's meaning to the largest possible audience, the generality of mankind:

> Make more
> the issue of those who worship more your ways, for as
> the gardener works in love, so love I best of all
> the unblighted generation of these upright men.
> All such is yours for granting. In the speech and show
> and pride of battle, I myself shall not endure
> this city's eclipse in the estimation of mankind.
>
> [909–15]

Athena's promise to the garden-city is a spacious one indeed, and we can find a responsive spirit in various kinds of achievement that range from the charge at Marathon through the *Oresteia* and beyond to the great temple of the goddess, high on the Acropolis.

BIBLIOGRAPHICAL NOTE

Aeschylus was born in Eleusis ca. 525 B.C. and died in Sicily in 456 B.C. The *Oresteia* trilogy was produced and performed in 458 B.C.

I have used Richmond Lattimore's translation of the *Oresteia* in *Aeschylus 1* of *The Complete Greek Tragedies*, ed. David Grene and Richmond Lattimore (Chicago: University of Chicago Press, 1953).*

170 THE DRAMATIC TRADITION

Other available verse translations include those by Philip Vellacott
(Harmondsworth: Penguin, 1956)* and Robert Fagles (New York:
Viking Press, 1975). For the serious student of Aeschylus, Eduard
Fraenkel's prose translation of the *Agamemnon* (3 vols. [Oxford:
Clarendon Press, 1950]) is indispensable, with its facing Greek text and
abundant commentary. Peter Green has written interestingly on various
translations of the *Agamemnon*, and an abbreviated version of his essay,
"Some Versions of Aeschylus: A Study of Tradition and Method in
Translating Classical Poetry," is in *Aeschylus: A Collection of Critical
Essays*, ed. Marsh H. McCall, Jr. (Englewood Cliffs, N.J.: Prentice-Hall,
1972).*

The McCall collection contains, in addition to a basic bibliography,
several essays to which my own is in debt: Robert F. Goheen's "Aspects of Dramatic Symbolism: Three Studies in the *Oresteia*"; N. G. L.
Hammond's "Personal Freedom and Its Limitations in the *Oresteia*";
C. J. Herington's "Aeschylus: The Last Phase"; and Richmond Latti-
more's fine "Introduction to the *Oresteia*." Herington's essay and E. R.
Dodds's "Morals and Politics in the *Oresteia*" in *The Ancient Concept
of Progress* (Oxford: Oxford University Press, 1973), both read after
completion of this essay, extend and deepen my general points. Eric
Havelock's *Preface to Plato* (Cambridge, Mass.: Harvard University
Press, 1963)* has stimulated my sense of fifth-century responses to
Homer.

For general background material on Greek tragedy, I would suggest
these important books: H. C. Baldry, *The Greek Tragic Theatre* (Lon-
don: Chatto and Windus, 1971);* Gerald Else, *The Origin and Early
Form of Greek Tragedy* (Cambridge, Mass.: Harvard University Press,
1965);* H. D. F. Kitto, *Greek Tragedy* (London: Methuen, 1939);* Jan
Kott, *The Eating of the Gods: An Interpretation of Greek Tragedy*
(New York: Random House, 1973);* and Albin Lesky, *Greek Tragedy*
(New York: Barnes and Noble, 1967).

*Paperbound available.

OEDIPUS THE KING

Paul H. Fry

Most interpreters of *Oedipus the King* have followed Aristotle in assuming that Oedipus falls because his character is marred by *hamartia*—that is, by a tragic flaw. Yet it is possible to resist this assumption, to feel that in truth Oedipus falls for reasons that are wholly independent of his will to stand. This is not at all to say that he is a hero without weaknesses, for indeed he has many; vividly evident in his past is the inherited weakness that later traditions would call original sin, and this weakness does have everything to do with his fall, his blinding, and his exile. But original sin is not what Aristotle meant by *hamartia*. "Oedipal" weakness cannot be cancelled or avoided through the strength of the will. Oedipal weakness is simply given: it exists potentially in all men, and if one happens to be the unlucky soul who is chosen by the gods to illustrate its presence, one will certainly suffer. To become the ritual scapegoat of the people, to absorb their sins as if they were all one's own, and to suffer for them—this is the fate of Oedipus.

We shall not detain ourselves long with the arguments commonly brought forward to show that somehow, through circumspection and piety, Oedipus could have avoided his crime and punishment. It could, however, be shown that at every stage of his life, at every turning of the narrated and enacted plot, Oedipus has had *withheld* from him, through no fault of his own, the information he or anyone would need to avoid mischance. For the moment, though, rather than spelling out this conspiratorial process we may content ourselves with the authority of Aristophanes, who evinces no doubt concerning the helplessness of Oedipus. In *The Frogs*, Aristophanes' character Euripides quotes from the prologue to one of his lost plays: "'Oedipus at the outset was a fortunate man. . . .'" To which the character Aeschylus rejoins:

> By god, he was not. He was most unfortunate from birth. Before birth, since Apollo prophesied, before he was even begotten, that he would kill his father. How could he have been, at the outset, *fortunate*?

"Of themselves things will come," says Tiresias in *Oedipus the King*, and Oedipus finally knows himself to be a puppet of necessity when he says, "It was Apollo, friends, Apollo did it all." *Oedipus the King* is not a tragedy of human freedom, in which the hero is captain of his fate, but a serious play of a different kind, a play on knowledge and a play on words; it is a portrait of a brilliant and affecting hero whose particular destiny is to be challenged by riddles and mocked by the omniscience of gods, diviners, and the audience. One of Sophocles' subtlest ironies lies simply in what happens when a universally familiar myth of human ignorance is repeated once more: only those who do not "already know the story of Oedipus" can understand spontaneously what it must be like to *be* Oedipus.

Readers who believe that Oedipus is his own victim will find much to agree with spoken by the chorus: "You're dangerous when you're out of temper"; "Natures like yours are justly heaviest for themselves to bear." But the chorus is not a reliably objective voice. Like the chorus of the *Agamemnon*, it represents the conservatism, the retrenchment of the city. It prefers safety to heroism. In the *Agamemnon*,

the chorus says it wants to avoid sex, conquest, and the accumulation of treasure. It is at the moment when its distrust
of heroism is called to account, when it recognizes that it
should run into the house and defend Agamemnon, that its
character is no longer choric at all, but a Babel of twelve
frightened voices. The chorus of the *Agamemnon* knows a
great deal more than it wants to know, and owing to its urge
toward quiescence it spends a lot of time, as in its otiose
responses to Cassandra, trying to resist foreknowledge. The
chorus of *Oedipus* is much the same, though it keeps its dignity (and therefore an unfortunate measure of plausibility
for the unwary reader) because its values are never perjured
by the necessity of action. To the very end the chorus is in
the rearguard of awareness, and resists knowing that which it
is the fate of Oedipus (and Jocasta) to know when it appeals
to the unheroic standards of moderation and piety: avoid
blasphemy during a plague, and try not to look at the under-
side of things even—and this is what the chorus appears significantly to forget—even in the interest of eliminating that
plague.

Impiety is another tragic flaw allegedly rampant in the
play. The chorus says:

> The oracles concerning Laius
> are old and dim and men regard them not.
> Apollo is nowhere clear in honor; God's service perishes.
> [906-09]

But the chorus here fails to distinguish between true oracles
and false oracles. To disbelieve a particular oracle is not to
disbelieve in Apollo or even in other oracles; it only exhibits
a reasonable scepticism about the fallibility of human interpretation. Around 427 B.C., when the play was first acted, the
priests of Apollo were out of favor in Athens because Apollo's
oracles concerning the Peloponnesian War were all pro-
Spartan. At that time, furthermore, the Athenian market-
place was full of itinerant dream-interpreters and augurs

from the East who were called magi and were commonly thought to be charlatans. It is to just such a person that Cassandra refers in the *Agamemnon* when she denies that she is "some swindling seer who hawks his lies from door to door," and to whom Jocasta refers when she says "there *came* an oracle once to Laius. . . ." Oedipus contemptuously calls Tiresias a *magus* or "trick-devising quack," and throughout the play, not just by Oedipus but by the pious Creon as well, Tiresias is called *sophos*, which had become by the fifth century a slightly derogatory term meaning "merely skilled." Euripides makes his Tiresias in *The Bacchae* an old pedant who is right about things more or less by accident and who admits, sheepishly, "I speak not prophecy. . . ." Nothing can be inferred safely about the piety of Oedipus, then, from his challenging the credentials of an interpreter of oracles.

Impiety has also been alleged against Jocasta. She has often been called a frivolous woman, and the following lines are quoted against her:

> Best to live lightly, as one can, unthinkingly.
> As to your mother's marriage bed—don't fear it.
> Before this, in dreams too, as well as oracles,
> many a man has lain with his own mother.
> But he to whom such things are nothing bears
> his life most easily.
>
> [979–84]

Far from being frivolous, I think, these lines are the seal of Jocasta's suicide. Granted, she uses the word *nothing* a lot. When she first comes onstage and tries to corral Oedipus and Creon into the house as if they were truant boys, she says, "Don't magnify your nothing troubles." But in the lines just quoted she does not say that ominous dreams and oracles are nothing to *her*; she says rather, in spite of herself, that life is easy for people to whom such things are "nothing." She is on the verge of catastrophic knowledge and she knows it; this speech is a prelude to her desperate plea that Oedipus call off his quest: "try not to keep in mind what has been said. It will be wasted labour." It is true that Jocasta has cut herself off from belief in oracles, but for her this is a tragic and knowing gesture, not a frivolous one.

To repeat: the lyrically evasive speeches of the chorus of the *Agamemnon* reflect its struggle to resist foreknowledge. In *Oedipus the King* this process becomes a theme, the end of which is the pathetic cry of Oedipus: "it is sweet to keep our thoughts out of the range of hurt." The point about what Jocasta says is not that she is a frivolous woman, but rather that the psychological necessity of denying oracles has made a nihilist of her. She is left not so much without belief—it must be remembered that she is on her way to the temples as a suppliant—as without the inclination to believe. It is in such devious ways that the play teaches piety, if it does at all. An anonymous and believing Greek author once said, "It would be eccentric for anyone to claim that he loved Zeus,"[1] and we should keep this in mind when we come to discuss the omnipresence of Apollo, who is to all intents and purposes a stand-in for Zeus in the play.

If the primary subject is neither impetuousness nor impiety, nor indeed any other failing on that order, let us try to describe the character and situation of Oedipus apart from these considerations. We shall indeed find his Achilles' heel, we shall find it graphically present, but it may not seem relevant to blame him for it when we do. To the priest and his young followers at the beginning of the play, Oedipus is on the threshold of deification as the savior and exemplary king of Thebes. We are meant to feel that it is most unusual for a priest to supplicate a king rather than the other way around, and the priest feels this too, apparently, since he makes a point of praising Oedipus for not wishing to be treated like an oriental god. Not only is he a good king, but as a seer he is credited with powers at least equal to those of Tiresias

---

1. Quoted from the *Magna Moralia* by E. R. Dodds, *The Greeks and the Irrational*, p. 35.

because of his success with the Sphinx: he is "the first of men in all the chances of this life." That is, he has *tyche*, luck. His luck has given him happiness and shows that he is *eudaimon*, he has a good demon. That demon is Apollo. Oedipus likes to think of himself as a favorite son of Apollo, but this is not a sign of exaggerated self-importance because in fact until now he *has* been a favorite son of Apollo. His only mistake, certainly a reasonable one, is to think that he has been singled out by Apollo for benevolent ends.

Most of the clashes in personality between Oedipus and the other characters in the play have to do specifically with his intelligence. To the end, Oedipus remains preoccupied with knowing; blinded, paranoid, and in despair, still he pauses to observe scientifically to the chorus, "I can *know* your voice, although darkness is my world." He loves guessing and clues. Like Sherlock Holmes, he loves the complexity, the method, of thinking, and talks often of wandering "many ways in thought." His riddle-solving ability is summarized in the word *gnome*, deductive wit, and he is apt to stretch this faculty to *xynienai*, intuiting. This is the word he uses when in accusing Tiresias he says, "I will not hold back a jot of what I think." His intuitive bent is what most of all draws the fire of the other characters, who place their faith in the cognitive verb *phronein*, being prudent. This is the word Creon uses when he says, rather sententiously, "My mind would not be traitor if it's wise." Roughly speaking, then, Oedipus on the one hand and Creon and the chorus on the other are at odds over the difference between conjectural and prudential wisdom.

But the prudential characters are nearly always wrong when they think that the conjectures of Oedipus are unreasonable. Surely, for instance, it is quite reasonable to believe that Creon is corrupt. He cants like a hypocrite about the folly of megalomania; it was he who sent for the "prophetic mumbler" Tiresias; and Oedipus knows that he is sitting on a throne of which Creon, brother-in-law of Laius, is the rightful possessor. It matters little that Creon gave him the throne;

after all, he might want it back again. In fact, one may find it quite unreasonable that Creon turns out *not* to be corrupt. As for Tiresias, what could be more reasonable than for a ruler concerned with the pollution of his lands to say, "How needlessly your riddles darken everything"? Why *is* Tiresias "quietly unmoved," as Oedipus observes? Can *we* answer that question even though we happen to know why the seer is speaking in riddles? And above all, as Oedipus wonders, why, if Tiresias is a true seer, did he not conquer the Sphinx himself? We are aware that Tiresias knew that Oedipus was destined to be the giant-killer in that myth and therefore kept out of it, just as now, in refusing to decode his riddles, Tiresias says, "It is not fate that I should be your ruin,/Apollo is enough." But Oedipus has no access to any of this information. By the time Tiresias actually makes the direct accusations that Oedipus refuses to countenance, the word of the seer is decidedly compromised by his behavior. It is quite unreasonable that Tiresias is not the fraud, the magus, Oedipus thinks he is.

Oedipus, again, is a victim of the gods, perhaps the victim par excellence in all of literature. Of course it is true that Oedipus makes a point of saying, in bitter triumph, that he has blinded himself with his own hands—that is, that at least Apollo cannot take the credit for his punishment; but even a belated self-determination seems rather unlikely. Early in the play Oedipus thinks of himself as a doer, a man of action: "Hear what I shall do then." But as the knot tightens he starts talking instead about *pathos*, or endurance: "What have you designed, o Zeus, to do with me?" It is unlikely that his blinding is gloriously self-inflicted. His weapons, the brooches of Jocasta, are like the two-pointed goad Laius struck him with at the crossroads. The brooches strike his eyes, the last in a series of thrustings and lungings: Laius thrust at him, he thrust back at Laius, the drunkard's innuendo at Corinth was thrust at him, Apollo's oracles are thrust at him, fortune thrust itself at the head of Laius, the chorus prays that Zeus will thrust his thunderbolt at "the War God" and then hopes that Apollo will thrust himself at the murderer; and at last, when Oedipus reenters blinded, the chorus says that his ill luck and evil demon have thrust themselves upon him.[2] In other words, the two brooches have carried out the orders of a higher power. "It was Apollo, friends, Apollo," says Oedipus, echoing Cassandra in the *Agamemnon.*

If Apollo is in many ways a stand-in for Zeus, so Oedipus has been in the past a stand-in for Apollo, an agent of the god. As in the *Agamemnon*, Apollo is at once Healer, Singer, and God of Light, but he is also the *apollon*, the destroyer, of whom only Cassandra had firsthand knowledge in the earlier play. At the climax of his suffering Oedipus is still an agent of the god, but now he is an agent-destroyer, and the thing to be destroyed is partly Oedipus himself. Another of Apollo's names, Loxias ("ambiguous one"), literally means "proceeding slantwise." In this name lies his particular affinity with Oedipus, whose name means "swellfoot" and therefore "stumbler." All the many feet in the play are stumbling feet except for *deinopous*, the "deadly-footed curse" which, according to Tiresias, will pursue Oedipus henceforward. The grandfather and father of Oedipus belong to this group of names: Labdacus, whose name is like the word for lameness, and Laius, whose name means "left-sided" (it may be recalled that in Homer spear-throwers are right-handed and auspicious bird omens always fly on the right). Crab-stepping, club-footed, lame: the Achilles' heel of Oedipus is the telltale name he shares with his ancestors and his divine patron.

In mythology, a number of men born from the earth—and Oedipus hamstrung and exposed on Mount Cithaeron is symbolically one of these—are physically deformed and often walk clumsily; but, like the blind Tiresias, they are given special powers of perception to compensate for their physical

---

2. The verbs governing all these actions are *enallesthai, paiein,* and *epenthroiskein*; see the commentary of Thomas Gould, in his translation of *Oedipus the King*, pp. 46–47.

disability.[3] Lameness, which symbolizes the imperfection of
mortal flesh, the moral asymmetry of man, is caused by the
struggle of emergence from the earth; clay sticks to the limbs,
or to a name, as in the case of Adam ("red clay"). As bespeaks
its general significance as tainted flesh, physical disability may
also be a retroactive punishment for sexual awareness: Tiresias
was turned into a woman when he saw two snakes coupling
and slew the female; when he saw another pair of snakes
coupling and slew the male he was turned back into a male;
finally he was blinded in punishment for having revealed the
Secret of Hera, a sexual mystery. A second feature of chthon-
ian or earthborn men is that during their heroic careers they
must slay an earth monster, the initiatory guardian at the
threshold between their status as clay and their status as man.
Cadmus, the founder of Thebes, slew the Dragon of Ares (the
"war god" personifying the plague in Oedipus's Thebes), who
guarded the future site of the city. In other words, Cadmus
subdued primordial conflict with the pledge of cooperative
community. He then sowed the teeth of the dragon in the
ground; from these teeth sprang up the Spartoi, one of
whom, Chthonia or "Earth Man," was a matrilineal ancestor
of Oedipus. Oedipus in person proved his descent from
Mother Earth by overcoming the female Sphinx, an earth
demon sent by Apollo to plague Thebes.

The question arises: why should mythmakers wish to dis-
prove the human and bisexual origins of their heroes? A first
reason is simply that his inhuman birth shows the hero to be
special, set apart to be a founder and savior, like Moses in
the bullrushes, or Christ in the manger. A second reason is
more complex: in retaliation for parental neglect, to which
they impute their frightening discovery of independent selfhood, children (mythmakers all) invent for themselves a

3. The ensuing discussion of mythic genesis draws heavily upon Otto Rank,
The Myth of the Birth of the Hero, trans. Robbins and Jelliffe, and Claude Lévi-
Strauss, "The Structural Study of Myth," in *Structural Anthropology*, trans.
Claire Jacobson and Brooke Grandfest Schoepf, pp. 202-28.

number of alternative, compensatory stories about their parentage. The purpose of such stories is to punish parents originally considered to be perfect—hence king and queen of the fancy—by illegitimizing them. The most extreme punitive story illegitimizes even invented alternative parents by announcing that the child is a foundling, like the Nile King's Daughter. The hero is left on a hillside, or in the bullrushes, or he is thrown into the sea. Children's stories, fairy tales, and epics abound with such figures: in the *Iliad*, for instance, Patroclus tells Achilles:

> the rider Peleus was never your father nor Thetis
> was your mother, but it was the grey sea that bore
> you and the towering rocks. . . .

What the infantile fantasy of the mythmaker actually does, in projecting a hero outward from the psyche, is to exaggerate the neglect of his parents to the point of saying that they deserted *him*, like Laius and Jocasta. Once depedestaled, parents are no longer kings and queens, and the child claims therefore to be raised by less noble foster parents. In *Oedipus* there are *two* herdsmen, wholly in excess of dramatic necessity, whose intermediate parental role is one of the things Oedipus must learn about. The Corinthian king and queen Polybus and Merope represent a more mature, magnanimous forgiveness on the part of the fantasizing child, his reunion with the noble parents who have remained, in his mind's eye, always his real parents. This four-stage cycle of rejection, denial, displacement, and restoration of parents has been made familiar to students of psychology through the work of Otto Rank. *Oedipus the King* is perhaps the only literary work in which all four stages are clearly present.

Oedipus' Achilles' heel is one of his virtues as a king. He has a natural antipathy for secrets and mystification. He loves openness and insists on thrashing everything out in public. He has come forward from the palace to listen to the suppliants. Creon comes back from Delphi and wants to go inside, but

Oedipus wants their conversation to take place onstage, where the people can listen. The first messenger, still apparently a stranger, wants to know if the Delphian disclosures are forbidden gossip, and Oedipus says, "O no! Once on a time Loxias said I should lie with my mother." After the suicide and the blinding, the second messenger reports that Oedipus still wants, in one mood at least, to stand revealed: "He shouts for someone to unbar the door and show him to all men of Thebes." This hatred of secrets and of concealment, this love of the sunshine of an objectively understandable world, is also the hatred of the very idea of an unconscious mind, and that is what makes his resolution to undergo an ordeal of self-revelation all the more courageous.

It is not at all interesting to say that *Oedipus the King* exemplifies the Oedipus complex. It is somewhat more interesting to notice that the structure of the play resembles a case study, a program in psychoanalysis. We may content ourselves here with one point of resemblance, of importance especially because it shows the relevance of substitute parents to the concerns of the play. A featured motif in the Theban genealogy of Cadmus is the idea of twin rulership, which is carried on in alternating years, usually with a great deal of mutual hostility. Amphion and Zetus are the first such pair; several regents, including Creon himself, alternate with legitimate rulers; and the final pair in the series are the sons of Oedipus, Polyneices and Eteocles. This makes intelligible the elaborate emphasis, the drawn-out quality, of the messenger's explanation of how he and the other herdsmen kept their flocks in alternation on Cithaeron. Later, true to their secret role, the herdsmen evince considerable mistrust of each other. (Their hostility is perfectly well motivated without this explanation; it will be argued in a moment, however, that the use of dramatic motivation as camouflage is part of Sophocles' "play on knowledge.") Not only does their mutual hostility echo the uneasy relation of Oedipus and Creon, his prospective regent, but it also temporarily reassures Oedipus, as "patient," that the real alternating rulers in his family are not royal after all, but peasants. If they are peasants he is a peasant too—at the last moment he even considers the possibility that he is a slave—and if he is a peasant, the king he has killed is obviously not his father. He goes on to "prove" that Laius was not his father by demonstrating that his real "Oedipal" hostility is directed toward the herdsman, whom he threatens to kill.

Those who take all this to be a specious embellishment of the text will raise the objection, among others, that in interpreting the scene this way one has more or less systematically inverted the dramatic quality, the overt motivation of the scene as a whole. It might be objected that just as Patroclus, in the passage quoted earlier from the *Iliad*, is accusing Achilles of inhumanity, not praising him as a superman, so here Oedipus does not *wish* to be a slave but is mortified at the prospect. This is quite true, but it is possible to read the scene *both* ways and to feel increasingly about the play as a whole that there really are two plays going forward at once.

Awareness of what we now call the Oedipus complex was widespread in Sophocles' time. Both maternal incest and parricide are prominent in a brief catalogue of evil dreams listed by Plato; and Jocasta, in the speech already quoted, attests that everybody has such dreams. The question then is, What is the attitude of Sophocles toward the psychological and taboo content of his play? Is he the naif Freud thought he was, concerned exclusively with the dramatic ironies of fated blindness, or is he a psychoanalytic thinker in his own right?

The play is quite plainly about riddles and the intellect. Each riddle is a mask of the truth. The mind of Oedipus, at each step along the way, decodes riddles with reference only to their surface or apparent content, and in each case his partial breakthrough is, or results in, a new riddle. A simple formula governs the whole process: each piece of evidence that is reasonable proves to be false. It is reasonable, for instance, as Oedipus suggests, that a king with a full and normal

traveling retinue of a dozen or more functionaries would be
set upon by "robbers," in the plural, who would be motivated by "money and bribery." This is false. It is unreasonable that Laius would travel with only six people, as Oedipus
shows in wondering whether he had "few with him . . . or
many servants, as would suit a prince." Furthermore, it is
unreasonable that a disinterested party would lie about the
number of his assailants, yet against all probability the herdsman turns out not to be disinterested. Every turn and twist
of the plot is an improbability come true, a riddle decoded.
Q: Who would fight against the odds? A: Oedipus. Q: Who
would have an uncorrupted motive for a dastardly deed?
A: Oedipus. Q: Who would bear false witness with nothing to
gain from it? A: An admirer of Oedipus. After all, Oedipus,
as a hero, is fated to do unusual things and call forth unusual
responses.

A riddle is a metaphor of the type "A is B: why?" We may
assume that riddles and metaphors exist in language for the
purpose of dressing up the nakedness of reality. In primitive
language, metaphor did the duty of euphemism by sidestep-
ping taboo words, words both extremely sacred and extremely
profane. Sacred rituals had to do with initiation into the
mysteries of sex, and all such rituals had a very impolite
meaning, knowledge of which in *most* cultures (of this qualification more in a moment) was taboo for everyone except
priests. Scholars are now fairly well agreed that all the more
polite myths having to do with sun kings and seasonal deities
are displaced versions of pornographic originals. All displaced
myths are euphemistic riddles, in other words, since they
refer back in code to their secret meaning. In accordance
with this train of thought, the modern poet Wallace Stevens
describes "the motive for metaphor" in a poem of that title:

shrinking from

The weight of primary noon,
The ABC of being,
The vital, arrogant, fatal, dominant X.

There is no more succinct critique of *Oedipus the King*. The fate of the hero, which is certainly to experience the primal ABC of being, is the motive for Sophoclean riddle, the process of the mind which resists and conceals the "facts of life," and which must be broken down, often tragically, by persistent interrogation, that is, by psychoanalysis.

This in itself does not prove that Sophocles was aware of his motive for metaphor, that he resembled the person we refer to now as "the Victorian Freud," privy to the darkest secrets but inhibited about them. In fact, the preceding argument, with its emphasis on taboo knowledge, is more apt to suggest the contrary. But the conditions of Greek culture present a special case. Until very late in the Golden Age of Greece, and then only for certain cabalistic rituals, there were no taboo priests. Pornographic myths flourished in the popular mind right alongside their polite and moralized displacements. Plato complained that the story of the castration of Uranos by Kronos, together with Kronos's unpleasant penchant for eating his children, was far too savage and indecent a story to be circulated among the people. But this only shows that the story did circulate, along with its somewhat more genteel equivalent, the human story of Thyestes. It must have been well known, then, that the prototype of the Oedipus story was the story of Uranos, father of Kronos. Uranos knew perfectly well that his wife was also his mother, the Earth, and he was himself, since he had no father, a victimized Laius castrated by his son. The human version of each of these theogonic stories is moralized or made palatable by the fact that both Thyestes and Oedipus are horrified by what they have done unwittingly—in contrast with the serene and insouciant gods. In each case, then, where there are two stories, both are known, and probably known equally well; Sophocles could assume on the part of his audience a thorough initiation in what other cultures would classify as taboo knowledge.

Oedipus the King is in a manner of speaking two plays. One play is a study of the heroic quest for truth decently curbed, made toothless and anti-Faustian by the via-mediism of the chorus. This play raises problems insusceptible of solution in terms of its own amply daylit categories, and invites us therefore to seek solutions in the second play, which is exclusively about primal sin and atonement. In other words, *Oedipus the King* is a riddle which has two answers. Q: "He slew his father but did not know it. He married his mother but did not know it. How can this be?" The first answer is unsecretive, like the character of Oedipus. A1: "It was the will of Apollo." The second answer is both different from and the same as the first. A2: "It was the archetype of male desire."

What is true in the abstract should be true in detail. If there are two plays, it should follow that every Sophoclean riddle has two answers; let us take one of the most innocuous-seeming riddles as a test.[4] Tiresias, in his maddening way, says something to Oedipus which does not appear to be a riddle at all: "You blame my temper but you do not see your own that lives within you." The word for temper is *orge*: it is the same word that describes the anger of Laius at the crossroads and the anger of Oedipus as he bursts in the double doors to his bedroom. The gender of this word is feminine, and since in the second line *orge* is referred to by its pronoun, "her," what Tiresias has really said is: "You blame my temper but you do not see her who lives with you." It is a cowardly hint. Later, when Tiresias is too thoroughly discredited to be believed, he says it straight out: "You have your eyes but see not where you are in sin, nor where you live, nor whom you live with."

It is also worth decoding the riddle of the Sphinx, a riddle which everyone knew and knows, but which is not featured in the play, very probably because its ominous content would have shattered the ambiguity of Sophocles' sustained double

4. Here I follow Gould's commentary, p. 56.

entendre. The Sphinx was sent against Thebes by Apollo to punish the sin of King Laius. Like Oedipus, Laius the left-sided grew up in the household of a king and foster parent, Pelops of Argos. Pelops had a handsome illegitimate son whom Laius forceably abducted. This was certainly a quintessential crime, like the rape of Helen, sexual but also violent and carried out in revolt against paternal authority. It is the availability of this legend which suggests that Oedipus is not just making phrases when he keeps harping on the fact that he is now proven "a child of impurity," "a sinner and a son of sinners," "impure and of the race of Laius."

The Sphinx's riddle in its attenuated form is best known: "What goes on four legs in the morning, two legs at noon, and three legs at evening?" The answer of course is man. But the full riddle of the Sphinx has another component: "but when the number of its limbs is largest, then it is weakest." The answer is still man, only now it is man in a pointedly moral sense rather than man simply as *homo ambulans*. We may readily assume that Oedipus, a reasonable and as far as he knows a pure man, responded only to this latter sense of the riddle, just as he caught only the primary meaning of Tiresias's remark about his bad temper. The answer "man" must have been obvious to Oedipus—who sees everything but himself—because in fact he is excluded from the species thus defined. We may imagine him onstage leaning on a staff: at the noon of his life he walks on three legs. Because of the alienation he owes to his physical deformity, he has stood far enough away from the species "man" to view it objectively—to know its anatomy; hence he could answer the riddle because he is not himself part of the answer. But it is also the evening of his life; he is about to be overtaken by fortune, and for that moment his three legs are appropriate. In addition, one of his legs is swollen. He is uniquely representative of "man" the answer to the more sinister meaning of the riddle: of whom could it be said more appropriately than of swellfoot Oedipus in bed with his mother that man is weakest when the number of his limbs is largest? Insofar as Oedipus knows his species, the appearance of man, he is a great king and savior, but insofar as his reasonableness seals off his own murkier inherited nature, the original sin of Laius which the Sphinx was sent to punish, Oedipus is a pollutant. He is a favorite son of Apollo the god of daylight and objective vision, but he is a favorite agent of apollon the destroyer.

Once Oedipus at the height of his fortunes, his noon, has come face to face with what Stevens calls the "primary noon" of reality, he perceives, as a psychoanalytic patient must, that all of his crimes are one and the same thing; and in his rage, as reported by the second messenger, everything he has done is summarized in the single image of the generative and destructive sword:

> Give me a sword, I say,
> to find this wife no wife, this mother's womb
> this field of double sowing whence I sprang
> And where I sowed my children!
>
> [1255–58]

He puts out his eyes, furthermore, in part because the Greek for eyeballs and testicles is the same word, and in choosing Jocasta's brooches for his self-effacement he has unfastened her robe for the last time. In the images of sowing and the contours of nature, one of man's most irresponsible fantasies, that of reunion with the mother, is transferred to the fields, where the Theban blight is still raging. It is important to notice, however, that the blight of the city is mentioned for the last time only halfway through the play, at line 665. Thereafter the blight is absorbed entirely by the body of Oedipus, where it originated.

As he begins to think about death, Oedipus sees that it will be a return to the natural womb of the field, a return to an exposure-fantasy of inhuman birth. As I mentioned earlier, an alternative to being exposed in a field is to be thrown into the water, and in late moments when he cannot bear to face

his ancestors underground, Oedipus seizes on this possibility:
"Kill me," he says, "or throw me into the sea, to be forever
out of your sight." He insists repeatedly that it is not fitting
for him to expose himself to the scrutiny of the sunlight,
but because he is an open person he has a natural horror of
the tomb, which resembles his blindness as "the horror of
darkness enfolding."

But there is a solution to these dilemmas. The fantasy of
inhuman birth leads finally to the prospect of inhuman
death, to the possibility, in other words, of atonement and
apotheosis. In his mounting hysteria Oedipus has claimed that
he is "the child of fortune," with "the months, his brothers"
for companions. The chorus, wishing half-consciously to
shelter him, has seized upon this idea and invoked for him a
variety of inhuman-birth myths, beginning: "Who was it bore
you, child?" One of the choral hypotheses is as follows: "was
she a bride of Apollo, your mother? The grassy slopes are all
of them dear to him." Indeed, symbolically, perhaps, Apollo
and Cithaeron are the most fitting parents of all for Oedipus,
and the latter may be his most fitting grave, even though it
is with ambivalence that he views the problem of whether or
not to be entombed. He has violated his mother; how can he
ever return even to her substitute, the Earth? At last, partly
as atonement and partly because he wants to rest in peace, he
accepts his exile and its implications:

> Leave me live
> in the mountains, where Cithaeron is, that's called
> *my* mountain, which my mother and my father
> when they were living would have made my tomb.
> So I may die by their decree who sought
> indeed to kill me.

> [1451–55]

Something resembling this will be his fate. In the *Oedipus
at Colonnus*, the death of Oedipus is hardly death at all. In a
grove sacred to the Eumenides, the earth simply opens up

and swallows him; there his spirit lives on in solitude and brings good fortune—*eudaimon*—to the city of Athens. Thus the pollution of Thebes is purged in a way that cheers an Athenian audience, for whom Oedipus becomes something like a presiding saint. In living through the "ABC of being," so primal that it has to be cloaked for decency's sake, or at least made concrete experience rather than universal fantasy, by means of the euphemism of riddle, metaphor, and myth, Oedipus has become more than the Everyman of the Sphinx's riddle; he has become through reenactment of first things the first man, whose wife and mother is no longer Jocasta but the very first deity of all, Gaia, the Earth. For Oedipus, in his dual role as earth monster and heroic savior, the cure of the land's pollution and atonement for human pollution must take the form of a single gesture. As scapegoat, in a single blinding reversal of fortune, Oedipus acts out the process of animal sacrifice, divine retribution, and human resurrection.

BIBLIOGRAPHICAL NOTE

Sophocles was born at Colonus ca. 496 B.C. and died in Athens in 406 B.C. *Oedipus Tyrannos* was performed ca. 427 or 426 B.C.

All quotations from *Oedipus the King* are from the David Grene translation in *Sophocles 1* of *The Complete Greek Tragedies*, ed. David Grene and Richmond Lattimore (Chicago: University of Chicago Press, 1970).* *Oedipus the King* has also been recently translated by Thomas Gould (Englewood Cliffs, N.J.: Prentice-Hall, 1970)* and by Philip Vellacott, *Sophocles and Oedipus* (Ann Arbor: University of Michigan Press, 1971). The Grene translation, quite justifiably, monopolizes the field. Gould's translation, being more literal, is not as readable as Grene's, but it is an indispensable aid to students of Sophocles. Although I use the Grene translation for this essay, both the translation and the commentary provided by Gould are more clearly biased than Grene's in favor of the sort of reading of the play I offer.

I am conscious of having drawn specific ideas from the following: Seth Benardete, "Sophocles' *Oedipus Tyrannus*," in *Sophocles: A Collection of Critical Essays*, ed. Thomas Woodward (Englewood Cliffs, N.J.: Prentice-Hall, 1966);* George Devereux, "Why Oedipus Killed

Laius," in *Psychoanalysis and Literature*, ed. H. Ruitenbeek (New York: Dutton, 1964); René Girard, "Tiresias and the Critic," in *The Structuralist Controversy*, ed. Richard Macksey and Eugenio Donato (Baltimore; Johns Hopkins University Press, 1972);* Bernard Knox, *Oedipus at Thebes* (New Haven: Yale University Press, 1957).*

The following works are also useful: C. M. Bowra, *Sophoclean Tragedy* (Oxford: Clarendon Press, 1944);* G. M. Kirkwood, *A Study of Sophoclean Drama* (Ithaca: Cornell University Press, 1958); Bernard Knox, *The Heroic Temper: Studies in Sophoclean Tragedy* (Berkeley: University of California Press, 1964); *Oedipus the King: A Collection of Critical Essays*, ed. Michael J. O'Brien (Englewood Cliffs, N.J.: Prentice-Hall, 1968);* A. J. A. Waldock, *Sophocles, The Dramatist* (Cambridge: Cambridge University Press, 1951);* Cedric Whitman, *Sophocles: A Study of Heroic Humanism* (Cambridge, Mass.: Harvard University Press, 1951).

For general material on Greek tragedy see the bibliographical note to Michael Holahan's essay on the *Oresteia* in this volume. For certain extraliterary notions that play a part in my argument, the reader is referred to E. R. Dodds, *The Greeks and the Irrational* (Berkeley: University of California Press, 1959);* Otto Rank, *The Myth of the Birth of the Hero* (New York: Brunner, rpt., 1957);* and Claude Lévi-Strauss, "The Structural Study of Myth," in his *Structural Anthropology* (Garden City, N.Y.: Doubleday, 1967).*

*Paperbound available.

THE BACCHAE

Charles Balestri

In 406 B.C., a year after its author's death, *The Bacchae* was first presented in Athens at the festival of Dionysus. Its production as part of a trilogy that included the *Iphigenia in Aulis* and the *Alcemon* (now lost) won first prize, one of Euripides' few victories in forty years of writing for the annual dramatic competition at the festival. The play survives today as Euripides' one assured masterpiece, still occasionally produced long after the theater and the society for which it was written have disappeared.

Euripides' plays are notably modern in their thought, combining a critical skepticism toward traditional beliefs with an almost obsessive fascination with the power irrational forces exercise in the lives of individuals and communities. Such themes exist uneasily within the formal conventions of Greek theater. The iconoclastic tendency of Euripides' thought clashes with a drama whose ritual origins remained clearly visible in its mythical subjects and its hieratic style. In many plays Euripides exploits this incongruity of form and content for strikingly new perspectives on human action; in some instances, notably with the choruses, the traditional forms seem merely vestigal. But the closest examination of *The Bacchae* will reveal the coherent and rich dramatic life Euripides has created from such conventional elements of Greek drama as the chorus, the messenger speech, debate and recognition scenes, and the visible presence of the gods in the action of the play. At the same time the tragic vision of *The Bacchae* is entirely Euripidean, a vision of the dark triumph of the irrational over the values of civilization. The archaic and the modern seem to meet on common ground and to become finally indistinguishable in this dramatic spectacle that closes the living tradition of Greek tragedy.

The Bacchae dramatizes the resistance of Pentheus, king of Thebes, to the worship of Dionysus, which leads to the destruction of the king at the hands of the god and his followers. The story, with these and other sets of human characters, had long been known. Aeschylus had much earlier written a play about the death of Pentheus, and there is an even earlier vase painting depicting the dismemberment of Pentheus by the Maenads, or Bacchae, the female worshipers of Dionysus. Dionysus is the god of communal ecstasy, divine possession, and the beauties and energies of natural life. Through the gift of wine and communal worship he offers an escape from moral inhibitions, rationality, and civic responsibility. Inevitably, in all cultures, the defenders of order and the city are enemies of anyone or anything that offers this kind of release. Parallels in our own culture to the ancient conflict, including clear resemblances in the means by which the divine ecstasy is sought or repressed and in the symbolic dress of the opposing forces, will be evident to any reader of *The Bacchae*, for instance, in the frenzy of a hard-rock festival, with Dionysus and his band of Maenads represented by the singers and their devoted groupies. In the myths dealing with Dionysus the god is usually presented as an outsider who descends on a community and demands that he be worshiped as a god. The story always includes a human opponent who refuses this recognition and is destroyed as proof of the god's absolute power. This deep-seated opposition seems to be the essence of the myths concerned with Dionysus's victories.

It is not surprising that Euripides ended his career with this

story. He had pursued the theme of the irrational from his
earliest plays. The Roman critic Longinus noted that Euripides incessantly returned to the subjects of eros and madness.
In the *Medea* (431), a discarded wife obsessed with jealousy
kills her husband's new love interest, the girl's father, and
finally her own children. In the *Hippolytus* (428), a play
very similar to *The Bacchae,* a virginal young man ignores the
power of eros. Aphrodite revenges herself by inflicting the
boy's stepmother with an irrepressible sexual desire for him
that results in her suicide and his destruction under the
curses of his father. In the *Heracles* (ca. 420), the greatest of
heroes is driven mad by Hera and kills his wife and children.
In his treatment of the House of Atreus legend, *Electra* (413)
and *Orestes* (408), Euripides presents the young avengers as
neurotics who, supported by Apollo, nurture homicidal ten-
dencies. In these plays the irrational in the form of passion or
madness takes possession of a person and compels him
(though often her) into a destructive act. The irrational force
is often embodied in an Olympian god or goddess. These
divinities are really demons, the gods viewed not as persons
but as *potencies* that exist within as well as without the
human characters. The gods in Euripides symbolize the
dominance these powers have over men. To understand
Euripides' tragic gods we must leave Judeo-Christian ideas
about justifying the ways of god to man behind us. In
Euripides the gods ignore human conceptions of goodness
and justice; the demons are vengeful and indifferent to the
suffering they inflict. Dionysus is Pentheus's demon in
Euripides' final study of the shape and energy of the irrational.

At the same time that *The Bacchae* is a continuation of a
central theme in Euripides' earlier plays, it is extraordinary
in its dramatic power and the archetypal intensity of its
action. The actions of the earlier plays impress us primarily as
the plots of stories, intrigues turning on inventions and deceptions, while the action of *The Bacchae* is unmistakably close

to the structure of ancient ritual. Indeed, it has been suggested that the fate of Pentheus is not simply a striking event in the mythical history of Dionysus but an inherent part of the worship of the god. Dionysus is a vegetation god; his worship encourages and celebrates the annual death and renewal of nature through the disappearance and return of the god. Students of ancient ritual tell us that an animal or human scapegoat was substituted for the god in the yearly sacrifice to insure the fertility of the land and the people. Pentheus midway through *The Bacchae* is dressed to resemble Dionysus, and, like the scapegoat figure of the ancient ritual, is led out by the god to be killed in the ceremonial hunt by his bacchic worshipers. After the death of Pentheus, Dionysus reappears, and reveals his immortality. The shape of the plot, then, corresponds closely to the primitive pattern of ritual sacrifice, the sacred killing of the god's scapegoat. Indeed, an earlier generation of Greek scholars accounted for the general form of Greek tragedy through its origins in just such a sacrificial ritual in honor of the god Dionysus. The presentation of the tragedies at the festival of Dionysus commemorated this continuity between ritual and tragedy. Despite the forceful attacks on this theory as a general account of tragedy, it does seem that Euripides, in the particular case of *The Bacchae*, connected tragedy with the ecstasy and terror of primitive human sacrifice and theophany, a connection that perhaps makes the action of *The Bacchae* as archaic as anything to be found in the plays of Aeschylus or Sophocles. There was no doubt an especially powerful effect gained by presenting in the theater of Dionysus, the sacred place of the god, a tragedy that enacted a ritual sacrifice to the god himself. But as the play draws emotional power from its resemblance to ancient sacrifice, it transforms ritual into drama. The audience finds itself not merely attending an imitation of the rite of Dionysus but questioning the nature of the demon and the significance of his action. Uniquely Euripidean is the complexity of emotional and intellectual response that *The*

Bacchae achieves in its transformation of the ritual of Dionysus. The tragedy's imitation of the ritual action is at least as ironic as it is celebratory; the demon is both worshiped and exposed.

The Bacchae's striking resemblances to ancient ritual should not distract us from what it essentially is: a tragic drama in which action, character, language, and spectacle arouse pity and fear in the audience and generate questions about the human condition. As in *Oedipus the King*, the central action of *The Bacchae* is an act of recognition. In the prologue of the play Dionysus tells us that, despite his wide following in Asia, the people of Thebes have refused to worship him as a god. This especially angers him because he is closely related to the ruling family of the city, Zeus having fathered him on Semele, a daughter of the city's founder, Cadmus. But Thebes, led by Agave, another daughter of Cadmus, and her son Pentheus, who is now king of the city, refuses to recognize the divine birth. The god tells us he has taken on the appearance of a man, a priest of Dionysus rather than the god himself, in order to present himself to Pentheus and Thebes. It is important to see that this is a significant disguise. Dionysus's human form, visible through the play, mocks the Theban rationalization that a man, not Zeus, was responsible for this birth. The "man" who proves he is a god by the violence he unleashes has already been anticipated in the myth by the fate of Semele, who was destroyed by lightning after insisting that her lover, Zeus, come to her in his divine form. Pentheus is incapable of seeing behind the priest's human form to the divine energy it embodies. As the play demonstrates, Pentheus's failure to recognize what the disguised Dionysus represents, the power of the demon, corresponds to his blindness about his own nature. Agave is subject to a similar failure. In her rational skepticism she refused to acknowledge Dionysus as the son of Semele and Zeus, now she is driven mad by the god and fails to recognize Pentheus as her son and murders him. In the conclusion of the play Agave regains her sanity and sees that it is her own son that she has killed; she and Thebes recognize Dionysus as he stands triumphant in the place of the gods above the palace. The action has revealed the demon to all. Through the catastrophe brought about by failed recognitions, Dionysus ironically accomplishes the recognition of his ultimate power.

As in *Oedipus the King*, a superficial rationalism is exposed as pitifully inadequate and even destructive when it challenges the mysteries of human existence represented in the power of the gods. This attack on rationalism is worth noting when we think about the acts of recognition in Greek tragedy. The recognitions are accomplished not by mental process but by emotional suffering, not through philosophical reflection but through tragic realization. In *The Bacchae* there is an evocation and purging of rational responses in anticipation of the final recognition. Cadmus and Tiresias follow Dionysus for calculated reasons and their worship is treated comically at the opening of the play and revealed as ineffective in the conclusion. With Agave and Pentheus recognition comes only after a rational denial has been overwhelmed by hysteria and madness, as if a psychic block had to be blown away, not simply disproven by evidence, before true recognition could occur. An analogous process can be assumed in the audience as we pass from mere knowledge of the events of the play to the recognition of their emotional significance. The myth of Pentheus's destruction by the forces of Dionysus would, of course, be well known to the audience before the beginning of the play, and the story is recalled in the prologue. But the power the god represents, the final sovereignty of the irrational demon, will be manifest to the audience only when it is imaged in the torn body of Pentheus and the grief of Agave and Cadmus at the end of the play. The audience, too, exchanges knowledge for recognition.

Recognition in *The Bacchae* is induced by the madness and suffering that results from Dionysus's revenge against the house of Cadmus. As in the *Agamemnon* the act of revenge is a family affair. We recall that Dionysus is grandchild to Cadmus, nephew to Agave, and first cousin to Pentheus; yet he works the destruction of Cadmus's entire line. Mother kills son and the remnant of the royal family is sent into exile. In the Greek theater to kill or be killed by the enemy or stranger is not tragic; to kill or be killed by a dear one is, and the closer that blood relationship the more terrible and pitiable the act. Greek tragedies posit such relationships as at once fundamental to the moral life of the individual and yet peculiarly susceptible to tragic violence. Heroic characters as different as Orestes and Oedipus, Clytemnestra and Agave, repeatedly enact their tragedy by violating one or another of these relationships. The dramatists depict the tragic antagonism between the family bond and such countervailing forces as heroic self-interest, public responsibility, sexual jealousy, eros, and the hysteria of religious ecstasy. Certainly the primal act in Greek tragedy is the murder, intentional or unintentional, of one's own parent or child. Heroic assertion again and again culminates in this darkest of deeds. The act of familial violation in the plays seems a subconscious communal metaphor for the act of ultimate self-destruction that is more terrible than personal death, the unmitigated violation of the sacred bonds that establish one's identity in the Greek world. The Greek hero identifies himself as the son of his father: Greek tragedy shows him tearing apart that definition.

The Bacchae, then, resembles the most frequent pattern found in the Greek tragedies as it fuses the act of violence against the primal relationships that guarantee the hero's identity and the act of recognition, the final perception of what the demon has brought to pass despite the hero's intentions. The play's action evolves out of the conflicts that are so prominently exposed in the world of *The Bacchae*. Some of the more general oppositions are fairly evident: energy and ecstasy versus order and repression, nature versus the city, Asian versus Greek, female versus male, the group and its collective emotion versus the pride of the individual and the great family. *The Bacchae* holds these and other polarities in tension, but the point is not that Euripides is writing a drama of ideas about the clash of such abstractions. He is depicting a world where human civilization and the primal energies of life have separated and stand in opposition to each other. Divinity, society, the family, and the individual are seen as divided and split, moving inevitably to destruction. It is a world about to fall into ruin, given over to bands of roving religious cultists, the empty formalism of old priests and fathers like Tiresias and Cadmus, inhibited women and mothers driven to madness, a conservative young man naively attempting to control this world by external and internal repression, and a liberated young god of ecstasy who presides over it all with a concern only for his own acknowledgment and a mocking indifference to humanity and its city. At the center is the antagonism between Pentheus, the new king of Thebes, and the mysterious priest of Dionysus, a tension which represents the wider social division between the orderly Greek polis ruled by the hero and the ecstatic religion of the Dionysiacs, the chorus of Asian women and their Theban counterparts.

Skillfully employing the conventional resources of the Greek theater, Euripides gives us early in the play a powerful visual image of this fatal opposition between the ecstasy of the chorus and the civic values of the king. As Dionysus leaves the stage after his prologue, we see across the empty dancing circle of the chorus to the palace of Pentheus, an architectural expression of public order and the power of the state. Suddenly the chorus of Bacchae begins to fill the orchestra in front of the palace. The choruses in Greek tragedies frequently represent the city in which the action occurs, but this chorus clearly does not belong to the civilized world represented by the palace. Dressed in fawn skins, crowned with ivy and serpentine forms, waving the thyrsus (the long pinecone-topped staff associated with the worshipers of

Dionysus), its members dance around the orchestra to the accompaniment of flutes and small drums. Their dress, as well as their songs, evokes the wild life of nature, a presence that also directly confronts the audience as it looks beyond the palace to the open landscape just beyond the theater of Dionysus. Against the solid stability of the palace and the city this is a life of compelling musical and dance rhythms, fluid, turbulent, yet graceful.

We still can grasp something of the meaning of Dionysiac experience by attending closely to the thought and imagery of each of the choral odes, even if we have lost, in translation, the verbal rhythms of the Greek. In the *parodos*, the entrance song of the chorus, the Asian Bacchae communicate the spirit of Dionysiac worship. Throughout this choral ode the emphasis is on movement, swift and compulsive, yet somehow free. The verbal imagery creates an identity between the choral dance and the swift flight of the fawn from the hunter in a natural world that is alternately thrilling and peaceful, frightening and reassuring. The chorus sings first of the pleasures and blessings that come in the service of the god. Above all there are the blessings of enthusiasm and ecstasy, understood in their ancient literal sense:

> Blessed is he who hallows his life in the worship of god
> he whom the spirit of god possesseth, who is one
> with those who belong to the holy body of god.

> [73–75]

In the ritual of the god, Dionysus enters into, possesses, his followers, enabling the individual to become one with the group of worshipers. The isolation of individuality and personal consciousness is absorbed by the god and the collective. The chorus emphasizes the sweetness of the ecstasy but also hints that the god will be hard on those who resist it. In the middle of the opening ode the Bacchae describe the miraculous birth of their god and call on those within the palace to enter his worship. At the close of the ode, when the energy of music, dance, and religious song have reached a peak, they describe the frenzy of their priest as he tears and eats raw the animal in the ritual hunt. This priest is suddenly transformed in the imagery to the miracle-performing god. At the end of the *parodos* the god himself cries out through the collective voice of his worshipers. Dionysus is within the dancing Maenads. The act of divine possession has been embodied before the closed doors of the palace.

In the later odes the chorus, under the pressure of Pentheus's threats to imprison it, turns from celebrating the ecstatic worship of the god to first threatening Pentheus and then celebrating the god's revenge against the king. These songs are filled with the traditional moral warning against kingly hubris and insolence. It may seem surprising to see the ecstatic chorus of the *parodos* settle into the moral sentiments of more conventional choruses. The usual function of the chorus, as in the *Agamemnon* and the *Oedipus*, was to express the traditional, generally conservative wisdom of the collective mind of the city. In *The Bacchae* the convention is fulfilled ironically: these sentiments come not from the city elders but from a band of possessed, invading Asian women. Partly this suggests that despite appearances, and despite Pentheus's insistence that these women and their god are the strangers in Thebes, the Dionysiac experience is both older and more fundamental to the life of the city than the king and his palace. Partly also it suggests the moral ambivalence of mob psychology. The chorus makes no distinction between the Dionysiac ecstasy of the *parodos* and the revenge justice against the infidel Pentheus. In both there is the hunt and the slaughter. The conventional wisdom of the community conceals a brutal urge for satisfaction against the individual; communal justice here is a civilized form of the scapegoat sacrifice. The release of mob energy in forms of violence is common to both. A number of commentators on *The Bacchae* have pointed to the play's investigation of wisdom, *sophos*, where its meaning ranges from true self-knowledge and knowledge of one's limited place in nature to the intellectual skill of the debater and the animal cunning of the hunter. The chorus at the height of communal hysteria expresses the most radical sense of "wisdom" in the play:

—What is wisdom? What gift of the gods
is held in honor like this:
to hold your hand victorious
over the heads of those you hate?
Honor is precious forever.

[877–81]

This crucial passage, a refrain sung as Pentheus falls into the hands of Dionysus, is mysterious, but it seems to suggest either that wisdom is meaningless in comparison to the pleasure of savoring an accomplished revenge, or that this itself is true wisdom, the power to realize one's deepest desire against an enemy. This is what is beautiful and what all men seek. Taken either way, the chorus expresses the primacy of irrational will over any kind of knowledge.

The Asian Bacchae chorus has a counterpart in the band of Theban women who have been possessed by the god and compelled to leave the city to worship Dionysus on Mount Cithaeron. We do not see the Theban Maenads on the stage, but their actions are described to us by the messengers. The religious frenzy imposed on the rationalizing women of Thebes is more terrible than the willing service the Asian Maenads perform. What the Asian women celebrate in dance and song, the hunt and the sacrifice, the Theban Bacchae act out in earnest. The two long messenger speeches, marvelous examples of truly dramatic narrative, are parallel stories describing the Dionysiac rituals of the women of Thebes and the inevitable consequences of obstructing or violating those rites. The first messenger reports to Pentheus the idyllic nature worship of the women on Mount Cithaeron, how this was interrupted by a group of men, led by a city fellow, who spy on and attempt to catch the women, and how the intrusion drives the Theban Bacchae into frenzied attack on the men. Point by point, Pentheus is listening to a foreshadowing of his own fate. The second messenger reports the death of Pentheus; again we have an opening description of the peaceful Theban Bacchae, followed by the intrusion of the king which turns the women into a destructive mob that hunts him down and kills him. In both speeches the narrative pattern is the same: joyful ecstasy suddenly transformed into destructive violence by the opposition of the man from the city. The two messenger speeches are really paradigms of the full action of the play. With the Theban women the god has located the destructive force not in a band of invading foreigners but within the city itself. Just as the Asian women in their choral odes show that a traditional moral conservatism can be absorbed into Bacchic experience, so the formerly civilized women of the Greek city enact the primitive ritual of human sacrifice. Similarly, Dionysus will destroy Pentheus, not by external force, but by exploiting an irrational impulse within the young king.

Dionysus is an ironic presence in a world as deeply divided as the Greek world of Pentheus. The symbolism associated with Dionysus suggests that he is above all a god who transcends and unites opposites. The human form the god assumes for the play is bisexual in appearance: he unites the polarities of male and female. Dionysus is a god who arises in Asia, but claims Greece as his ancestral home: he is both the stranger and the rightful inheritor. Initiates in his worship discover both great gentleness and terrible cruelty. Preeminently the god of ecstasy and emotional release, Dionysus is calm and controlled in his exchanges with Pentheus. At the end of the play in his response to the human suffering he seems almost devoid of emotions. Throughout the performance we see the eerie smile fixed on the mask of the god. The smile is the face the god turns to the human tragedy of Pentheus and Thebes. The mask represents Dionysus's assurance that his power is absolute, that he is the necessity of the play. But the smile also suggests that the god of paradoxical unions transcends the divided and conflicting impulses of human nature. He confronts the anxiety of Pentheus with the face of total self-possession. Dionysus, the god of tragedy, wears the mask of comedy.

Over against this smiling image of the demon, Pentheus is the image of our essential humanity, outwardly assertive but inwardly weak. King of Thebes and scion of its royal family, he remains insecure of his authority and acts with the brutality and insolence of a tyrant toward his family and the worshipers of Dionysus. Pentheus prides himself on his male physique and character; he is presented as an athlete and a warrior, quick to take offense and call for his troops and armor. Yet he keeps returning to his fantasies about the sexual license of women, fantasies he projects as charges against the god. The young hero's fatal curiosity about the private rites of the women suggests that he lingers in the stage of adolescence, with his own sexual identity not yet fully established. Or is the overwhelming obsession and insecurity the inevitable reaction to his own and his culture's insistence on the completeness of his masculinity? Pentheus offers himself as the defender of Greek order, the hero of reason and restraint, but it is clear from his opening scene that he is the most irrational character on the stage. The young man seems always nervous and anxious. Unlike the god who unites opposites in his person, Pentheus is pulled apart by the polarities in his life. You can hear the tension in his footsteps, Cadmus says (213–14).

Dionysus's triumph over Pentheus is accomplished with great economy in a sequence of three scenes at the center of the play. In the first scene the king sets out to interrogate and charge the foreign priest with crimes against the city, but the action quickly turns into a verbal wrestling match, an agon, between the two young men. Although Dionysus with his coolness and cleverness easily gets the best of the argument, Pentheus commands the physical power of the state. The agon here can be compared with that between Oedipus and Tiresias, between the power of the king and the truth of the priest. With masculine arrogance Pentheus mocks the feminine appearance of Dionysus, contemptuously seizing the blond curls and the thyrsus. Pentheus's assault on the physical symbols of the Dionysiac priesthood barely conceals a fascination with what he is attacking. But here he overtly scoffs at the weakness of those symbols and relies on the forms of his political and masculine power, his military police, the chains that will bind the priest, and the prison that Pentheus thinks will hold him. Confronted with the supple and flowing images of Dionysus and his chorus, Pentheus can only think of rigidity and restriction. The absurdity of this effort of containment is quickly demonstrated after Pentheus takes Dionysus into the palace. The god's shape-changing and fluid existence proves impossible to bind down; the confinement results in an explosion that tears the royal palace apart. What happens to Pentheus's palace here, of course, foreshadows what happens next to his mind, then to his body, and finally to his family.

In the second scene Pentheus learns of the destruction performed by the Theban women on Mount Cithaeron and calls for his armor and army. He ignores what has happened to him inside the palace and the physical ruin of his house. The verbal exchange between Dionysus and the angry king is now cast not as a debate but as a temptation scene, similar to the scene in the *Agamemnon* where Clytemnestra lures Agamemnon across the carpet to his doom inside the palace. Dionysus dangles before Pentheus the opportunity of watching the secret rites his mother has joined, provided the young man allows himself to be disguised as a Bacchante. The god swiftly uncovers and exploits the irrational condition that lurks just beneath the surface in this champion of order. He calls attention to Pentheus's eagerness to observe the women's rituals. "Why are you so passionately curious?" (813). Curiosity is a quality on which ancient Greek men prided themselves, the detached, objective quest for knowledge that lay behind their great achievements in art, science, and philosophy. Pentheus stresses the purely intellectual nature of his inquisitiveness: he wants to be able to see the women without being seen, to remain apart from the orgiastic ritual which he will observe. But the god knows this detachment is only the subterfuge of shame, and that the man's curiosity is driven by a perverted eros. Pentheus, like anyone on the board of censors, is deeply attracted to what scandalizes him. He shies away from Dionysus's suggestion that he go back into the palace and disguise himself as a woman. "You want me, a man, to wear a woman's dress. But why?" (822). Yet he quickly reveals a fascination with the idea. The young man's insistence on his absolute masculinity only conceals a deeper, more ambivalent sexual curiosity. As king he tried to deny the darker, irrational forces of emotional life, powers that can overwhelm the conventional distinctions on which men construct their rational, moral, and civic orders. Pentheus's attempt at a simplistic order is twisted by the life force until he willingly becomes the opposite of what he imagined himself to be. As he enters the palace we can see that the man is driven by an inner compulsion that will command him to act out Dionysus's plan.

The final scene between Dionysus and Pentheus is an exhibition of the proud king's helplessness as the irrational force embodied in the god possesses him. Pentheus emerges from his palace costumed as a Bacchante, with long dress, fawn skin, a wig of long blond curls, and the symbolic thyrsus in one hand. The man seems in a hypnotic trance; instead of the human priest he sees Dionysus now in animal form, as a powerful bull. The god tells the king that he now sees more truly than he did before. As well as a costume change, there has been a psychic alteration in the young man. Pentheus displays a feminine anxiety about the neatness of his hair and long dress. The transvestite metamorphosis of the virile young king brings to the surface the female principle he has rejected. The rigid distinctions the king tried to enforce between reason and emotion, order and ecstasy, male domi-

nance and female submission, have collapsed within his own
psyche. Cruelly guided by the god, the king reveals what he
has carefully hidden, especially from himself. Dionysus
makes of this scene a ritual exposition of human helplessness
and blindness. He leads Pentheus through a grimly ironic
dialogue through which the transformed king is made to embrace his own destruction before he is led off to his death.

The three brief scenes whereby the doom of Pentheus is
encompassed are extraordinary in their theatrical power. We
can see that the third scene is carefully designed as an exact
reversal of the first. In that first meeting Pentheus seems to
triumph over the priest, and in the last Dionysus has absolute
power over the king. The opening exchange resembles a
rational debate, the final one seems a nightmare. Pentheus's
mockery of the god's feminine appearance and dress is
answered by his obsessive concern with his own female
apparel in the last scene: now he wears the blond curls and
waves the thyrsus he earlier threatened. The swiftness of this
ironic reversal underlines how close Pentheus's opening
hubris was to his final blindness. The action is less a development or transformation of Pentheus's character than a revelation of what has always lurked inside him. The reversal of the
action is adumbrated in the major image pattern of the play.
Early in the play Pentheus frequently proclaims himself the
hunter of frenzied Bacchae: in the second half of the drama
the hunter turns out to be the hunted, and the metaphor of
the animal hunt is transformed by the Theban women into a
brutal reality. Such quick turns and reversals are characteristic of Greek tragedy, but with Euripides they seem to represent a fundamental principle of his dramatic world. In *The
Bacchae* the multiple reversals are presided over by a god who
cannot be limited to a single form, constantly changes shape,
and manifests himself only in momentary disguises. Rational-
ists like Pentheus who try to pin him down inevitably follow
one illusion after another. The reversals of *The Bacchae*
evoke a universe governed by an uncertainty principle, a

world where instability afflicts the city, family, and individual. Even what appears the most secure fact about Pentheus, son of Echion—his masculine identity—is exposed as unstable.

There are traditional elements in the scenes between Pentheus and Dionysus: the agon between two opposed characters, the temptation, the employment of ironic reversal as a structural principle can all be found throughout the plays of Aeschylus and Sophocles. What is original with Euripides is his focus on a psychological action. This is suggested in the first scene when Dionysus accuses Pentheus of a specific kind of ignorance: "You do not know who you are" (507). In *Oedipus the King* Tiresias charges Oedipus with a similar blindness. Both exchanges stress the limits of human knowledge, but in different ways. Tiresias accuses Oedipus of not knowing who his true parents are and, hence, what he has done. Oedipus's ignorance concerns the meaning of the acts he has performed; there is nothing to suggest that Tiresias means that Oedipus has failed to understand his own nature, the kind of man he is. The charge has to do with external relationships, not internal ones. Pentheus gives an Oedipus-like answer to Dionysus's taunt that he does not know who he is. He says, "I am Pentheus, son of Echion and Agave" (508). This is a traditional Greek answer, that a man's identity is determined by his lineage, that he is who he is because of who his father and mother are. But this is clearly not what the accusing god has in mind. What Dionysus charges Pentheus with is a lack of self-knowledge, a failure to grasp the emotional makeup of his own nature. What the god then exposes in the subsequent temptation and possession is the profound irrational impulse within Pentheus that he had failed to recognize as part of his identity. The dramatic emphasis here is on the psychology of character, the layers of internal life that make up the character's identity, not, as in Aeschylus and Sophocles, on actions that define character.

The ancient Greeks thought that any radical change in a man's character was explicable only in terms of divine inter-

ference. In a culture that believed deeply in the permanent
identity of character the sudden emergence in a man of a
hitherto unforeseen passion seemed to require some kind of
external explanation. We retain something of this view when
we say of our own acts, "I don't know what came over me."
Euripides, although the myth he employs in the play conveys the traditional idea of external possession, breaks with
it and creates a psychological tragedy. The demon is within
Pentheus as surely as it is embodied in the human disguise of
the god who confronts him. Despite Pentheus's insistence,
Dionysus is not a foreigner in Thebes; he is native-born and a
rightful inheritor, the god from within. In their final scene
together there is a powerful visual connection between
Pentheus and his demon. Up to this point Pentheus and
Dionysus have been sharply distinguishable by dress and bearing. The muscular king in royal or military dress is the visual
antithesis of the stranger with his curls and Bacchic costume.
In their last scene, however, with Pentheus transformed in
mind and appearance, the two strangely bisexual young men,
with blond curls, fawn skins, and thyrsus, stand before the
palace door almost indistinguishable, like double images of a
single reality. What appeared to be an opposition turns out
to be an identity.

The scene is at once psychological and ritualistic. What still
makes Euripides' dramaturgy unique is that he presents
his explorations of the psychological forces in the hieratic
form of Greek tragedy. No subsequent dramatist has com-
bined the kind of psychological complexity we find in
Pentheus with those conventions of ancient tragedy—the
myths, the presence of the gods, the chorus, the masks,
ritual dress and acting style of the performers—that raise the
action to an impersonal, universal level.

In relocating the drama of fate within the psychology of
his characters, Euripides also transformed the traditional
view of the tragic hero. Pentheus is not merely overcome
by Dionysus, he is humiliated as his inner weakness is ex-

posed and savagely mocked by the god. The exhibition of the king in female dress is designed to rob the hero of what remains of his dignity. Indeed, the bizarre costume change is a theatrical device more appropriate to comedy than to tragedy, to the burlesque tradition of Aristophanes than to the heroic drama of Aeschylus and Sophocles. For Euripides, the representative man is not the larger-than-life hero of the older tragedy. Aristotle in the *Poetics* quotes Sophocles as saying that Euripides presented men as they actually were, not magnified into heroic greatness. Pentheus, as his name in Greek implies, is the hero as sufferer; he points away from an older conception of the hero and toward the more complicated, less monolithic heroes of modern tragedy.

In the messenger's speech reporting Pentheus's fate on the mountain there is a passage that vividly expresses both the character of Pentheus and the larger power that destroys him. This is the description of the miracle Dionysus performs just before Pentheus is attacked and torn to pieces by the Maenads:

> And now the stranger worked a miracle.
> Reaching for the highest branch of a great fir,
> he bent it down, down, down to the dark earth,
> till it was curved the way a taut bow bends
> or like a rim of wood when forced about the circle
> of a wheel. Like that he forced that mountain fir
> down to the ground. No mortal could have done it.
> Then he seated Pentheus at the highest tip
> and with his hands let the trunk rise straightly up,
> slowly and gently, lest it throw its rider.
> And the tree rose, towering to heaven, with my master
> huddled at the top. And now the Maenads saw him
> more clearly than he saw them.

[1063–75]

The Dionysiac power is in the hand of the god but also in the sap and spring of the tree. Note how the double simile

also locates that mysterious, indwelling energy in the tools
of civilization, the bow and the wheel. It is the life force,
present everywhere and symbolized in Dionysus, that Pentheus
blindly sought to repress. Pentheus, seated at the highest tip,
huddled and pathetic as the tree springs upright, is the image
of man diminished by forces that he cannot understand and
that dwarf him in size. The messenger still sees him as "master"
but his present position is clearly an ironic comment on the
king's former hubris. The phallic implication of the image
mocks Pentheus's male superiority. As in the psychological
action of the dramatic scenes, the description shows man entirely dominated by the irrational energies of life that thrust
up from beneath him. At this moment it is the Maenads in
their Dionysiac ecstasy who see accurately, not the man who
wanted to see without being seen. The man is swiftly pulled
into the frenzied orgy of the Bacchae. Here all personal identity is lost; he is now the animal to be hunted, torn apart,
and devoured, the victim of the god he resembles in the ritual
of human sacrifice.

If the play were to end with the reported death of Pentheus,
the final image would be the chorus of Bacchae singing jubi-
lantly in front of the fallen king's palace. The theater would
again be filled with the collective ecstasy that we saw and
heard in the *parodos*. This might be a conclusion appropriate
to sacred ritual, but the human drama does not end here. The
choral hymn of triumph is interrupted by the entrance of a
single, frenzied Bacchante. It is Agave, daughter of Cadmus
and mother of Pentheus. She has been mentioned throughout
the play but now makes her first appearance. She has mounted
on her thyrsus the head of her son, still crowned by the wig
of blond curls. Agave thinks it is the head of a long-maned
lion that she and her Bacchae have hunted and killed. She
caresses the head as a trophy of her female victory, surpassing
in heroic skill what the male members of her family could
accomplish. This deluded chant is broken by the entrance of
Cadmus. In contrast to Agave he moves slowly, partly from

age but also partly because he attends a burden that is being carried onto the stage. It is a bier holding the torn remnants of Pentheus's body, minus the head. The fragments of the once proud king are carefully placed in front of the palace door where we last saw Pentheus.

Cadmus gently leads Agave out of her madness into an understanding of what she has done and the true nature of the prize she carries. She gradually regains her perception of individual relationships and identities until she can recognize the trophy on her thyrsus as the head of Pentheus. Pathetically she carries on the reintegration by piecing together the torn body of her son and restoring his head. Agave's return to sanity in the last part of the play reverses the process her son underwent and completes the total psychological action in the play. Pentheus's skeptical rationalism developed into hubris and then into madness; Agave emerges from madness into sanity, not Pentheus's rationalism, but an understanding of her weakness against the power of Dionysus. Unlike Pentheus earlier, she now knows who she is.

Dionysus now appears in his true form. He stands above the palace in the place reserved for the immortal and all-powerful gods. He no longer appears on the stage with the human actors, and the physical distance between the god and the family of Cadmus underlines the final inhumanity of the god. He pronounces the doom of the entire family. The surviving members are to be separated and driven off into exile from Thebes. Cadmus and his wife will wander into Asia and be transformed into serpents, thus reversing and undoing the civilizing act, the slaying of the serpent, by which Cadmus founded the city. What Dionysus is prophesying is the end of the family and the city, the dismemberment of civilization. When Cadmus suggests that this excessive punishment is unjust, the god can only repeat that he has been blasphemed by this family, thus its end is fated. This is the kind of answer that comes when there are no moral reasons for what is happening, only the recognition of force. The supple, fluid figure of Dionysus has stiffened and hardened into a brute necessity. What he does is so inhuman that he cannot even use human language to explain it, and his speech dwindles into silence.

Ironically, the theophany of the god corresponds with the most movingly human moment of the play. At the end Cadmus and Agave are no longer looking at the god but at each other. The profound pity the father and daughter show for each other and the dead Pentheus is the dramatic center of the play's final moments and draws our attention away from Dionysus. The contrast between the compassion of father and daughter here and Pentheus's harsh treatment of his grandfather and mother at the opening of the play is surely intended. The destruction of the house of Cadmus has restored, just before the final dissolution of the family, the love that its members had lacked. As so often happens in the Greek theater, the internal action is given physical presence in a series of visible gestures. Agave, filled with the Dionysiac spirit and waving the thyrsus with Pentheus's head impaled on it, had boasted of her victory accomplished by "the white and delicate hands of women" (1205–06). A moment later when she realizes what she has done, the hands that had torn her son apart are the hands that gently lift and caress the parts of his body as she sings her mother's lament. Then she clasps Cadmus in her white arms like a "white swan warding its weak old father" (1365). At last the arms are forced apart and the final embrace between father and daughter ends as each goes separately into a life of exile. In the midst of total disaster, the changing gestures of the woman's arms act out the recovery of her human identity as mother and daughter.

Euripides' final image of tragic man was not simply of one who was doomed to suffer but of one who was also capable of feeling the suffering of others. The pity felt by the characters for each other and by the audience for all the characters is the human complement to the terror inspired by the indifferent god above the palace. Within the suffering Agave and Cadmus experience at the end of the play, the familial love expressed by their compassion for each other's fate makes

them recognizably human and saves them from being like the
god. It is as if the tragedy has evoked and exorcised the spirit
of Dionysus. Like all Greek tragedy *The Bacchae* enacts the
deepest kinds of truly human behavior as it reveals the re-
morseless power of the demons from which no man can
escape.

BIBLIOGRAPHICAL NOTE

Euripides was born ca. 484 B.C. in Attica and died in Macedon in
406 B.C. *The Bacchae* was performed posthumously in 406 B.C.

I have used the William Arrowsmith translation of *The Bacchae* in
Euripides 5 of *The Complete Greek Tragedies*, ed. David Grene and
Richmond Lattimore (Chicago: University of Chicago Press, 1959).* I
have also consulted the translation and commentary by Geoffrey Kirk,
The Bacchae (Englewood Cliffs, N.J.: Prentice-Hall, 1970).

This essay is heavily indebted to the introduction and notes of E. R.
Dodds, *Euripides: Bacchae* (Oxford: Clarendon Press, 2d ed., 1960),
and to Dodds's *The Greeks and the Irrational* (Berkeley: University of
California Press, 1959).* I am also generally and specifically indebted
to D. J. Conacher, *Euripidean Drama: Myth, Theme and Structure*
(Toronto: University of Toronto Press, 1967); G. M. A. Grube, *The
Drama of Euripides* (London: Methuen, 1941); Gilbert Murray, *Euripi-
des and His Age* (London: Oxford University Press, 2d ed., 1965);
Essays on Euripidean Drama, ed. Gilbert Norwood (Berkeley: University of California Press, 1954); *Euripides: A Collection of Critical
Essays*, ed. Erich Segal (Englewood Cliffs, N.J.: Prentice-Hall, 1968);*
T. B. L. Webster, *The Tragedies of Euripides* (London: Methuen, 1967);
and R. P. Winnington-Ingram, *Euripides and Dionysus* (Cambridge: University Press, 1948).

For general material on Greek tragedy see the bibliographical notes
to Michael Holahan's essay on the *Oresteia* and Paul Fry's essay on
Oedipus the King in this volume. For further background on the nature
of Dionysiac worship, see Walter F. Otto, *Dionysus: Myth and Cult*
(Bloomington: Indiana University Press, 1965);* for the possible ritual
origins of the drama see Gilbert Murray, "Excursus on the Ritual Forms
Preserved in Greek Tragedy," in Jane Ellen Harrison, *Themis: A Study
of the Social Origins of Greek Religion* (Cambridge: Cambridge University Press, 1912), and Sir Arthur Pickard-Cambridge, *Dithyramb, Tragedy and Comedy* (Oxford: Clarendon Press, 2d ed. rev. T. B. L. Webster,
1962).

*Paperbound available.

A MIDSUMMER NIGHT'S DREAM

Clifford Earl Ramsey

The history of interpretation, and misinterpretation, of Shakespeare's *A Midsummer Night's Dream* demonstrates more strikingly than that of most works a deep truth of literary history: changes in critical fashion, changes in the theory of literature and in approaches to particular literary works, virtually alter those works themselves. Criticism shapes our fundamental responses to the works of art it contemplates. Whatever *Iliad* we hear, it surely is not the poem Homer sang.

In our time we have come increasingly to accept the idea, notably articulated by T. S. Eliot and Northrop Frye, that the "primary context" of any individual work of literature is other literature, that all literature—not just that we call neoclassical—is inherently and inescapably traditional. We are also beginning to see that criticism itself is an intrinsic part of this "primary context," that the history of literature is deeply interfused with the history of interpretation. Thus the *Aeneid*, as well as growing out of the *Iliad*, also recoils upon it. Virgil is involved in an act of criticism as well as an act of creation. Criticism, hardly less than creation itself, is a consequence of and gives expression to our deepest needs—needs that are often unacknowledged. Euripides could not write plays like Sophocles any more than he could accept Homer's gods. The Middle Ages had to moralize Ovid. Shakespeare's plays will mean what we need them to mean.

The *Midsummer Night's Dream* we see and study today is, in an almost literal sense, not the play Coleridge saw and studied, not the play Johnson saw and studied, perhaps not even the play Shakespeare wrote. My point is not simply that modern criticism of *A Midsummer Night's Dream* differs from that of earlier periods. We expect that. The point I want to stress is that the differences are more striking in the case of this play and therefore that a consideration of it may have much to tell us about the way we think critically today; certainly as much as the way we think critically today has to tell us about *A Midsummer Night's Dream*.

It might be imprudent to claim that today's audiences enjoy *A Midsummer Night's Dream* more than audiences of previous eras, but it does seem clear that today's scholars and critics—and teachers—pay it far more attention. We do know that a shrewd member of one audience three centuries ago could not enjoy it. On Michaelmas Day in 1662 Samuel Pepys wrote this comment in his diary:

> To the King's Theatre, where we saw "Midsummer Night's Dream," which I had never seen before, nor shall ever again, for it is the most insipid ridiculous play that ever I saw in my life. I saw, I confess, some good dancing and some handsome women, and which was all my pleasure.

To give Pepys and the play their due, we can assume that he is likely to have witnessed a very uninspired and truncated version. But a century and a half later we can catch an unquestionably great Shakespearean critic—Coleridge, discussing the dating and sequence of the plays—observing that *A Midsummer Night's Dream* "hardly appeared to belong to the complete maturity of his genius" because when writing that comedy Shakespeare was "ripening his powers" for such works as *Julius Caesar*, *Troilus and Cressida*, *Coriolanus*, and *Cymbeline*. As late as 1951, in a standard *Introduction to*

Shakespeare, one could find the then still fairly common opinion that the play was mostly a glittering fabric of "moonlight, with a touch of moonshine." But by 1961, in an essay provocatively entitled "The Mature Comedies," Frank Kermode was "prepared to maintain that *A Midsummer Night's Dream* is Shakespeare's best comedy."

If we take *A Midsummer Night's Dream* more seriously than former eras did, it is partly because the idea of comedy, the genre itself, is now taken more seriously. (The same point might be made about romance and about pastoral, the other genres most prominent in *A Midsummer Night's Dream.*) We have begun to glimpse the profound suggestiveness lurking in Socrates' oracular assertion, made in the presence of the drowsy Aristophanes at the close of Plato's *Symposium,* that the genius of comedy and the genius of tragedy is the same. So in our time we find Northrop Frye perceiving a ritual pattern of death-and-resurrection lying behind both comedy and tragedy, and thence arguing that two things follow from this: "first, that tragedy is really implicit or uncompleted comedy; second, that comedy contains a potential tragedy within itself."

Such arguments are briefs for the parity of comedy and tragedy, not their identity. The genius of comedy and tragedy may be the same, they may be equally serious or equally profound, but their forms, their characteristic structures, will be different. The comic muse and the tragic muse dance to different rhythms. So Frye and modern critics like him stress the shape, the characteristic movement, of each genre: whereas the characteristic movement of tragedy is toward isolation, they theorize, that of comedy is toward integration. C. L. Barber describes "saturnalian" movement in Shakespearean comedy, a movement "through release to clarification." Frye, in "The Argument of Comedy," an account now so famous as to have become a shibboleth, speaks of Shakespeare's "drama of the green world" and defines the archetypal pattern of that drama as one of "withdrawal and return": the characteristic action of a Shakespearean comedy, Frye hypothesizes, "begins in a world represented as a normal world, moves into the green world, goes into a metamorphosis there in which the comic resolution is achieved, and returns to the normal world." Perhaps the common thread in such theories is a willingness to take seriously the wish-fulfillment pattern of all comedy. Comedy may only present the "beautiful lie," but for all our cynicism and secularism there is something in each of us that wants to believe in those happy endings. What the modern theorists of comedy are finally claiming is that the comic muse responds to the renewing cycles of time, and so refreshes time.

What of the structure of this particular comedy? I will suggest that the elements of external form in *A Midsummer Night's Dream* correspond to its internal elements, that the play's structure is precisely commensurate with its argument, that its shape *is* its vision. The play's "scenic" structure articulates its thematic design. (By "scene" I mean a formal unit that is both dramatic and spatial.) What we shall find, if we examine the scenic structure of this play, is that the organization of scenes—the juxtaposition and interplay of scenes, the movement between and through them—is everywhere expressive of diversity and variety and opposition, and yet at the same time paradoxically everywhere expressive also of harmony and concord and integration; that is, everywhere expressive of the play's twin themes, the power of love and the power of the imagination.

In focusing on the scenic structure of *A Midsummer Night's Dream*, I am following out the implications of a suggestion made by Madeleine Doran, who reminds us that the original quarto was not divided into acts and scenes. Taking the quarto as the authoritative text and taking a clear stage to represent a change of scene, Doran concludes that there are only seven scenes in the whole play (no other play by Shakespeare has so few scenes). According to Doran's scheme, the

play begins and ends, respectively, with two scenes outside
the wood (the same two, but in reverse order). Podlike, these
first two and last two scenes enclose the core of the play, the
three scenes in the wood. If we place the first and last scenes
in the court of Theseus, and the second and sixth somewhere
inside Athens where Peter Quince and his crew of patches can
rehearse (possibly Quince's house), we could diagram the
play's scenic structure like this: T;Q// W, W, W //Q;T. Such a
scheme crystallizes the fundamental thrust of the play. Thus
anatomized, there can be little doubt that its central action
is the movement into and out of the wood. Such a scheme
also crystallizes our awareness that there are three major
domains within the play: the play occurs in three places only,
occupies only three landscapes. Each of these three landscapes constitutes what might be called a separate "world."
Such talk of "worlds" seems more persuasive than usual because it is solidly rooted in the spatial and dramatic facts of
the play's setting and organization. In *A Midsummer Night's
Dream*, there is the world of the court, presided over by
Theseus; there is the world of the hardhanded amateur actors,
presided over by Peter Quince (this second world, like the
first, is inside Athens); and there is the world of the magical
wood, presided over by Oberon (this world is outside Athens
and obeys none of its rules). These three places or landscapes,
these three separate environments or milieus, constitute three
different "worlds" in the sense that each projects different
values and styles, each offers a different slice or dimension of
experience. These three worlds of the play define three separate aspects of reality; they provide three *perspectives on
reality*. Each world of the play gives "a local habitation and
a name" to, a different way of looking at, apprehending, or
organizing human experience. Furthermore, the way the play
holds these worlds up against each other, makes them balance
and mirror and qualify each other, how the play moves between and through these worlds, is at the heart of its comic
meaning.

For a brief and partial illustration, observe the movement of the young lovers through these "worlds": they flee the court or normal world; they enter the wood or "green" world, for them a scene first of confusion, then of resolution; and they finally return to the court where, having been changed, they can be assimilated. Admittedly, this is a rather facile account of the young lovers' experience in the play; experience never reduces itself to a diagram. I ought to indicate that the lovers, after their assimilation into the court world, are entertained by a parody of their incongruous nighttime experience in the wood (one way to take the mechanicals' presentation of the Pyramus and Thisby story). Too, I ought to acknowledge the possibility that the court has changed more than the lovers (all the members of the court did, after all, finally enter the wood), and the possibility that the court —having relaxed its laws and solemnized three weddings—is now free and flexible enough to make room for the young lovers. But even such a facile account can suggest how, by the end of *A Midsummer Night's Dream*, the young lovers, having shuttled between worlds, have undergone a change of perspective; and, in contemplating them, so have we. Matters are not so crystal clear as our diagram because the play throughout manifests an extraordinary diversity, but the notion of perspective may help guide us through the diversity. Indeed, I would be willing to maintain that almost everything in this play can be understood as either the comically incongruous clash, or the richly inclusive fusion, of perspectives.

Together, the first three scenes of *A Midsummer Night's Dream* initiate its first major movement—the entrance into the wood. Individually, each scene defines one of the play's major worlds, one of its main perspectives on reality. The opening lines of the first scene quickly reveal an imposing world, the court of Athens. The first nineteen lines of the play introduce many of its most important concerns; these lines suggest what Theseus and his queen are like, and they

orient us in the kind of world Theseus inhabits and controls,
the kind of perspective he embodies. Theseus and Hippolyta
open the play by speaking of their imminent nuptials:

> *Theseus.* Now, fair Hippolyta, our nuptial hour
>   Draws on apace. Four happy days bring in
>   Another moon; but O, methinks, how slow
>   This old moon wanes! She lingers my desires,
>   Like to a stepdame, or a dowager,
>   Long withering out a young man's revenue.
> *Hippolyta.* Four days will quickly steep themselves in
>   night,
>   Four nights will quickly dream away the time;
>   And then the moon, like to a silver bow
>   New-bent in heaven, shall behold the night
>   Of our solemnities.

Then Theseus instructs his master of revels, Philostrate, to
stir the Athenian youth to merriment, to

> Awake the pert and nimble spirit of mirth,
> Turn melancholy forth to funerals;
> The pale companion is not for our pomp.

After Philostrate exits, Theseus again addresses his Amazon
bride-to-be:

> Hippolyta, I wooed thee with my sword,
> And won thy love doing thee injuries;
> But I will wed thee in another key,
> With pomp, with triumph, and with reveling.

Here in these opening lines we already have the motifs of
the moon, desire and dreams, mirth and solemnity. We have a
sense of time as both a fructifying and a withering force, as
something linked with the rhythms of nature and with the
rhythms of human feeling and ceremony. Striking a dominant tone for the whole work, the first line's "nuptial hour"
provides an overarching frame, an enveloping action, for the

entire play. Partly a Renaissance prince, partly the great hero of antique fables, very much the Theseus of Plutarch and Chaucer, the lord of Athens seems established in these opening lines as a man of action and of reason, of authority and maturity and eloquence, as a figure of measured and civilized dignity. He seems very much in control of his world. Theseus knows what he feels and says what he means. Perhaps what most makes Theseus and Hippolyta imposing here is the cadence of their speech, their poised and urbane idiom. They seem to represent an achieved mastery of experience realized in great magnificence of style.

Here, and in the last scenes of the play too, Theseus is a figure of self-proclaimed potency. Pulsating just under the elegant surface of these first lines are Theseus's assertive energies: he wooed his Amazon queen with his sword, and he can't wait to get her into bed. Control may be less easy than it first appears. Such energies could have a darker, more threatening aspect. They could issue in injuries. In each of the play's first three scenes, we can observe a tendency for irrepressible desires to break out in quarreling or confusion. As modern critics unfailingly point out, these first scenes are haunted by the threat of contention.

Thus, immediately after the opening nineteen lines, Egeus comes in "full of vexation" (1.1.23) and appeals—against his daughter—to "the sharp Athenian law" (1.1.162), which "by no means" may be extenuated, according to Theseus (1.1.117 ff.). What is the "complaint" of Egeus?—simply that Hermia loves someone other than her father's choice. Theseus, less flexible than we might have hoped, leaves the stage ruling that Hermia must accept her father's choice or suffer the penalty of death or "single life." Within a hundred lines, the court—at first a world ruled by thoughts of an imminent "nuptial hour"—has been revealed as a world inimical to young love, a world with little tolerance for "feigning" love or "feigning" verses (1.1.31). The rest of the play will be required to integrate the young lovers into the court. The rest of this first scene alternates, without resolution, between images of love as special pain ("The course of true love never did run smooth," line 134) and images of love as special vision ("Things base and vile, holding no quantity,/Love can transpose to form and dignity./Love looks not with the eyes, but with the mind," lines 232-34). Let me pause over one image where, as it were, the "pain" and the "vision" come together. I speak of Lysander's description of his plan to flee Athens with Hermia. The urgings of unfulfilled desire drive them out of Athens, one presumes, but an image of beauty and repose—of glittering moonmade reflections—is used to describe the moment of their fleeing; the young lovers intend to flee the city when Phoebe beholds "her silver visage in the wat'ry glass,/Decking with liquid pearl the bladed grass" (1.1.209-11). In the image, if not yet in the action, frustration resolves itself into a dew.

From Theseus's court—a stately, aristocratic world of elegance and authority (though a world not yet elastic enough to accommodate the young lovers)—we pass to another, and startlingly different, version of the "normal" or "first" world. Athens is also the domain of Peter Quince and his handicraftsmen. The second scene of *A Midsummer Night's Dream* takes us into a more "barren sort" (3.2.13) of world. Quince and his "crew of patches" are "hempen homespuns," "rude mechanicals" (3.1.74 and 3.2.9). Quince the Carpenter (and playwright), Snug the Joiner, Bottom the Weaver, Flute the Bellows-Mender, Snout the Tinker, and Robin Starveling the Tailor are "hard-handed men" that "never labored in their minds" until their interlude for Theseus's nuptial (5.1.72-75). In their world one must "hold" or "cut bowstrings" (1.2.111). Their language (unlike that of Theseus and Hippolyta or that of Oberon and Titania) consistently betrays disjunctions between intention and expression, fact and idiom. Today's critics see the mechanicals as well-intentioned literalists and stress the parodic value of their failure to comprehend the nature of dramatic illusion. The mechanicals repair plays much as they might repair houses. Quince's hope that "here is a play fitted" (1.2.66)—"Here is the scroll of every man's name which is thought fit, through all Athens, to play in our interlude before the Duke and the Duchess, on his wedding day at night" (1.2.4-7)—receives this judgment from Philostrate in the last scene: "in all the play/There is not one word apt, one player fitted." Philostrate does admit, however, that he laughed until he cried (5.1.61-70).

Prosaic as the perspective of the mechanicals is, they project a world of sprawling energies. There is something vital about their good will and their rude wit. Like the young lovers, the mechanicals are headed for the wood too, where they expect to "rehearse most obscenely and courageously" (1.2.108). Yet at this point there is a sense in which the mechanicals, compared with the rather stiff, conventional, and undifferentiated lovers of the first scene, convince us that a "paramour" is, indeed, "a thing of naught" (4.2.14). Of course Bottom has his irrepressible desires too—he wants to play every role in Quince's interlude. No one ever had a stronger histrionic appetite than Nick Bottom. In fact, Bottom's irrepressible desires might have led to contentions like those of the first and third scenes (his desires do lead to a modest degree of confusion, one can safely say), if Quince were not able to "manage" his realm better than Theseus does his. Certainly Bottom well deserves the title "my mimic" that Puck gives him (3.2.19).

In a curious sense, Flute's hilarious pronouncement later that Bottom "hath simply the best wit of any handicraft man in Athens" (4.2.9-10) does not seem entirely unjustified. In his inadvertent way, Bottom often stumbles into some of the play's most trenchant utterances. In the third act, for example, Bottom tells Titania that she can "have little reason" for loving him and then utters lines that some critics find definitive of the play's theme:

And yet, to say the truth, reason and love keep little company together nowadays; the more the pity, that

some honest neighbors will not make them friends. Nay,
I can gleek upon occasion. [3.1.129–33]

In a fine recent essay, J. Dennis Huston has demonstrated
that one of Bottom's earliest "gleeks" is one of his most
trenchant. When Peter Quince tells Bottom that he is set
down for Pyramus, Bottom asks, "What is Pyramus? A lover,
or a tyrant?" (1.2.22). Apparently Bottom believes that these
two parts, lover and tyrant, subsume all the roles a man could
play; curiously enough, as Huston demonstrates, the play's
opening scenes suggest that Bottom is virtually correct. Egeus
surely acts like a tyrant. The behavior of Oberon and Titania
in the next scene to some degree convicts them of the charge
of tyranny. If we extend the idea of tyranny to include the
caprice of passion's oppressive hold on us when infatuated,
then the young lovers tell us something of tyranny too. Perhaps Bottom's query most revealingly recoils upon Theseus
himself. Having entered the stage in the first scene as a lover,
Theseus leaves it as a tyrant. But Egeus may not be on the
stage at the end of *A Midsummer Night's Dream*, and as one
of its final delights the play will appear to banish tyranny.

From the homely and literalistic yet strangely life-filled
world of the mechanicals, we pass to yet another extraordinarily different scene, the green world of the wood and the
exotic perspective of the fairies. Possibly expecting a world
of fertility, we find a world of misrule. Oberon and Titania are
contentious indeed. Their irrepressible desires for the "sweet"
changeling boy have produced the most violent and pervasive
disorder of the play, a "distemperature" throughout the
natural world. Titania accuses Oberon of love for Hippolyta.
Oberon in turn accuses his queen of love for Theseus. Titania's
retort to Oberon's charges describes a world upside down, a
scene of "brawls," of the "forgeries of jealousy," of "con-
tagious fogs," of flooding rivers, rotting grain, and diseased
flocks:

The human mortals want their winter here;

> No night is now with hymn or carol blest.
> Therefore the moon, the governess of floods,
> Pale in her anger, washes all the air,
> That rheumatic diseases do abound.
> And thorough this distemperature we see
> The seasons alter. . . .
> .   .   .   .   .   .
> . . . The spring, the summer,
> The childing autumn, angry winter, change
> Their wonted liveries; and the mazèd world,
> By their increase, now knows not which is which.
> And this same progeny of evils comes
> From our debate, from our dissension;
> We are their parents and original.
>
>   [2.1.101–17]

The cause of this "progeny of evils," the "little changeling boy," seems out of all proportion to the consequences.

   The speech in which Titania explains her fervent determination to keep the changeling boy (2.1.121–37) is one of the most elusive and suggestive in *A Midsummer Night's Dream*. Titania tells Oberon to set his heart at rest; all fairyland cannot buy the child from her because she felt a deep attachment for his mother. Titania's remembrance of the delicately playful, affectionate relationship she had with the boy's mother seems at first to call up a happier and more perfect world:

> His mother was a vot'ress of my order,
> And, in the spicèd Indian air, by night,
> Full often hath she gossiped by my side,
> And sat with me on Neptune's yellow sands,
> Marking th' embarkèd traders on the flood;
> When we have laughed to see the sails conceive
> And grow big-bellied with the wanton wind;
> Which she, with pretty and swimming gait
> Following—her womb then rich with my young squire—
> Would imitate, and sail upon the land,

> To fetch me trifles, and return again,
> As from a voyage, rich with merchandise.

What Titania provides in these lines is a paradigm of visionary perception, a model of how the optics seeing generate the objects seen, a glimpse of poetic consciousness actively at work. Too, like Bottom, Titania and her votaress have rich histrionic sensibilities. Like Bottom, the votaress is a "mimic," and with her at least imitation becomes transformation. But unlike Bottom, Titania and her votaress cannot be accused of literalness; they laugh all the while. Their visionary consciousness is suffused with self-consciousness.

Perhaps what is most important in Titania's speech is how she subtly, and yet very explicitly, interweaves love and the imagination. She and her big-bellied votaress playfully imagine the ships' sails to be big-bellied: "we have laughed to see the sails *conceive*/And *grow* big-bellied with the *wanton* wind." The pun here on "conceive" is especially suggestive, and pertinent to the whole play. The lover and the poet both "conceive" a world, bring a world into being; each, being a visionary, returns from the voyage of experience "rich with merchandise." But at this very moment Titania pulls us up short with what may be the most sobering and poignant lines in the play. Almost with casualness she reveals that this haunted grove is no paradise, reminds us that we inhabit a mutable, indeed a mortal, world. Titania tells the rest of her votaress's story:

> But she, being mortal, of that boy did die;
> And for her sake do I rear up her boy,
> And for her sake I will not part with him.

For the Renaissance, death is a corollary of the principle of plenitude. A world of growth is a world of change. A fecund world must be a mutable world. Does *A Midsummer Night's Dream* also hint that the reverse might be true? Is a world without change less fecund? Do Titania and Oberon possibly regret their immutability? Are they, like the Wife of Bath, possibly childless? Does their passionate desire for the *changeling* boy suggest that the creatures of eternity are in love with time?

In any event, Titania's loving remembrance of her votaress enforces an awareness of the human need to mythologize experience. Oberon continues in the same vein. He provides his own mythological remembrance of the powers of love and the imagination. Immediately after Titania leaves, Oberon asks Puck if he remembers the time

> I sat upon a promontory,
> And heard a mermaid, on a dolphin's back,
> Uttering such dulcet and harmonious breath,
> That the rude sea grew civil at her song,
> And certain stars shot madly from their spheres,
> To hear the sea maid's music.
>
> [2.2.240–45]

Oberon has given us a compelling image of art making rude nature harmonious. At the same time the image suggests that the source of the harmony—the sea maid's music—was also a source of disruption. What Oberon then saw from his promontory (we are told that Puck could not see it) was Cupid's empurpling of the pansy—"maidens call it love-in-idleness"— with "love's wound" (2.1.155–74). What Oberon saw, in effect, was a myth about the power of love (a myth designed to recall the change of the mulberry from white to crimson in Ovid's account, in the fourth book of the *Metamorphoses*, of the tragic love of Pyramus and Thisby). And just as certain stars shot "madly from their spheres" to hear the mermaid's song, the juice of love-in-idleness, laid upon sleeping eyelids, will make "man or woman madly dote/Upon the next live creature that it sees." Oberon orders Puck to fetch him this herb, and at this point in the play the invasions of the wood by the Athenians begin.

The rest of the play's movement through this haunted grove will reveal it as simultaneously a scene of confusion and fertility, a place where folly is manifested and constancy is discovered, a place of midsummer madness and magical meta-morphoses, of hateful fantasies and most rare visions; the play's movement, all this is to say, will reveal this "green plot" as the natural home of love and the imagination. In these first three scenes, *A Midsummer Night's Dream* has in-troduced three distinct realms, each radically different from the others, each thoroughly alive. What is most remarkable of all, by playing these three worlds off against each other, Shakespeare has somehow managed to affirm simultaneously their partialness and their integrity. Somehow the play's embrace of incompleteness assures its coherence. Building better than Peter Quince, Shakespeare "fits" all three worlds together on his stage.

These first three scenes get us into the wood. I would like to focus now on the precise moment when we begin to come back out; and then I would like to discuss the way we come out. The pivotal moment in *A Midsummer Night's Dream*, the moment where the movement back out of the wood begins, is that wonderful moment—almost a visual oxymoron —where Titania and Bottom embrace and fall asleep in each other's arms. Thoroughly enamored, Titania makes rapturous love to her ass:

> Sleep thou, and I will wind thee in my arms.
> Fairies, be gone, and be all ways away.
> So doth the woodbine the sweet honeysuckle
> Gently entwist; the female ivy so
> Enrings the barky fingers of the elm.
> Oh, how I love thee! How I dote on thee!

> [4.1.43–48]

Shakespeare has indeed made his world "fit" together. This "sweet sight," as Oberon calls it (4.1.49), is a moment of ex-treme incongruity, yet also a moment of great inclusiveness. The most diverse, indeed antithetical, perspectives have been fused in this single moment. The wood has done its utmost magic. I find it significant that Titania's language at the moment of her embrace of Bottom echoes precisely that of the earlier moment at the close of the third scene when Oberon had described her bower. Puck has returned with the love-in-idleness, and Oberon declares that he knows where to find Titania:

> I know a bank where the wild thyme blows,
> Where oxlips and the nodding violet grows,
> Quite overcanopied with luscious woodbine,
> With sweet muskroses, and with eglantine.
> There sleeps Titania sometime of the night,
> Lulled in these flowers with dances and delight;
> And there the snake throws her enameled skin,
> Weed wide enough to wrap a fairy in.
>
> [2.1.249–56]

Taken together, these two passages go far toward defining the reconciling and transfiguring power that the wood, at its best, is said to possess. After the pivotal embrace of Titania and Bottom, every Jack can begin to have his Jill (as Puck puts it, 3.2.448 ff.), and "all things shall be peace" (as Oberon puts it, 3.2.370–77). Then, but only then, the play's resolutions begin to occur. After the pivotal embrace, but only after this, a sense of inclusiveness begins to dominate the play. After this, but only after this, Oberon can "begin to pity" Titania's "dotage" (4.1.49 ff.). Now the other members of the court can enter the wood. Now all the sleeping lovers can begin to awaken. Now the play begins to drive toward that great final scene in Theseus's hall where love seems to be the common will.

Fundamentally, we get out of the wood by watching a series of dreaming lovers awaken from their visions. First, right after Titania winds Bottom in her arms, Oberon (he now has the changeling boy) releases the fairy queen from her vision. He and Titania dance, and then the "king of shadows" (3.2.347) declares that he and his queen, now "new in

amity," will "tomorrow midnight" solemnly and triumphantly
dance in Duke Theseus's house and "bless it to all fair pros-
perity": "There shall the pairs of faithful lovers be/Wedded,
with Theseus, all in jollity" (4.1.90–95). At this exact moment the altogether palpable rulers of Athens enter the
wood. Theseus and Hippolyta have been engaged in May Day
rites, and they have decided to spend the rest of the morning
hunting. Anxious to impress Hippolyta, Theseus orders the
attendants to uncouple his hounds in the western valley so
that his love can hear their "music":

> We will, fair Queen, up to the mountain's top,
> And mark the musical confusion
> Of hounds and echo in conjunction.

This prompts Hippolyta to remember some rather spectacular
hounds and hunts in her own past:

> I was with Hercules and Cadmus once,
> When in a wood of Crete they bayed the bear
> With hounds of Sparta. Never did I hear
> Such gallant chiding; for, besides the groves,
> The skies, the fountains, every region near
> Seemed all one mutual cry. I never heard
> So musical a discord, such sweet thunder.

Not to be outdone, Theseus makes strong claims for the extraordinary muscularity, and musicality, of his hounds:

> My hounds are bred out of the Spartan kind,
> So flewed, so sanded; and their heads are hung
> With ears that sweep away the morning dew;
> Crook-kneed, and dew-lapped like Thessalian bulls;
> Slow in pursuit, but matched in mouth like bells,
> Each under each. A cry more tuneable
> Was never holloed to, nor cheered with horn,
> In Crete, in Sparta, nor in Thessaly.
> Judge when you hear. . . .

                                              [4.1.112–30]

Theseus must want to convince Hippolyta that he is as physically impressive, as potent, as his hounds. I suspect this passage puzzled many earlier critics, but modern critics exult over these lines as a remarkable illustration of the play's habitual concern to make concordant music out of potential clamor. This talk of the hounds' "sweet thunder" also serves an important structural function. Here in the third scene from the end of the play we have the enactment of a perceptual and poetic activity very similar to that which occurred in the third scene from the beginning of the play; much as the fairy king and queen had done earlier (in 2.1.121–74), the human king and queen are mythologizing experience. It is entirely characteristic of *A Midsummer Night's Dream* that in one of the passages where the characters most overtly revel in dynamism, the play itself—as an artifact—calls covert attention to its own symmetries.

Theseus and Hippolyta came to the wood to hunt; expecting one kind of "sport," they find another and better game: they find the four young Athenians. Seeing that the young lovers have now more amicably paired up ("Saint Valentine is past./Begin these woodbirds but to couple now?"), Theseus wonders, "How comes this gentle concord in the world?" (4.1.142 ff.). None of the four young lovers is able to answer him with confidence. All their replies are full of wonder and amazement. For each of them the visionary experience of the moonlit night in the haunted grove now seems blurred and indistinguishable.

The reply of the one lover most changed during the midsummer night deserves attention. Demetrius confesses that he followed Hermia and Lysander into the wood "in fury," but he now affirms his love for Helena. Anticipating the exchange between Theseus and Hippolyta at the beginning of the last scene, and echoing Hermia's defiance of her father in the first scene ("I know not by what power I am made bold," 1.1.59), Demetrius assures Theseus that, no matter how indefinable, something real has happened to him:

> . . . I wot not by what power—
> But by some power it is—my love to Hermia,
> Melted as the snow, seems to me now
> As the remembrance of an idle gaud,
> Which in my childhood I did dote upon. . . .

Possibly magical, certainly indefinable, but for Demetrius his change of heart seems as natural as growing up. Now that Demetrius has been in the wood, all his faith, all the virtue of his heart, the entire object and pleasure of his eye is "only Helena"; to her

> Was I betrothed ere I saw Hermia:
> But, like a sickness, did I loathe this food;
> But, as in health, come to my natural taste,
> Now I do wish it, love it, long for it,
> And will for evermore be true to it.
>
> [4.1.163–79]

Does Theseus recognize the power Demetrius speaks of? We can never be certain, but it is at this precise moment that he decides to overbear the will of Egeus; he sets aside the "purposed hunting" and rules that "these couples shall eternally be knit" in the same ceremony with him and Hippolyta (4.1.180–88).

The last "lover" to awaken seems the least touched by his vision. Just when we might have allowed ourselves to believe that the stage had emptied, Bottom—irrepressibly histrionic as always—starts up and cries, "When my cue comes, call me, and I will answer" (4.1.2.3 ff.). At first Bottom does not seem to recall his amorous experience with Titania. Not hearing his next cue, he searches frantically all over the stage for his lost companions. But Bottom has been "translated" (3.1.120), and the "change" (3.1.115) wrought in the haunted grove is too intense for even Bottom to ignore. Glimmerings of remembrance begin to steal over him:

> I have had a most rare vision. I have had a dream, past the
> wit of man to say what dream it was. Man is but an ass, if

he go about to expound this dream. Methought I was—
there is no man can tell what. Methought I was—and methought I had—but man is but a patched fool if he will
offer to say what methought I had. The eye of man hath
not heard, the ear of man hath not seen, man's hand is
not able to taste, his tongue to conceive, nor his heart to
report what my dream was. . . .

Predictably, Bottom misquotes, but one of his sources here is
Saint Paul (1 Corinthians 2:9). Realizing that, we can realize
that we have just seen still another of the play's "translations"; we have watched the comically irrepressible slide into
the profoundly inexpressible.

Bottom's dream may be too unfathomable to expound, but
it seems too rare to waste; so having himself made his dream
into "material for a performance," as Alexander Leggatt puts
it, Bottom will give it to Peter Quince as material for a work
of art:

I will get Peter Quince to write a ballet of this dream. It
shall be called "Bottom's Dream," because it hath no
bottom; and I will sing it in the latter end of a play, before the Duke. Peradventure, to make it the more gracious, I shall sing it at her death.

Bottom rebounds quickly. He is "a patched fool," but his
vitality is, indeed, bottomless.

After Bottom's momentary uncertainties, we return to the
daylight world of Athens. After the brief scene (the sixth in
the Doran scheme) of the reunion of Bottom with Quince
and the other handicraftsmen, we turn to the poised urban-
ities of Theseus's famous pronouncement on love and the
imagination (5.1.2–22). Bottom and Theseus—so unutterably
different, yet so curiously alike. Each has the desire, and the
capacity, to play many parts. Each is extraordinarily alive,
and yet each achieves a kind of repose—each is, in today's
vernacular, "unflappable." For all that he is "but a patched
fool," Bottom is in some respects a more beguiling interpreter
of visionary experience than the rational and detached and

self-possessed Duke. Of course Bottom speaks from firsthand experience, whereas the Duke has only been a spectator; but then the Duke may not need magic spells to realize his desires.

Still, for us the Duke is almost too cool a customer. For all Theseus's eloquence, almost no critic today sees his speech as the play's last word on love and the imagination. His pronouncement, from one perspective, is cool reason's cogent demonstration that, as Rosalind disarmingly puts it in *As You Like It* (3.2.376), "Love is merely a madness." Yet, from another perspective, Theseus's pronouncement recoils upon him (he is himself an "antic fable"), and today's critics relish the way Shakespeare has insidiously used this speech to defend his own imaginative achievement. Perhaps imagination and love are forms of lunacy, but as Orlando had just said to Rosalind before she called love a mere madness, "Neither rhyme nor reason can express how much" he loves. Surely *A Midsummer Night's Dream* has apprehended "more than cool reason ever comprehends." Surely Shakespeare wants us to see the value of Theseus's common sense, but just as surely he wants us to see that, behind common sense and beyond cool reason, his imagination has bodied forth the "forms of things unknown," his "pen" has given palpable shape to such "strange" things and given "airy nothing" a "local habitation and a name."

Theseus does not even get the last word here; Hippolyta does:

> But all the story of the night told over,
> And all their minds transfigured so together,
> More witnesseth than fancy's images,
> And grows to something of great constancy;
> But howsoever, strange and admirable.

                                                                    [5.1.23–27]

It is Hippolyta's speech, not that of Theseus, that today's critics have grown to love. At the very moment of her final words, as if to prove the queen's point, the newly married young lovers, "full of joy and mirth," stroll onto the stage, and the whole last scene is a compelling emblem, visual as well as verbal, of consummation and communion.

A bit later in the scene Theseus *will* get a last word. Just as Hippolyta has amended his view of love and the imagination, he amends hers of plays and players. Wearying of Quince's "tedious brief" interlude, Hippolyta growls, "This is the silliest stuff that ever I heard" (5.1.211). Theseus's response to her remark, and their subsequent exchange, is often perceived today as one of Shakespeare's most incisive comments on the necessary contribution of the audience to the power of any dramatic illusion:

> *Theseus.* The best in this kind are but shadows; and the worst are no worse, if imagination amend them.
>
> *Hippolyta.* It must be your imagination then, and not theirs.
>
> *Theseus.* If we imagine no worse of them than they of themselves, they may pass for excellent men.

Now more amenable to the imagination than he appeared to be 180 lines earlier, Theseus seems to be acknowledging that we half create what we perceive. The idea of "amendment" will continue to reverberate throughout this final scene (most emphatically at the close in Puck's epilogue), and it might be said that *A Midsummer Night's Dream* is ultimately about the power of love and the imagination to amend the human condition. We might draw a moral for critics, as well as one for audiences, and speculate that criticism, too, must be a history of continuing amendment.

Have we, I wonder, finally accounted for this play's deep hold on the contemporary imagination? I have been trying to suggest that it is the dynamism and perspectivism of the play that fascinate modern critics. I would like further to suggest that the play's affirmations—self-conscious and guarded and mellow as they may be (Shakespeare never wears his heart on his sleeve)—engage us deeply too. The play may speak of things more "strange than true," as Theseus declares (5.1.2); yet as well as being "strange," such things, as Hippolyta urges, are also "admirable." For the play's many ripe sports have abridged at least one evening, have forestalled and perhaps softened the "iron tongue of midnight" (5.1.39 and 365). Even Theseus, about to get Hippolyta into bed at last, slips and can be heard to exclaim "'tis almost fairy time." Shakespeare does not of course expect us to believe literally that the fairies can keep "the blots of Nature's hand" from the "issue" of the newlyweds (5.1.403 ff.), but he may well expect us to agree that his "palpable-gross play hath well beguiled/The heavy gait of night" (5.1.368–69). Wouldn't Shakespeare ask of us, and have us ask in turn, "How shall we beguile/The lazy time, if not with some delight" (5.1.40–41)? We now regard *A Midsummer Night's Dream* as an authentic masterpiece because in it, better than in most works we know, we are persuaded that (to borrow words from Wallace Stevens) "Life's nonsense pierces us with strange relation."

BIBLIOGRAPHICAL NOTE

William Shakespeare was born in Stratford-upon-Avon in 1564; he died in Stratford in 1616. *A Midsummer Night's Dream* was probably performed in 1594–95. It was first published in 1600.

I have used the Signet edition, edited by Wolfgang Clemen (New York: New American Library, 1963),* but also recommend the Pelican edition for Madeleine Doran's excellent introduction (Baltimore: Penguin, 1959).* I am in debt throughout this essay to the felicitous and comprehensive study by David Young, *Something of Great Constancy: The Art of "A Midsummer Night's Dream"* (New Haven: Yale University Press, 1966). His book continues to the point of departure for all serious study of this play. Most valuable for me among other studies have been essays by J. Dennis Huston, "Bottom Waking: Shakespeare's 'Most Rare Vision,'" in *Studies in English Literature* 13 (1973): 208–22; Frank Kermode, "The Mature Comedies," in *Early Shakespeare*, Stratford-upon-Avon Studies 3, ed. John Russell Brown and Bernard Harris (London: Edward Arnold, 1961);* and Paul A. Olson,

"*A Midsummer Night's Dream* and the Meaning of Court Marriage," *ELH* 24 (1957):95-119. I owe the point that Demetrius seems to grow up in act 4 to Alexander Leggatt's useful chapter in *Shakespeare's Comedy of Love* (London: Methuen, 1974). On comic structure I refer to C. L. Barber, *Shakespeare's Festive Comedy* (Princeton: Princeton University Press, 1959);* to Northrop Frye, *Anatomy of Criticism* (Princeton: Princeton University Press, 1957);* and to Frye, "The Argument of Comedy," *English Institute Essays, 1948* (New York: Columbia University Press, 1949).

For general background material on Shakespeare see E. K. Chambers, *William Shakespeare: A Study of Facts and Problems* (London: Oxford University Press, 1930); S. Schoenbaum, *Shakespeare's Lives* (New York: Oxford University Press, 1970); S. Schoenbaum, *William Shakespeare: A Documentary Life* (New York: Oxford University Press, 1975). For Shakespeare's sources see Geoffrey Bullough, *Narrative and Dramatic Sources of Shakespeare*, 6 vols. (New York: Columbia University Press, 1957–). For Elizabethan stage history see E. K. Chambers, *The Elizabethan Stage*, 4 vols. (New York: Oxford University Press, 1923; rpt., 1945); and Enid Welsford, *The Court Masque* (New York: Macmillan, 1927). For additional material on Shakespeare see the bibliographical note to Mark Rose's essay on *Hamlet* in this volume.

*Paperbound available.

HAMLET

Mark Rose

Classical and Elizabethan tragedy represent polar opposites in dramatic structure, the one tightly focused with few characters and a sharply defined action, the other loose and sprawling with many characters, multiple locales, and complex plots which may span years of narrative time. And yet all tragedies tend to share certain central concerns. Sophocles' Oedipus fled Corinth to prevent the oracle's prophecy from coming true, but in the process of trying to escape his fate he only succeeded in fulfilling it. Sophocles' play is concerned, we might say, with the degree to which our lives are not in our own control. The words of the player king in *Hamlet* are apposite:

> Our wills and fates do so contrary run
> That our devices still are overthrown;
> Our thoughts are ours, their ends none of our own.
>
> [3.2.217–19]

Hamlet, too, is concerned with the limits imposed upon mortal will, with the various restrictions that flesh is heir to; and it is upon this central tragic theme that I wish to dwell, suggesting how Shakespeare employs a characteristically

This essay originally appeared in slightly different form under the title "Hamlet and the Shape of Revenge" in *English Literary Renaissance* 1 (1971): 132–43.

Renaissance self-consciousness to transmute a popular Elizabethan dramatic form, the revenge play, into a tragedy the
equal of Sophocles'.

Early in the play Polonius speaks to Ophelia of the "tether"
with which Hamlet walks. The image is a useful one to keep
in mind, for it suggests both that the prince does have a degree of freedom and that ultimately he is bound. Laertes
cautions Ophelia in a similar manner and develops more explicitly the limits on Hamlet's freedom. The prince's "will is
not his own," Laertes says,

> For he himself is subject to his birth,
> He may not, as unvalued persons do,
> Carve for himself; for on his choice depends
> The safety and the health of this whole state.
>
> [1.3.18–21]

What Laertes means is simply that Hamlet as heir apparent
may not be free to marry Ophelia, but he says much more
than he realizes. Hamlet is indeed subject to his birth, bound
by being the dead king's son, and upon his "carving"—his
rapier and dagger-work—the safety and health of Denmark do
literally depend. Possibly Shakespeare has in mind the imagery of *Julius Caesar* and Brutus's pledge to be a sacrificer
rather than a butcher, to carve Caesar as a dish fit for the
gods, for, like Brutus, Hamlet is concerned with the manner
of his carving. But the word is also Shakespeare's term for
sculptor, and perhaps he is thinking of Hamlet as this kind of
carver, an artist attempting to shape his revenge and his life
according to his own standards. Yet here, too, Hamlet's will
is not his own: there is, he discovers, "a divinity that shapes
our ends,/Rough-hew them how we will" [5.2.10–11).

From the first scene in which the prince appears, Shakespeare wishes us to perceive clearly that Hamlet is tethered.
He contrasts the king's permission to Laertes to return to
France with his polite refusal of Hamlet's request to return
to Wittenberg. Denmark is in fact a prison for Hamlet, a kind

of detention center in which the wary usurper can keep an eye on his disgruntled stepson. Claudius acclaims Hamlet's yielding as "gentle and unforced" and announces that he will celebrate it by firing his cannon to the heavens, but what he has done in fact is to cut ruthlessly the avenue of escape that the prince had sought from a court and a world he now loathes. One other, more desperate avenue still seems open, and as soon as the stage is cleared the prince considers the possibility of this course, suicide, only to remind himself that against this stands another sort of "canon," one fixed by God. Hamlet is tied to Elsinore, bound by his birth; on either side the road of escape is guarded and all that remains to him is his disgust for the world and the feeble wish that somehow his flesh will of itself melt into a puddle.

Hamlet's real prison is of course more a matter of mental than physical space. "Oh God," he exclaims to Rosencrantz and Guildenstern, "I could be bounded in a nutshell and count myself a king of infinite space, were it not that I have bad dreams" (2.2.258–60). The erstwhile friends suppose Hamlet means he is ambitious for the crown, but the bad dream the prince is thinking of, the insubstantial "shadow" as he calls it, is evidently the ghost and its nightmarish revelation. If Claudius has tied him to Elsinore it is of little consequence compared to the way the ghost has bound him to vengeance. Hamlet's master turns out to be even a more formidable figure than the king. Ironically, Laertes' and Polonius's remarks upon what they conceive to be the limits placed upon Hamlet's freedom immediately precede the scene in which the prince at last encounters the ghost and discovers what it means to be subject to one's birth. "Speak," Hamlet says to the ghost, "I am bound to hear," and the ghost in his replay picks up the significant word *bound* and throws it back at the prince: "So art thou to revenge, when thou shalt hear" (1.5.6–7). Hamlet cannot shuffle off his father's spirit any more than he can the mortal coil. The ghost's command is "Remember me," and after his departure Shakespeare dramatizes how from this charge there is no escape. Hamlet rushes about the stage seeking a place to swear his companions to secrecy, but wherever he makes his stand the ghost is there directly—"Hic et ubique," the prince says—its voice crying from the cellarage: "Swear!"

The ghost binds Hamlet to vengeance, but there is another and more subtle way in which the spirit of his father haunts the prince. It is one of the radical ironies of the tragedy that the same nightmarish figure who takes from Hamlet his freedom should also embody the ideal of man noble in reason and infinite in faculties—the ideal of man, in other words, as free. The ghost of King Hamlet, stalking his son dressed in the same armor he wore in heroic combat with Fortinbras of Norway, becomes a peripatetic emblem of human dignity and worth, a memento of the time before the "falling-off" when Hamlet's serpent-uncle had not yet crept into the garden, infesting it with things rank and gross in nature. It is no accident that Hamlet bears the same name as his father: the king represents everything to which the prince aspires. Hamlet, too, has his single-combats, his duels both metaphorical and literal, but the world in which he must strive is not his father's. The memory of those two primal, valiant kings, face to face in a royal combat ratified by law and heraldry, haunts the tragedy, looming behind each pass of the "incensed points" of the modern "mighty opposites," Hamlet and Claudius, and looming also behind the final combat, Hamlet's and Laertes' poisoned play, swaddled in a show of chivalry as "yeasty" as the eloquence of Osric, the waterfly who presides as master of the lists.

Subject to his birth, tethered by Claudius, and bound by the ghost, Hamlet is obsessed with the idea of freedom, with the dignity that resides in being master of oneself. One must not be "passion's slave," a "pipe for Fortune's finger / To sound what stop she please" (3.2.72–74)—nor for that matter a pipe for men to play. The first three acts are largely concerned with the attempts of Claudius and Hamlet to play upon each other, the king principally through Rosencrantz and Guildenstern, Hamlet through "The Mousetrap." It is Hamlet who succeeds, plucking at last the heart of Claudius's mystery, pressing the king to the point where he loses his self-control and rises in a passion, calling for light. "Dids't perceive?" Hamlet asks, and Horatio replies: "I did very well note him" (3.2.293, 296). I should like to see a musical pun in Horatio's word *note*, but perhaps it is farfetched. At any rate, Hamlet's immediate response is to call for music, for the recorders to be brought, as if he thinks to reenact symbolically his triumph over the king. What follows is the "recorder scene" in which Rosencrantz and Guildenstern once again fail with Hamlet precisely where he has succeeded with the king:

> Why, look you now, how unworthy a thing you make of me! You would play upon me; you would seem to know my stops; you would pluck out the heart of my mystery; you would sound me from my lowest note to the top of my compass; and there is much music, excellent voice, in this little organ, yet cannot you make it speak. 'Sblood, do you think I am easier to be played on than a pipe? Call me what instrument you will, though you can fret me, you cannot play upon me. [3.2.371–80]

Immediately after speaking this, Hamlet turns to Polonius, who has just entered, and leads the old courtier through the game of cloud shapes, making him see the cloud first as a camel, then as a weasel, and finally as a whale. Though Claudius and his instruments cannot play upon him, Hamlet is contemptuously demonstrating that he can make any of them sound what tune he pleases.

Hamlet's disdain for anyone who will allow himself to be made an instrument perhaps suggests his bitter suspicion that he, too, is a kind of pipe. One of the most interesting of the bonds imposed upon Hamlet is presented in theatrical terms. Putting it baldly and exaggerating somewhat for the sake of clarity, one might say that Hamlet discovers that life is a poor play, that he finds himself compelled to play a part in a drama that offends his sense of his own worth. Hamlet is made to sound a tune that is not his own, the whirling and passionate music of the conventional revenger, a stock character familiar to the Elizabethans under a host of names, including Thomas Kyd's Hieronomo, his Hamlet, and Shakespeare's own Titus Andronicus. The role of revenger is thrust upon Hamlet by the ghost, and once again it is profoundly ironic that the figure who represents the dignity of man should be the agent for casting his son in a limited, hackneyed, and debasing role. That Hamlet should be constrained to play a role at all is a restriction of his freedom, but that it should be this particular, vulgar role is especially degrading.

Lest I should seem to be refashioning Shakespeare in the modern image of Pirandello, let me recall at this point that he is a remarkably self-conscious playwright, one who delights in such reflexive devices as the play within the play, the character who is either consciously or unconsciously an actor, or the great set speech on that favorite theme of how all the world is a stage. Of all Shakespeare's plays, perhaps the most reflexive, the most dramatically self-conscious, is *Hamlet.* This is possibly due in part to the circumstance not unprecedented but still rather special that Shakespeare is here reworking a well-known, even perhaps notorious, earlier play, a circumstance which permits him to play off his own tragedy and his own protagonist against his audience's knowledge of Kyd's *Hamlet.* In any case, the self-consciousness of Shakespeare's *Hamlet* is evident. Here the play within the play is not merely a crucial element in the plot but a central figure in the theme. Here Shakespeare actually introduces a troop of professional actors to discuss their art and give us examples of their skill onstage. Here even a figure like Polonius has had some experience on the boards, acting Julius Caesar to a university audience, and nearly every character in the play from the ghost to the king is at some time or other seen metaphorically as an actor. So pervasive is the play's concern with theater that, as many critics have noted, simple terms like *show*, *act*, *play*, and *perform* seem drawn toward their specifically theatrical meanings even when they occur in neutral contexts.

If *Hamlet* is Shakespeare's most self-conscious play, the prince is surely his most self-conscious character. An actor of considerable ability himself, he is also a professed student of the drama, a scholar and critic, and a writer able on short notice to produce a speech to be inserted in a play. The prince is familiar with the stock characters of the Elizabethan stage—he lists a string of them when he hears that the players have arrived—and he is familiar, too, with at least two Elizabethan revenge plays (not counting *The Murder of Gonzago*), for at various times he burlesques both *The True Tragedy of Richard III*, that curious mixture of revenge play and chronicle history, and *The Spanish Tragedy*. Moreover, Hamlet habitually conceives of his life as a play, a drama in which he is sometimes actor and sometimes actor and playwright together. We recall immediately that in the third soliloquy ("O, what a rogue and peasant slave am I!") he speaks of having the "motive and the cue for passion" (2.2.571). Only slightly less familiar in his description of how on the voyage to England he devised the plot of sending Rosencrantz and Guildenstern to their deaths with a forged commision:

> Being thus benetted round with villains,
> Or I could make a prologue to my brains,
> They had begun the play. I sat me down,
> Devised a new commission, wrote it fair.

[5.2.29–32]

And we remember that in the final scene the dying Hamlet addresses the court—and probably the actual spectators in the Globe as well—as you "that are but mutes or audience to this act" (5.2.336).

Hamlet's first reaction to the ghost is to leap enthusiastically into the familiar role. "Haste me" to know the truth, he cries, that I may "sweep to my revenge" (1.5.29–31). And a few lines later he launches into his vow of vengeance, the furious second soliloquy ("O all you host of heaven!") in which he calls upon heaven, earth, and hell, addresses his heart and his sinews, and pledges to wipe from his brain everything except the commandment of the ghost. It is a tissue of rhetoric passionate and hyperbolical in the true Senecan tradition, a piece of ranting of which Kyd's Hieronomo would be proud. Hamlet's self-consciousness as a revenger is suggested by the speech he requests when the players arrive, the story of Pyrrhus's bloody vengeance for his father's death. What he sees in this story is an image of his own father's fall in the crash of father Priam and, in the grief of Hecuba, the "mobled queen," an image of how Queen Gertrude ought to have behaved after her husband's death. But he also sees in Pyrrhus a horrible reflection of his own role, and, significantly, it is the prince himself who enacts the first dozen lines describing the dismal heraldry of the revenger.

Art for Hamlet is the mirror of nature, designed to provoke self-examination. Very reasonably, then, his interview with the players prompts him in the third soliloquy to consider his own motive and cue for passion, to examine how well he has performed as a revenger. Excepting his stormy vow of vengeance, Hamlet has so far controlled himself rather strictly in his duel with Claudius; he has not, by and large, indulged in much cleaving of the general ear with horrid speech in the normal manner of a revenger, and his contempt for such a manner is implicit in his description of what the common player would do with his cue: amaze the very faculties of eyes and ears and drown the stage with tears. Hamlet's aristocratic taste is for a more subtle species of drama, for plays like the one from which the story of Pyrrhus comes, which he praises to the players for being written with as much "modesty"—by which he means restraint—as cunning. Yet now, with the stock role he is to play brought home to

him by the actors, Hamlet falls into the trap of judging himself by the very standards he has rejected and is disturbed by
his own silence. Theatrically self-conscious as he is, Hamlet
is naturally preoccupied by the relationship between playing
and genuine feeling. He touches upon this in his first scene
when he speaks to Gertrude of his outward "shapes of grief":

> These indeed seem,
> For they are actions that a man might play,
> But I have that within which passes show;
> These but the trappings and the suits of woe.
>
> [1.3.83–86]

How is one to distinguish mere shape—in theatrical parlance
the word means costume or role as well as form—from the
real thing? Or conversely, if the usual shape is lacking, how
can one be sure of the substance? After the interview with
the players, it is the latter problem which concerns Hamlet,
for now he wonders whether his refusal to play the revenger
in the usual shape, his reluctance to drown the stage with
tears, means simply that he is unpregnant of his cause. As if
to prove to himself that this is not so, he winds himself up
again to the ranting rhetoric of the revenger, challenging
some invisible observer to call him coward, pluck his beard,
tweak his nose, and finally hurling at Claudius a passionate
stream of epithets:

> Bloody, bawdy villain!
> Remorseless, treacherous, lecherous, kindless villain!
> O vengeance!
>
> [2.2.591–93]

But this time, at any rate, the role playing is conscious, and a
moment later the aristocrat in Hamlet triumphs and he
curses himself for a whore, a drab. To rant is cheap and vulgar; moreover, what is presently required is not the player's
whorish art but action. And so, with superb irony in his
choice of means, Hamlet decides to take his own kind of

action: "I'll have these players/Play something like the murder of my father/Before mine uncle" (2.2.606–08).

Hamlet's difficulty is aesthetic. His problem is one of form and content, of suiting the action to the word, the word to the action—that is, of finding a satisfactory shape for his revenge. Inevitably he is drawn to the preexisting pattern of the familiar revenge plays: life imitates art. Inevitably, too, his sensibility rebels, refusing to permit him to debase himself into a ranting simpleton. I find no evidence that the idea of revenge, of taking life, is itself abhorrent to Hamlet—he is not after all a modern exponent of nonviolence—rather it is the usual style of the revenger that he disdains. He objects to passionate rhetoric because to him it typifies bestial unreason. The conventional revenger, the Hieronomo or the Titus Andronicus, responds mechanically to circumstances, beating his breast in grief and crying wildly for revenge. Such a man is Fortune's pipe, the puppet of his circumstances, and the prisoner of his own passion. When Hamlet praises the man who is not "passion's slave," he is not merely repeating a humanist commonplace; he is commenting on an immediate problem, asserting a profound objection to the role in which he has been cast. At stake, then, for Hamlet is an aesthetic principle, but it is a moral principle as well: the issue is human dignity. In a play in which earsplitting rhetoric becomes the symbol of the protagonist's burden, it is suitable that "silence" is the final word from his lips as he dies. "The rest," he says, referring to all that must be left unspoken but also to the repose of death, "is silence."

The nature of Hamlet's objection to his role is elaborated in his address to the players—a speech too frequently overlooked in interpretations of this play—which Shakespeare has included because it permits the prince to comment indirectly on his most vital concern, how one ought to play the part of a revenger. Hamlet's demand is for elegance and restraint—in a word, for dignity in playing. Lines are to be spoken "trippingly on the tongue"—that is, with grace—rather than clum-

sily "mouthed" in the fashion of a town crier. Nor should the
player permit himself gross gestures, as sawing the air with his
hand; rather he must "use all gently," and even in the very
torrent, tempest, and whirlwind of passion—the moment of
extremity when the temptation to strut and bellow is greatest—
must "acquire and beget a temperance that may give it smoothness" (3.2.7–8). The actor who tears a passion to tatters may
win the applause of the groundlings who are only amused by
noise, but he is worse than Termagant or Herod, those pro-
verbially noisy stock characters of the old mystery plays
which Hamlet disdains as ignorant and vulgar drama. It is interesting that Hamlet mentions Herod and the mythical infidel god Termagant: he means to suggest that undisciplined
acting is not merely poor art, an offense against the "modesty
of Nature," but an offense to all that a Christian gentleman,
a humanist like himself, stands for. "O, there be players," he
says a few lines later, "that I have seen play . . . that neither
having th' accent of Christians, nor the gait of Christian,
pagan, nor man, have so strutted and bellowed that I have
thought some of Nature's journeymen had made men, and
not made them well, they imitated humanity so abominably"
(3.2.30–37). To rage and rant is to make oneself into a monster. The crux of the issue is this: like his father—"'A was a
man, take him for all in all" (1.3.187)—Hamlet intends to be
a man.

   The player answers Hamlet's indictment of vulgar acting by
assuring him that his company has improved its style: "I
hope we have reformed that indifferently with us, sir." This
complacency irritates Hamlet. "O, reform it altogether"
(3.2.39–40), he snaps in reply. Hamlet's concern is intense
and personal precisely because his own life has taken the
shape of a vulgar play, a crude and commonplace tragedy of
revenge. The prince's response—tantalizingly like Shakespeare's, working over what must have seemed to him the
crude and commonplace material of Kyd's *Hamlet*—is to "reform it altogether." Since he cannot escape the role, Hamlet

intends at least to be a revenger in a style that offends neither the modesty of nature nor his sense of human dignity. He intends to exercise discipline. I do not mean to suggest that Hamlet, like the singing gravedigger, has no feeling for his work. On the contrary, much of the drama lies in Hamlet's war with himself, his struggle to reduce his whirlwind passion to smoothness.

Hamlet and *Lear* are the only two of Shakespeare's tragedies with double plots. The Gloucester plot in *Lear* provides a relatively simple moral exemplum of one who stumbled when he saw and lost his eyes in consequence. This is a commonplace species of Elizabethan moral fable designed to set off the more complex and ambiguous story of the king. The story of Polonius's family works analogously in *Hamlet*. Each member of the family is a fairly ordinary person who serves as a foil to some aspect of Hamlet's extraordinary cunning and discipline. Polonius imagines himself a regular Machiavel, an expert at using indirections to find directions out, but compared to Hamlet he is what the prince calls him, a great baby. Ophelia, unable to control her grief, lapses into madness and a muddy death, reminding us that it is one of Hamlet's achievements that he does not go mad but only plays at insanity to disguise his true strength. And Laertes, of course, goes mad in a different fashion and becomes the model of the kind of revenger that Hamlet so disdains.

Hamlet knows he is playing a role, but Laertes is blissfully unselfconscious about his part. The prince boasts to his mother that his pulse "doth temperately keep time" (3.4.141), but Laertes' brag is of his stereotyped rage: "That drop of blood that's calm proclaims me bastard" (4.5.117). Laertes— to adapt Nashe's famous allusion to Kyd's old *Hamlet*—if you entreat him fair in a frosty morning, will shamelessly afford you handfuls of tragical speeches, ranting in the best manner of English Seneca:

> To hell allegiance, vows to the blackest devil,
> Conscience and grace to the profoundest pit!

> I dare damnation. To this point I stand,
> That both the worlds I give to negligence,
> Let come what comes, only I'll be revenged
> Most thoroughly for my father.
>
> [4.5.131–36]

What comes is not quite the revenge Laertes expects, for the situation is not so simple as he supposes; rather he finds himself on account of his unthinking passion an easy instrument for Claudius to play, becoming, in his own word, the king's "organ." The advice that Polonius gave Laertes might have stood the young man in good stead if he had followed it: "Give thy thoughts no tongue,/Nor any unproportioned thought his act" (1.3.59–60). Ironically, Polonius's words perfectly describe not Laertes' but Hamlet's approach to revenge. From the very first Hamlet has understood the practical as well as the aesthetic importance of controlling his rage. "But break my heart, for I must hold my tongue" (1.2.159), he says at the end of the first soliloquy, and it is interesting in the light of the play's general association of lack of discipline with noise, with rant, that even here control is connected with silence.

Shakespeare contrives to have his two revengers, the typical Laertes and the extraordinary Hamlet, meet at Ophelia's grave, where the prince finds Laertes true to form tearing a passion to tatters, bellowing to be buried alive with his sister. Hamlet steps forward and the technical rhetorical terms he uses, *emphasis* and *phrase*, together with the theatrical simile of making the stars stand like "wonder-wounded hearers," like an audience, reveal his critical attitude, his professional interest in the quality of Laertes' performance:

> What is he whose grief
> Bears such an emphasis, whose phrase of sorrow
> Conjures the wand'ring stars, and makes them stand
> Like wonder-wounded hearers?
>
> [5.1.256–59]

According to the probably authentic stage direction of the first quarto, Hamlet at this point leaps into the grave alongside Laertes, suiting outrageous word to outrageous action by challenging the young man to a contest of noise, of rant. What will Laertes do to prove his love for Ophelia, weep, tear himself, drink vinegar, eat a crocodile? Hamlet will match him. Does Laertes mean to whine, to prate of being buried under a mountain higher than Pelion? Why, then Hamlet will say he'll be buried too, and let the imaginary mountain be so high that it touches the sphere of fire and makes Ossa by comparison a wart. "Nay, an thou'lt mouth," the prince says, using the same word with which he had earlier described the manner of vulgar actors, "I'll rant as well as thou" (5.1.285–86).

Hamlet is mocking Laertes' style, but the bitterness of his mockery, the nastiness of it, derives from his own sincere grief for Ophelia. In a world of overblown rhetoric, of grotesque elephantine shows, how can a man of taste and discernment be understood? Moreover, since the usual sound and fury so often signify nothing, how will a man of genuine feeling be believed? This burlesque of Laertes is Hamlet's last act of bitter rebellion against the vulgarity of his world and the role he has been constrained to play in it. Moreover, it is a reversion to his earlier and fiercer mood, the proud, contemptuous spirit of the prince before the sea voyage; for, as most critics observe, the prince who returns from sea is a changed man, resigned, detached, perhaps "tragically illuminated." Having refused to kill the king when the time was every way propitious—that is, when he found Claudius kneeling in empty not genuine prayer—and then, having chosen his own moment to act only to find that instead of the king he has murdered Polonius, Hamlet seems to have allowed his sinews to relax. He has let himself be thrust aboard ship, let himself in effect be cast onto the sea of fortune that is so common an image in Shakespeare and the Elizabethan poets, an image recalling that "sea of troubles"

against which he had earlier taken arms. When the opportunity to escape the king's trap arises, Hamlet seizes it, leap-
ing aboard the pirate ship, but what he is doing now is reacting
to circumstances rather than trying to dominate them wholly.
The prince returns to Denmark at once sad and amused, but,
except for the single flash of "towering passion" at Ophelia's
grave, relatively impassive. He has ceased to insist that he
must be above being played upon by any power.

And yet, before Hamlet consents to the duel with Laertes,
about which he has justified misgivings, he plays a scene with
that impossible fop, Osric, the emblem of the empty courtesy
of Claudius's court. Just as Hamlet earlier led Polonius
through the game of cloud shapes, so now he toys with Osric,
leading him to proclaim first that the weather is warm, then
that it is cold, and finally warm again. At the penultimate
moment, Hamlet is demonstrating that if he wished he might
still play upon the king and his instruments like so many
pipes. Hamlet's mocking Osric, like the scene with Laertes in
the grave, recalls the early proud manner of the prince; nevertheless, Hamlet no longer seems to be in rebellion: rather
than bitter contempt he displays amusement that at the end
he should be forced to share the stage with a waterfly. The
prince's motto is no longer "heart, lose not thy nature," but
"let be." He has ceased to struggle for absolute freedom in his
role, ceased to insist that he alone must be the artist who, in
all senses of the term, shapes his life. He understands now
that, in Laertes' words, he cannot carve for himself. One can
at best be a collaborator in one's life, for there is always another artist to be taken into account, "a divinity that shapes
our ends,/Rough-hew them how we will."

The Hamlet who speaks of special providence in the fall of
a sparrow is not perhaps so exciting a figure as the earlier
Hamlet heroically refusing to be manipulated. There is something almost superhuman in the discipline, consciousness,
and cunning of the earlier Hamlet: certainly he makes superhuman demands upon himslef, insisting that he be in action

like an angel, in apprehension like a god. But Hamlet has discovered that, finally, he is subject to his birth, that he is
neither angel nor god, and, in an ironically different sense, it
can now be said of him what he said of his father, "'A was
a man, take him for all." King Hamlet fought his single combat in an unfallen world of law and heraldry; his son must
seek to emulate him in a corrupt world of empty chivalry and
poisoned foils; and yet, in its way, Hamlet's duel with Laertes
is as heroic as his father's with Fortinbras, and in his own
manner Hamlet proves himself worthy of the name of soldier.

"Bear Hamlet like a soldier to the stage" (5.2.397) is the
command of Fortinbras which concludes the play, a command which not only ratifies Hamlet's heroism by using the
term *soldier*, but in its theatrical allusion reminds us that
much of his achievement has been in the skill with which he
has played his inauspicious role. If all the world is a stage and
all the men and women merely players, then the reckoning of
quality must be by professional standards. By these standards
Hamlet has proven himself a very great actor indeed, for he
has taken a vulgar role and reformed it so that it no longer
offends the modesty of nature or the dignity of man. Even a
man on a tether, to pick up Polonius's image again, has a
certain degree of freedom. One may be cast in a vulgar role
and still win distinction in the manner the role is played. Or
one may be tied to the story line of a crude melodrama and
still produce a *Hamlet*.

BIBLIOGRAPHICAL NOTE

William Shakespeare was born in Stratford-upon-Avon in 1564 and
died in Stratford in 1616. *The Tragedy of Hamlet, Prince of Denmark*
was first performed in 1601–02 and first published in the "bad" quarto
of 1603.

Quotations from the play in this essay are from Edward Hubler's
readily available Signet edition (New York: New American Library,
1963).* I am conscious, as are all essayists on *Hamlet*, of the enormous

body of critical material on this play. I can only cite several studies that have been useful to me. A. C. Bradley's *Shakespearean Tragedy* (London: Macmillan, 1904)* is a classic work containing an important discussion of *Hamlet*. A useful collection of original essays is *Hamlet*, Stratford-upon-Avon Studies 5, ed. John Russell Brown and Bernard Harris (London: Edward Arnold, 1963).* *Hamlet: A Collection of Critical Essays*, ed. David M. Bevington (Englewood Cliffs, N.J.: Prentice-Hall, 1968)* also contains some major essays by important scholars and critics.

Other useful studies are the following: Stephen Booth, "On the Value of *Hamlet*," in *Reinterpretations of Elizabethan Drama*, ed. Norman Rabkin (New York: Columbia University Press, 1969); Maurice Charney, *Style in Hamlet* (Princeton: Princeton University Press, 1969); Howard Felperin, "'O'erdoing Termagant': An Approach to Shakespearean Mimesis," *Yale Review* 63 (1974): 372-91; Northrop Frye, *Fools of Time* (Toronto: University of Toronto Press, 1967);* Ernest Jones, *Hamlet and Oedipus* (New York: Doubleday, 1954); H. D. F. Kitto, *Form and Meaning in Drama* (London: Methuen, 1956);* Harry Levin, *The Question of Hamlet* (New York: Oxford University Press, 1959);* Maynard Mack, "The World of *Hamlet*," *The Yale Review* 41 (1952): 502-23; Eleanor Prosser, *Hamlet and Revenge* (Stanford: Stanford University Press, 2d ed., 1971);* Norman Rabkin, *Shakespeare and the Common Understanding* (New York: Free Press, 1967); Anne Righter, *Shakespeare and the Idea of the Play* (London: Chatto and Windus, 1962); Mark Rose, *Shakespearean Design* (Cambridge, Mass.: Harvard University Press, 1972); Theodore Spencer, *Shakespeare and the Nature of Man* (New York: Macmillan, 1942);* D. A. Traversi, *An Approach to Shakespeare* (Garden City, N.Y.: Doubleday, 1956);* J. Dover Wilson, *What Happens in "Hamlet"* (New York: Macmillan, 1935).*

For general background material on Shakespeare and on Elizabethan drama see the bibliographical note to Clifford Earl Ramsey's essay on *A Midsummer Night's Dream* in this volume.

*Paperbound available.

THE MISANTHROPE

Maria DiBattista

In *A Midsummer Night's Dream* we became acquainted with the Comic Muse and found her often to be a goddess of mischief. She loves cosmetics and disguises, intrigues and revels (usually sexual), jokes and puns (usually sexual). The Muse's obsession with sex, however, is a function of her larger obsession with the unconscious or suppressed motives of human behavior. Under the direction of the Comic Muse, the stage becomes the place where those irrational impulses a society may wish to suppress as a collective unit but wishes to indulge as individuals are played out without fear of censure. In *A Midsummer Night's Dream*, for example, the woods are the licentious preserve of Puck, the irrepressible trickster. Society as audience, like the bemused Theseus, tolerates these dark terrains, indulges these outbursts of midsummer night's madness, secure in the knowledge that the wildest passion pleads but a *temporary* insanity. The audience knows that in the comic scheme of things a sane reality will not only reveal, but assert, itself. What is clothed will be stripped, what is masked will be unmasked, what is confusing and unruly will be clarified and set in order.

Like tragedy, comedy dramatizes the instability of human life, but comedy exacts its perspective from below rather than on high. Tragedy despairs of its central situation as a demonstration of an inexorable fate beyond the control of the individual or collective will. Comedy, on the other hand, delights in its situations, laughing at the blindness of its heroes and the vagaries of their fortune, for comedy feels in control. The comic catharsis, unlike the tragic catharsis, consists in a renewed confidence that society can control its own future. In comedy, hubris or impiety becomes irresponsibility, a human failing that can be corrected by human means. *A Midsummer Night's Dream* is only an apparent exception, since the fairy world works with and not against the desires of the community for a stable social order. As Hippolyta observes of the doting lovers:

> And all their minds transfigured so together
> More witnesseth than fancy's images,
> And grows to something of great constancy. . . .

In this transfiguration of the inconstant to the constant lover, comedy asserts its triumph over the corruptible human will. The rebellion of man's instincts is quelled, but the victor proves lenient. The proper emblem of this truce between man's sexual and social nature is marriage, the socialization of the libido. The bias of comedy, then, is fundamentally conservative, for all its flirtations with the anarchy of uninhibited instinctual life. The end in comedy is not self-integration in and for itself, but as a means to social integration. Social harmony and right relations are comedy's predetermined goals. That is why comedy usually ends with twin emblems, marriage and a harmonious social or political order. Theseus is both husband and benign ruler. The comic hero, in turn, is defined at the end of the play in terms of his acquired social responsibilities rather than through his isolated, distinct, or lofty sense of self.

It may seem that these preliminary remarks on the action of comedy do not coincide with the experience of reading *The Misanthrope*. The play's comic brilliance does not lie in its manipulation of the standard comic formulas: absurd complications and resolutions, alienation of lovers and their reconciliation. There are no festivals, dirty jokes, disguises, or happy endings either. Nor is anyone's mind changed in the course of the play. Alceste remains a frustrated lover, Célimène is still a coquette, Arsinoe still a prude, the suitors just as silly and foppish as ever. If, then, Molière's comic genius does not express itself in these forms, what kind of comedy is he writing?

One answer can be found in the plot of the play. The action of *The Misanthrope* is minimal, serving to connect scenes whose dramatic interest resides in the conflict between highly individualized characters rather than the inherent absurdity of their situation. One may confuse Hermia with Helena, Lysander with Demetrius, but one can easily distinguish Alceste from Oronte, Célimène from Arsinoe. The staging of *The Misanthrope*'s first performance in 1666 illustrated, unwittingly, this distinction between a situation comedy and a character comedy. In that production Molière played Alceste, Célimène was played by his wife, Eliante by his mistress, and Arsinoe by an actress who, prudishly or not, had repulsed Molière's advances. The comic potential in the casting of the play is in this confusion of relationships with its hints of bedroom farce in which Molière leaps from one bed to another until he either finds the right bed or collapses from sexual exhaustion. The scenario of the play is somewhat different. There is, of course, the comic competition of the suitors—Alceste, Oronte, and Acaste—for the hand of Célimène. But the real focus of the comedy is on Alceste, the misanthrope. He, not a situation, is the controlling center of the play. When he is first seen, he is seated, encamped in Célimène's house, and when he first speaks, it is to insist on his solitude: "Leave me alone," he barks to Philinte. He is a comic variant of Achilles, preferring to sit apart, cherishing solitude and brooding over his grievances against society. If the controlling center of the play chooses to make nothing happen, nothing will happen. The antisocial, alienated hero will block the social-oriented, reintegrating action of comedy.

"I'll do nothing," Alceste tells Philinte when questioned about his lawsuit.

But Alceste's passivity is, paradoxically, extremely militant. When he says he'll do nothing, he means he'll do nothing but rail. He is even willing to pay damages on his lawsuit for the pleasure of denouncing the injustices of a corrupt and hypocritical society. His function is not to advance the action of the play, but to criticize the world presented in the play. Alceste represents the satiric spirit—the spirit of criticism, of denunciation, of ridicule. For Alceste, the moral takes precedence over the social, not the other way around. There are in the play two forces set in contention—the satiric spirit and the comic spirit—and this clash animates the action of the drama.

Some critics have focused on Alceste's antisocial, anti-comic instincts and have condemned him for his moral egotism. Those who subscribe to this view of his cantankerous nature are fond of citing Alceste's ultimatums to Célimène and to the judges who are presiding over his trial. "I choose to be chosen," Alceste insists, a remark that sums up the high-minded attitude he takes in his personal and public affairs. This argument seems unnecessarily reductive. Alceste as satirist has a right to pronounce moral judgments because he is invested with supreme moral authority in the play. Unlike Thersites, the ugly, surly satirist of the *Iliad*, Alceste is the acknowledged, esteemed, and at times *attractive* conscience of his society. Everyone agrees with the substance of his remarks; what is in dispute is the *tone* of his remarks. Most of the play is concerned, in terms of its social dynamics, with distinguishing the true satirist—Alceste—from the *médisants* (those who speak ill or maliciously of others) like Célimène and Arsinoe. Motive seems to be the decisive test of authenticity. Célimène's satires on the follies and hypocrisies of her suitors have all the malice, the stinging particularity, the merciless truth of legitimate satire. But her satires serve her self-interest rather than the public interest. They enhance her reputation as a lady of wit and thereby enhance her social status and appeal. Arsinoe presents, psychologically, a more complicated case. Arsinoe is a prude, and in this case the usually reductive Freudian explanation may be the truest one. Arsinoe is sexually frustrated, and her spleen, unlike Alceste's, is composed of vital juices that have turned sour. Célimène is acute in attributing Arsinoe's "sermonizings and sharp aspersions" to her "loveless solitude":

> Madam, I think we either blame or praise
> According to our taste and length of days.
> There is a time of life for coquetry,
> And there's a season, too, for prudery.
>
> [3.5.975–78]

Célimène sees no cause to be a prude at twenty, but her boast of youth may be fated for disaster. Arsinoe may be a projection of a future Célimène who, unable to choose among suitors, will eventually be forced to conceal her loneliness behind a facade of piety. Both Célimène's and Arsinoe's "blame and praise" are a function of their time of life. Célimène's coquettish banter is a function of her irrepressible youth, Arsinoe's righteousness a sign of her Indian summer, while Alceste's ire is, as he says, "never out of season." Arsinoe thus poses a formidable threat to comedy's summery mood and to satire's disinterested, impersonal severity. Importantly, Alceste rejects not only Arsinoe's personal advances but her satiric judgments as well. He resists her flattery, refuses her offer to secure him favors at court, and rejects her criticisms of society. Alceste may realize that Arsinoe is a negative image of himself as satirist, just as she is a negative projection of Célimène as comic heroine. Alceste's wrath may not originate in, but it is certainly aggravated by, his sexually frustrated pursuit of Célimène. And certainly Arsinoe's loveless solitude comments on Alceste's alienation at the opening of the play.

That Alceste's righteous anger is never out of season suggests that the true satirist must be disinterested. Of course, Alceste's wrath is inflexible because he believes mankind is always wrong, but in trying to set mankind right he does not seek to be "fashionable." The true satirist, unlike Célimène and Arsinoe, who usurp his proper function, should convey in his satires an implicit commitment to an ideal. And that ideal is a more virtuous, honest mankind. If Alceste is the blocking agent to the comic action of reconciling individual man to mankind, he is also the conscience of his community, railing at his peers to let their better selves shine through. He does represent the social ideals of the play: honesty and plain-dealing, integrity and fair play, status and honor predicated on merit rather than on social connection. A hundred years after Molière, Jean-Jacques Rousseau protested that the women of Geneva would be corrupted by going to the theater to see Molière satirize the virtuous Alceste. Rousseau, in thinking that *The Misanthrope* was the work of a profoundly immoral genius, may have miscalculated the positive function of Alceste in the play—the satirist as social reformer. The question is, how is this reformation or restoration of the social virtues to take place?

And this is where the action of the comedy blends with its subject, the satiric spirit, and suggests to us as readers and audience how to receive the play. The only action taken in the play is legal action. In the paralyzed world it depicts, viscounts spend their leisure spitting into wells and courtiers compose ghastly sonnets as their calling cards into ladies' salons. *The Misanthrope* does reflect a specific historical milieu, the world of Louis XIV. Clitandre can dally at Célimène's until the king's *coucher.* The French aristocracy, of which the noble Alceste is a member, is portrayed as an idle, gossipy, complacent elite whose social obligations are discharged by seeing the king put to bed. Moreover, we only see Alceste, Alceste only lives, in the world circumscribed by Célimène's salon. His case against mankind is made by criticizing this world and then extrapolating from his judgment of a specific class a sweeping condemnation of mankind.

Like the rest of his class, Alceste's only public activity is litigation. He sets out to prove the accuracy of his misanthropic vision through the courts:

I'll discover by this case
Whether or not men are sufficiently base
And impudent and villainous and perverse
To do me wrong before the universe.

[1.1.197–200]

Alceste wants to lose his case to justify his misanthropic vision—and his spleen. But before he submits to this martyrdom, he submits to the established procedures of adjudication. The satirist, like the law, is concerned with the truth and nothing but the truth, the satirist nominally, the courts ideally. Satire and the law, however, share more than this common commitment to the truth. They also share common procedures. In ancient Rome, for instance, satire liberally borrowed the forms of jurisprudence as the basis of its literary structure. The satirist or speaker appeared as a plaintiff who presented his case against society. He in turn was opposed by the figure of the *adversarius*, who defended society against the satirist's virulent attacks. In *The Misanthrope* this speaker/adversarius format is reflected in the structure of individual scenes, especially those which feature Alceste. The scenes observe this forensic structure of argument and counterargument, affirmative case and negative rebuttal. Think of the debate between Alceste and Philinte, Alceste and Oronte, or the frequent cross-examinations of Célimène by that merciless prosecutor, Alceste. In fact, the entire action of the comedy can be seen as a legal proceeding in which Alceste presents his case and waits for the verdict of the comic jury.

Historically, there is a reason for Alceste's caution. Satire has had to know the law to insure its own survival. There is internal evidence in the play as to why this should be so. Alceste's criticism of Oronte's literary productions constitutes a legitimate satire, as anyone with taste would agree. But his remarks are construed as libelous. Later in the play, Alceste

is both furious and frightened by rumors spread by his enemies:

> The dog now seeks to ruin me by stating
> That I composed a book now circulating,
> A book so wholly criminal and vicious
> That even to speak the title is seditious.

[5.1.1500–04]

Satire as a form of severe social or personal criticism walks
the razor's edge of libel and treason. The satirist is always
having run-ins with the law. Molière as comic satirist is no exception. His *Tartuffe* was banned for its incisive assault on
religious hypocrisy. Molière wrote a famous defense of his
comedy in which he explained society's hostility to satire:

> Criticism is taken lightly, but men will not tolerate satire.
> They are quite willing to be mean, but they never like to
> be ridiculed. [Preface to *Tartuffe* 1669]

Molière was fond of citing this anecdote to drive home his
point:

> Eight days after *Tartuffe* had been banned, a play called
> *Scaramouche the Hermit* was performed before the court;
> and the king on his way out said to a great prince: "I
> should really like to know why the persons who make so
> much noise about Molière's comedy do not say a word
> about *Scaramouche*." To which the prince replied, "It is
> because the comedy of *Scaramouche* makes fun of Heaven
> and Hell, which these gentlemen do not care about at all,
> but that of Molière makes fun of them, and that is what
> they cannot bear."

The satirist holds a mirror up to mankind and the spectators
laugh and applaud the ridiculous figure reflected as long as
they do not recognize their own faces. To see what kind of
mirror Alceste holds up to mankind, let us turn to the play
itself.

The substance of Alceste's complaint against mankind is presented in the opening scene of the play. The target of his satire is society's tendency to divorce private feelings from public behavior. He uses Philinte as his test case for social hypocrisy:

> I see you almost hug a man to death
> Exclaim for joy until you're out of breath
> And supplement these loving demonstrations
> With endless offers, vows and protestations;
> Then when I ask you "Who was that?" I find
> That you can briefly bring his name to mind.
>
> .   .   .   .
>
> By God I say it's base and scandalous
> To falsify the heart's affections thus.
> If I caught myself behaving in such a way,
> I'd hang myself for shame, without delay.
>
> [1.1.17–22; 25–28]

To falsify the heart's affections is a capital crime for which Alceste recommends hanging—rather cruel and unusual punishment. It is characteristic of Alceste that he is always confusing vices and folly with crimes. When Philinte, the comic advocate of moderation, suggests that hypocrisy is not a hanging matter, Alceste insists that it is and goes on to establish his moral absolutes:

> I'd have [men] be sincere and never part
> From any word that isn't from the heart.
>
> [1.1.35–36]

The dramatic context of this speech is essential. Alceste has come to Célimène's house to get her to declare her love openly and to reject her numerous suitors. Thus when he enjoins Philinte, "Let the heart speak," his words are earmarked for Célimène, too. His call for plain-dealing and honesty is made more urgent because of the crisis in his personal life. This may also explain Alceste's strident criticism of Oronte's sonnet, written, no doubt, for Célimène, a fact Alceste probably knows. Significantly, he responds to Oronte's challenge by reciting a primitive ballad whose theme is a lover's choice of his beloved over the attractions of Parisian life, a choice he wishes Célimène would make. Philinte, probably sensing Alceste's private feelings, answers with a counterview of society. He argues against Alceste's unmitigated honesty by proposing what can be termed a contract theory of social life:

> When someone greets us with a show of pleasure
> It's but polite to give him equal measure
> Return his love the best that we know how
> And trade him offer for offer, vow for vow.
>
> [1.1.37–40]

Philinte uses an economic metaphor for his model of social life. Social forms are means of social commerce that operates on principles of fair trade. Social gestures, like money, are mediums of exchange. Money, of course, has no intrinsic value. Money does not represent or recognize personal worth. Money only recognizes itself. The repeated references to bribery in the play suggest how a society founded on such "economic" principles leaves itself wide open for corruption. Alceste, the thoroughly honest man, rejects these social formulae as "false and hollow," a series of empty exchanges. Philinte responds by modifying the contract theory as an example of social rather than economic law:

> But in polite society Custom decrees
> That we show certain outward courtesies.
>
> [1.1.65–66]

In these terms the dialogue between Alceste and Philinte clarifies itself. Philinte cites as his precedents the usages of custom, what society as a part of its social contract has decreed. Alceste cites as his precedent "Nature"—the uncorrupted heart. His real criticism of Oronte's sonnet is, after all, that "Nature never spoke in such a way."

In his dislike of convention Alceste is the romance hero who would join the inward with the outward heart. And as a romance hero he is somewhat of an anarchist. Philinte is right in saying that no society could apply Alceste's injunction to "let the heart speak," especially when that heart seems to hold mainly negative feelings. It is hard to conceive of a society peopled by Alcestes; it would be a society totally lacking in charity, the key social virtue of the play. Even Alceste can only invoke as an alternative to Philinte's society a desert—his hyperbolic vision of the provinces:

> Sometimes I swear I'm moved to flee and find
> Some desert land unfouled by humankind.

> [1.1.143–44]

Deserts may be unfouled, but they are nonetheless wastelands, perilously like Arsinoe's loveless solitude. And as much as Alceste is moved to flee to this desert, he can never bring himself to do so. Alceste can never really act out his drama of departure. "I can't stay," he keeps telling Célimène, while the truth is that he can't leave. "Are you still here," she says to him. For Alceste, the stage has no exits. The real alternatives open to him are not conceived in terms of place—Célimène's house versus the desert. There is a suggestion that the alternative may be in terms of time. Critics who applaud Philinte's notion of a "pliant rectitude" simplify the case. Even as Philinte makes his case for philosophic phlegm, he remembers "the rigid virtues of the ancient days." It is not just that Alceste is stuck in the wrong place; he is living in the wrong time. Philinte's society is composed of aristocrats of diminished moral stature who have substituted good sense for high ideals. This lingering memory of the good old days is, however, purely nostalgic. Alceste can no more return to some golden age than he can flee to a desert. He is a man without any options, or, at least, without the options as he conceives them.

Molière satirizes Alceste's extreme vision by exposing his secret fantasies. I have in mind that scene in which Alceste, trying to woo Célimène, wishes that she were terribly poor so that he could repair the great injustice of her plight. Alceste's fantasies parody more than his romantic longings. They also parody the very idea of romantic notions in an age when the normative values of romance—lofty virtue and magnanimous action—are dead. Alceste's predicament is that he is a romance hero displaced and trapped in a comedy of manners. And instead of resolving Alceste's dilemma with yet another fashionable formula, Molière insists on making it the center of his play. Alceste the passionate moralist wishes to renounce the world. Alceste the passionate lover longs to be the center of the world—Célimène's world, the world of the play. The divided emotions of the satirist—his loathing and his love—are dramatized in his relationship to Célimène.

At the close of his debate with Alceste, Philinte points out that Alceste's case is compromised by an inconsistency—his love for Célimène. The surface irony is that a misanthrope is in love at all. The deeper irony is that Célimène typifies, as Philinte observes, "the manners of our days," the very object of Alceste's attacks. How is it, he goes on to ask, "that the traits you most abhor/Are bearable in this lady you adore?" That is the most interesting question of the play. Alceste offers an explanation when he says that Célimène's charms outweigh her faults. The best way to define her charms is to see Célimène in action with Alceste:

> *Célimène.* And what d'you mean by those dramatic sighs
>   And that malignant glitter in your eyes?
> *Alceste.* I mean that sins which cause the blood to freeze
>   Look innocent beside your treacheries;
>   That nothing Hell's or Heaven's wrath could do
>   Ever produced so bad a thing as you.
> *Célimène.* Your compliments were always sweet and
>   pretty.
>
>   [4.3.1277–85]

Alceste is always blowing up moral issues into metaphysical

ones. Weak people become moral monsters, incarnations of evil. Célimène takes his responses out of the realm of metaphysics into the human sphere and by that means triumphs over him. He is the master of tragic inflation, she of comic deflation. As a pair they are perfect complements, each supplying what the other lacks. Alceste finds the social sense his intelligence lacks, Célimène the moral sense her wit needs.

However, that Alceste and Célimène are perfectly matched in wit and satiric intelligence does not really answer the question, a question that is still plaguing Philinte later in the play.

> What most intrigues me in our friend Alceste
> Is the grand passion that rages in his breast.
> The sullen humors he's compounded of
> Should not, I think, dispose his heart to love;
> But since they do, it puzzles me still more
> That he should choose your cousin to adore.
>
> [4.1.1169–74]

Philinte addresses his question to Eliante, who usually has all the right answers in the play. But in this case Eliante can only concur with Philinte that Alceste's grand passion does belie the favored theory that love "is born of gentle sympathy." Well, if it belies one theory, it must suggest others, one of which I would propose. Alceste the passionate moralist is outraged by the world so charmingly represented in Célimène. Alceste the passionate lover wants to transform the world. "I can but aim," he says, "to cleanse her spirit in my love's true flame." The satirist's consuming love of the world drives him to redeem it. The constructive role of the satirist as social critic is a function not of his hatred but his love. Love is the true transforming power in Alceste's universe, just as love is the transforming power in the comic universe. Love is what redeems his negative vision of desert lands with a more positive image of "unfouled humankind"—a purified or cleansed Célimène.

It is Eliante, that prudent, even-tempered soul, who indicates how love can purge Alceste's misanthropic vision:

> Love, as a rule, affects men otherwise,
> And lovers rarely love to criticize.
> They see their lady as a charming blur
> And find all things commendable in her.
> If she has any blemish, fault, or shame,
> They will redeem it by a pleasing name.
>
> [2.5.711–16]

"Rule" is Wilbur's translation for *loi*, law. The law of love, unlike the moral law Alceste upholds, is to love your lady for her faults, even for, not in spite of. Eliante does not claim that love is blind; Cupid just suffers from astigmatism. Alceste would see his lady and the world she represents as a naked truth with every flaw and blemish revealed. Alceste, in seeking Arsinoe's help, seeks "ocular proof" of Célimène's deceptions in the form of written proof. Letters play an important part in complicating the action of the play. Under the rule of best evidence, they certify Célimène's treachery beyond the shadow of a doubt. Célimène stands condemned by them in the eyes of Alceste the moralist. But not in the eyes of Alceste the lover. When he confronts her with his "ocular proof," she makes her "mocking and perverse" confession. This admission of guilt should satisfy Alceste the moralist—perhaps it does—but Alceste the lover is exasperatd:

> Take back that mocking and perverse confession;
> Defend this letter and your innocence,
> And I, poor fool, will aid in your defense.
> Pretend, pretend, that you are just and true,
> And I shall make myself believe in you.
>
> [4.3.1186–90]

Alceste pleads with Célimène to redeem her behavior with "a pleasing name." He begs to be deceived. The clear-eyed moralist of the opening scenes is not only willing but anxious to overlook the failings of his lady. Alceste forfeits his ideal woman cleansed of all vice for the "charming blur" of the real person. His willingness to submit to love's rule, the rule of illusion and euphemism where failings are concealed by pleasing names, marks the point where the misanthrope rejoins mankind, that species that relies on illusion to save it from the truth.

Comedy aims to unmask pretensions, expose the self-deceived. Alceste's plea to Célimène is one instance of comic exposure, revealing as it does the depths of his "unrewarded, mad and bitter love." But *The Misanthrope* has two recognition scenes, the second more bitter—Célimène's exposure. That extraordinary scene in which Alceste confronts Célimène with letters that prove her treachery upsets the comic tone of the play. Comic exposure becomes satiric exposé. Célimène's enterprise backfires and exposes not only the foppishness of her suitors but the duplicity of their critic. Célimène's malicious wit in characterizing others is turned against her so that in painting their pictures she eventually produces, as the embittered Acaste remarks, "a sublime self-portrait." In this scene the two satiric strategies at odds in the play converge: Alceste's, who always criticizes people to their face, and Célimène's, who always criticizes people behind their backs. Célimène's elitist satires depend on the distinction between outsider and insider. In this scene those "not here" are brought onstage and let in on the inside joke on themselves. The end result is that everyone is exposed and everyone is repudiated. The triumph of Alceste's honesty is in this collapse of Célimène's clique, with Célimène left presiding over an empty salon. As a satirist satirized, her fate is harsher than Alceste's. He can defect. She is deserted.

This darkening of tone in *The Misanthrope* continues to haunt the rest of the play. With the verdicts in, Célimène exposed, Arsinoé rejected, the suitors gone, the comic jury is ready to pass a sentence. Molière teases us with the hope of a suspended sentence in Alceste's proposal to Célimène:

Woman, I'm willing to forget your shame
And clothe your treacheries in a sweeter name.

[5.7.1757–58]

But this time Alceste puts a condition on his "blindness" to
her faults, and a severe stipulation it is:

> My one condition is that you agree
> To share my chosen fate and fly with me
> To that wild, trackless, solitary place
> In which I shall forget the human race.
>
> [5.7.1761–64]

One may criticize Célimène for refusing Alceste's offer, but
such a judgment is inappropriate. Célimène's comic instincts
in this, as in all cases, are the right ones. Comedy never re-
nounces the world, but is reconciled to it. It is Célimène who
offers Alceste the proper solution to his problems—her hand
in marriage. By persisting in his misanthropic spleen, Alceste
finally realizes his wasteland, not offstage, but on. As Stendhal
acutely remarked of the comedy's *dénouement:* "Célimène's
salon would at once have been compromised and soon have
become a desert. And what would a coquette find to do in a
deserted salon?"

Alceste's reputed triumph over Célimène—and the social
vices she represents—is, then, a questionable one. Alceste
has pursued two suits in the play: his lawsuit and his suit to
win Célimène's hand. He loses both, but feels justified in
doing so. In losing his lawsuit, he is consoled in finally exposing the injustices of a corrupt society; and if he fails to secure
Célimène's hand, he has assured that no one else will do so.
"Justice," remarked Pascal, "is just as much a matter of
fashion as charm is." Alceste's justice, like Célimène's charm,
is subject to the whims of fashion. But *The Misanthrope* in
verifying Pascal's dictum, cannot move beyond its inherent
cynicism. Of course, Molière's comedy does conclude with an
impending marriage, augury of the new society to be called
into being, but a marriage of the wrong pair—Eliante and
Philinte. It could be argued, and many critics have done so,
that Eliante and Philinte represent the forces of moral and
social moderation, and, as such, are the appropriate pair for

comic union. But such an explanation is certainly too facile. Eliante's initial role in the play is to be a substitute for Céli- mène as Alceste's love object. And Philinte offers himself as a substitute for Alceste when he declares his love for Eli- ante. Molière doesn't "marry" the moral and the social. He can only suggest a substitute or compromise for the expected comic solution of love and law united in marriage.

The comic reprieve comes, if it comes at all, in the last lines of the play:

> Come, Madam, let's do everything we can
> To change the mind of this unhappy man.
>
> [5.8.1807–08]

To change Alceste's mind would be to effect the desired comic transformation. This hint of a possible conversion con- soles, but only momentarily. Alceste has no life off the stage. If he is to be converted, it must be in the play, not out of or beyond it. The fact remains that Alceste's satiric vision is never absorbed or transformed by the comic action of the play. He begins the play in solitude, seeking a place unpeopled and apart. For Alceste it is the same world with the same fools from beginning to end and so he and the world must part on grounds of irreconcilable differences. Philante had warned Alceste (and here I translate literally from the French) that for all his pains the world will never change, "le monde par vos soins ne se changera pas." In the course of the play only fashion changes. The play concludes with the same un- regenerate society with which it began. This persistence of the satiric vision at the end of the comedy is disturbing. Theseus banished satire from his court entertainments at the conclusion of *A Midsummer Night's Dream*, giving as his reason that "satire, keen and critical" was "not sorting with a nuptial ceremony." Moliére does not observe such strict comic decorum. The comic vision and the satiric vision co- exist at the end of the play, observing an uneasy truce. Be- tween Alceste's vision of desert lands of loveless solitude and

the comic vision of solitudes redeemed by love, *The Misanthrope* remains in suspension.

BIBLIOGRAPHICAL NOTE

Molière was born in Paris in 1622 and died in Paris in 1673. *Le Misanthrope* was first performed in 1666 by Molière's own acting company.
Molière played Alceste in the production.

I have used Richard Wilbur's translation, *The Misanthrope and Tartuffe* (New York: Harcourt, 1965).* Wilbur's is the most accessible as
well as the most inspired version in English verse couplets. Another,
relatively recent, translation of the *Misanthrope* by Miles Mallcson
(New York: Coward-McCann, 1960) is available, but it does not rank
with Wilbur's. The French text of the play can easily be checked in
many current editions, but a useful set of notes and commentaries is
included in *Oeuvres Complètes de Molière*, 11 vols., ed. Gustave Michaut
(Paris: Richelieu, 1947).

My essay is indebted to many commentaries on Molière, but I owe
special debts to Robert Elliott's essay on the *Misanthrope* in his *The
Power of Satire* (Princeton: Princeton University Press, 1960)* and to
Martin Turnell's treatment of the play in *The Classical Moment: Studies
in Corneille, Molière, and Racine* (New York: New Directions, 1948).
I am also indebted to Jacques Guicharnaud, *Molière; une aventure
théâtrale: Tartuffe, Don Juan, Le Misanthrope* (Paris: Gallimard, 1963);
Judd D. Hubert, *Molière and the Comedy of Intellect* (Berkeley: Uni-
versity of California Press, 1962); *Molière: A Collection of Critical
Essays*, ed. Jacques Guicharnaud (Englewood Cliffs, N.J.: Prentice-Hall,
1964);* *Molière, Stage and Study*, ed. W. D. Howarth and Merlin Thomas
(Oxford: Clarendon Press, 1973); and Will G. Moore, *Molière, A New
Criticism* (Oxford: Clarendon Press, 1949).*

My general remarks on comedy are indebted to C. L. Barber's *Shake-
speare's Festive Comedy* (Princeton: Princeton University Press, 1959);*
Northrop Frye's *Anatomy of Criticism* (Princeton: Princeton University
Press, 1957);* and Wylie Sypher's *Comedy: An Essay on Comedy by
George Meredith and Laughter by Henri Bergson* (Garden City, N.Y.:
Doubleday, 1956).

*Paperbound available.

PHAEDRA

Paul H. Fry

Phaedra is about a certain kind of rarefied heroic imagination for which there is no greater passion than the desire to suppress passion. This theme is given an added dimension by form; for Racine the frenzy of moral restraint finds a perfect vehicle in the constraining conventions of neoclassical theater, the three unities—together with a number of subordinate rules called *bienséances* or proprieties. If we tend to feel that much classical theater succeeds in spite of its dramaturgical conventions, we feel equally that *Phaedra* succeeds because of them. Racine's play is the happy ending—and there will be more to say about happy endings—of a piece of historical drama that might be called "Three Unities in Search of a Subject"; but in this happy ending there lurks a frustrating ending for Racine himself.

The unities, for the record, had their origin in suggestions by Aristotle, more descriptive than prescriptive, concerning the procedure of a good play; but between Aristotle and Racine's critical climate there had intervened the belief that the unities were not just suggestions but inviolable rules. The unity of time came to dictate that the plot of no play should encompass more than twelve or at most twenty-four fictional hours (the most extreme unitarian, one d'Aubignac, insisted on three hours); the unity of place, that the action should never shift to a locale at any great distance from the

starting point; and the unity of action, simply that the characters should never veer in thought or deed from the tragic
issue at hand. Let us try to see how these rather severe limitations could come to be assets in Racine's imagination, beginning with an indirect approach to the unity of action in
Phaedra.

Theseus has been a monster-slayer by vocation whose first
wish is to live and rule in a monsterless world, but he is
obliged more than anyone else, finally, to admit that there
are still monsters everywhere. The eighteen instances of the
word *monstre* in *Phaedra*, very often as an epithet for persons,
recall certain passages in the *Pensées* of Racine's contemporary,
Pascal. Thinking about life in a human jungle resembling
Racine's Trozenian forest, Pascal wrote:

> If an animal did rationally what it does by instinct, and if
> it spoke rationally what it speaks by instinct when hunt-
> ing, or warning its fellows that the prey has been lost or
> found, it would certainly go on to talk about matters
> which affect it more seriously, and it would say, for in-
> stance: "Bite through this cord; it is hurting me and I
> cannot reach it."

The cord that hurts the Racinian hero is tied into a *noeud*
or knot; this is the name in the theory of tragedy of Racine's
time for the complication of the plot. The hero is chafed at
by this knot for the first four acts; the more he struggles the
tighter it gets:

> These useless ornaments [says Phaedra]
> These veils oppress me. What officious hands
> Have taken care to knot upon my head
> My heavy hair? How all conspires to hurt,
> Hurt and afflict me.
>
> [1.3.7–10]

Then comes the *dénouement*, which means the unravelling or
severing of the knot, a severing which is violent in tragedy

and causes an ultimate but mercifully brief anguish. Pascal says that the greatness of man, his heroism, consists solely in his knowing that he is "wretched," a deliberately ambiguous word signifying both "unhappy" and "corrupt." That is the greatness of Phaedra: her acute awareness of being wretched; and it is the measure of tragic stature in Racine.

As in the passage quoted above from Pascal, the Racinian character's knowledge of wretchedness can find an outlet only through his ability to speak. Language in *Phaedra* goes forward by means of an ebb and flow of subterfuge and confession, and running beneath it all is one wistful imperative: Bite through this cord, love me, kill me, authorize my suicide, but bite through this cord, it is hurting me and I cannot reach it. The *noeud* in Racine is not the coiling monster of sin that severs the knot of Hippolytus but rather the language itself which confesses the existence of the monster. Thinking to release herself prematurely, Phaedra grabs for the sword of Hippolytus, but her fate for the time being is to go on confessing, to expose herself thoroughly so that she may be released at a point of full lucidity, to "restore . . . purity" to Trozene at the end of a fine and luminous sentence. The first and most comprehensive unity in the play, then, consists in an unusual near-equivalence of action and language. Thus we miss the degree to which external form is part of the meaning of *Phaedra* unless we look for that form *as* the plot itself.

Owing to the unity of time, the single day during which the play takes place brings together and repeats a series of memories in new forms. The bull-dragon of Neptune supersedes the old Minotaur of Crete; the passion of Phaedra recapitulates her mother Pasiphaë's monstrous love for a bull; the conquest of Hippolytus by Aricia replays the conquest of the Amazon Hippolyta by Theseus. On this one day each character reenacts the leading features of his own past and of the past of his ancestors, but this time the enactment is terminal, because it is accompanied by the frequently fatal shock which Aristotle called reversal. For instance, Theseus orders his son to hide from the light beyond the Gates of Hercules, and calls him a monster. When at last the light enters his own mind, Theseus implies his own monstrosity by calling down the same banishment on himself: "Hounded forever by this memory,/From the whole universe I long to hide/And banish me." For the first three acts Theseus has already been hidden, we are uncertain for a time whether in the underworld, a prison, or some new love-nest. Then he appears, like a blurted-out confession, and, like so many confessors in the play, once he has seen the oft-invoked daylight (Phaedra's entrance cue was also her desire to see the sun), he soon enough longs for concealment. It is a vain wish, his lot is to be "hounded forever by a memory," and his curse is that although he is fully subject to reversal, nevertheless the unity of time for him will not be terminal; it will not cut his knot. In vain he utters a talismanic phrase for sufferers in Racine, "pour la dernière fois"—for the last time. "For the last time, begone out of my sight," he says to Hippolytus, yet though he may bury a corpse he will never bury "the image of my mangled son."

Although Phaedra is perhaps a more acute sufferer than Theseus, she is a more fortunate victim of the unity of time: "Oh Thou, great Sun!" she says, "I come to look on thee for the last time." And this proves true. The unity of time defines tragedy as a collision between two modes of suffering, the ache of duration and the shock of reversal. Both modes meet in Phaedra when she discovers that Hippolytus is a lover after all; for her the single day of tragedy reserves a special agony: "Ah! Anguish as yet untried! What more? For what new tortures am I still reserved?" The single day is at last the focus of her torment:

> Alas, if I had died
> This morning I had died at least, at least
> Deserving pity . . . Oh gods,

What have I done this day?

[3.3.14–15; 17–18]

By 1677, and earlier too, as *The Misanthrope* shows, the unified place of a play had narrowed itself from a region to a room. Since the characters of tragedy are royal, that room is perforce a room in a palace. Its walls confer both privilege and bondage; the privilege involved is a thorough isolation from what royal characters call the "universe," that temporizing world of lesser mortals beyond and beneath the scope of tragedy; but the bondage imposed by a royal antechamber is more crucial. "My mind's made up," says Hippolytus in effect as the play opens, "I'm going." But he stays. News arrives that Theseus must be presumed dead; hence the interests of Aricia should be looked after in Athens. The ships are ready, I'm going, says Hippolytus, yet he does not sail. Phaedra makes her advances and Hippolytus recoils: "Let us fly, Theramenes!" He stays on. Phaedra's son rather than Hippolytus is named king of Athens. Let's go anyway, says Hippolytus, but he still lingers. He is like Molière's Alceste, always on the verge of fleeing to his "Desert," yet chained to a salon. Having failed repeatedly to take his leave, Hippolytus is finally banished: he departs and is promptly destroyed just outside of Trozene; at the edge, as it were, of the place of the play.

It should be noticed, indeed, that the space to which Hippolytus has been confined is literally the stage-room, but descriptively and reportorially the larger circumference of the town of Trozene. What for him was "beautiful" Trozene in the morning has become by the afternoon "a doomed and filthy place where virtue breathes a poisoned air." The play is not set in Athens (as it was in Seneca's *Hippolytus*), because, as Oenone suggests, the provincial immanence of Trozene is consistent with an ominous moral atmosphere:

Oh crime! Unhappy land, reached at the end
Of what ill-fated voyage! Why are we

   Doomed ever to approach your dangerous shores?
                                                    [1.2.124–26]

In a small town like Trozene one is on display, gossip spreads
fast, everyone rushes down to greet a ship; in such a tiny
place, concealment both from sin and in order to sin is virtually impossible, at most a forest revery. One is trapped
imaginatively on the edge of things, on a shore, that is, under
the hard, sternly judging eye of a Mediterranean sun which
makes the contrast of dark and light the dominant visual
motif of the play. Thus the manifold image of Trozene is a
verbal Cinemascope that broadens the literal stage; particularly it adds the darkness of revery, the forest with its labyrinthine glades and windings. Description also adds the rest
of the palace, the corridors along which it is possible to run
or wander distractedly, only to encounter suddenly onstage
whomever one has been avoiding, there to confess in the
shock of the moment what in the rest of the palace was hidden. The unity of place, then, like that of time, measures
suffering, measures it as an aspect not of duration and reversal, but of proximity. When Phaedra in the past was able
to banish Hippolytus to another region, she began to breathe
more easily, and now Oenone suggests the possibility of escape into the "nobler cares" of rule in Athens. Theseus too,
listening to Oenone's false history of the lust of Hippolytus,
is appalled by the confining accident of neighborhood:
"Then this fire broke out again at Trozene? Is that it?"
   Although the palace room is a moral and emotional prison,
at center stage it is actually a physical void. One of the *bienséances* dictates that ladies and gentlemen onstage are never
to touch each other, either in love or hate. We know how
very nearly Phaedra violates this propriety—Hippolytus
snatches his arm away from her and she grasps only his sword—
but this near-violation only calls attention to the wall of
space between characters, corresponding as it does to their
own several walls of heart and will. Seneca's more lax and ineffective handling of this scene, in which Phaedra more or

less assaults Hippolytus, tumbles into farce with Hippolytus's reaction' "Keep off those wanton hands from my chaste body! What! Does she fling herself into my arms?" Racine's use of convention, then, actually focuses passion, and avoids the collapsing bathos of lust enacted. The rule against physical contact, made more excruciating by the rule of proximity, reduces action to the sphere of vision, language, and silence, that is, action is unified not just by content but by a systolic rhythm and manner. The unities, finally, are tragic snares conspiring to produce a theater of unbroken crisis; there is no digression, no oblivion, and no exit.

No theater so closely anticipates that of Samuel Beckett. One finds in *Endgame* that Beckett scrupulously observes not only the unities but the proprieties: no one ever touches, there is a constant threat of violence but no actual violence, the action of Beckett's literally immobilized characters consists entirely of alternating confessions and "Pauses," and his speakers, who are driven by the need to dominate, might as well be called royal, since no one but the speakers is left on earth to dispute their accession-by-default. Like the Racine of *Phaedra*, Beckett appears to confirm Pascal: man is glorious in proportion to his knowledge of wretchedness.

Of course the austerity of this view is open to challenge as a commentary on Racine. The language and self-conception of his characters would appear to suggest a much greater range of human possibility. What about the nobility of Hippolytus, the well-disciplined sweetness of Aricia? Racine does differ from Pascal in one obvious respect. Although the *Pensées* are only notes for an intended book of sustained prose, it is still significant that Pascal and La Rochefoucauld and many other pessimistic writers of the seventeenth century chose the genre of fragments or epigrams as the one most suited to their outlook. This may be explained in part by arguing that even in sustained prose, and much more so in theater, the uninterrupted development of an idea of human character will begin to attach to that character a certain grandeur, or at least sympathy, solely as a result of its articulate persistence, its doggedness in the face of its author's condescension. In Racine there is an elusive and variable gulf between the exhilaration of his theater and the grimness of his moral philosophy.

The mainstream of seventeenth-century moral philosophy in France was far more compatible with the uplift of theater. Far from assuming a fixed chasm, since the Fall, between divine perfection and human vanity, as Pascal and Racine did, the ethics approved in polite circles described a "Ladder of Virtue" whereby in gradual steps the human character was capable of approaching the divine, leaving its pathetic animality far behind. The goal of this upward spiritual mobility was called by one popular author "the City of True Voluptuousness," and he designated the rungs of the ladder as Art, Science, Reputation, Fortune, and Virtue, in that order.[1] The last three of these categories are the chivalric norms that inform the theater of Racine's great rival Corneille, who customarily chose two virtues and then wrote a play in which they were hopelessly at odds. In *Phaedra*, though, a chief torment is the fact that heroic virtues do exist in one's habitual language, they are said to exist and they are certainly attractive, yet the self-knowledge that comes with suffering shows heroic virtue in any form to be well out of reach.

The most subversive part of Racine's contribution to the tragic theater is his analysis of ideal love; one can get at this by considering the relationship of the noble Hippolytus and the sweet Aricia. Perhaps Hippolytus's leading trait in his hatred of subjugation, and the special irony with which he struggles is that during the course of the play, like Chaucer's Troilus (another whose pride was that he "no devocioun/Hadde . . . to noon"), he is enslaved and conquered in every imaginable way. I have suggested that he is imprisoned by the unities; in addition, he submits to the slavery of which he disapproves in his father, the yoke of Venus. He prides himself on his

---

1. The author of these phrases is Desmarets de Saint-Sorlin, whose *Délices de L'Esprit* is discussed in Bénichou, *Mind and Ethics*, noted below.

uniqueness, both in chastity and filial piety, yet it is a dawn-
ing resemblance to his profligate father which makes him, as
Theramenes points out, a "rebel." When Hippolytus finally
has a chance to imitate his father and kill a monster, he
manages to destroy the bullish contamination of Phaedra's
family, but he is himself vanquished by the formerly tamed
horses which had been the symbol in his quite conscious
mind of his triumphant dominion over the animal in himself.
He has admitted earlier that in the laziness caused by love he
has neglected his horsemanship. His parade of virtue is
stampeded by his own deeper nature. His resemblance to
Phaedra does not stop at the fact that both of them think
love is "poison." His unconscious mind is the same as hers
also. Phaedra dreams aloud of the image of Hippolytus racing
through the woods in his chariot, and we recognize that the
forest resembles the Minotaur's labyrinth, the underworld of
Theseus, and the recesses of the palace. The forest is a tryst-
ing place shaped by the unconscious and representative of the
unconscious. To this erotic substratum Hippolytus refers also
when he tells Aricia:

> Your image haunts
> Me in the forest's depth. The light of day,
> The shades of night, all bring back to my view
> The charms that I avoid.

> [2.2.84–86]

Hippolytus is an unwilling prisoner of sex, to be sure, but
then so is Phaedra.

There are not two kinds of love in the play, but one. It has
its origin in hostility: consider Theseus and the conquered
Amazon; Theseus and Phaedra, viewed as the betrayal of
Ariadne and marriage with the daughter of an enemy;
Phaedra and Hippolytus, the enemy of her son's political
future; and Hippolytus and Aricia, the political enemy of his
father. The love which begins in hostility comes to be celebrated in the metaphors of rape and conquest. The sweet
Aricia's command of metaphor is especially startling:

. . . to make stoop a heart inflexible;
To touch a soul insensible to love;
To take a captive startled by his chains,
Vainly a mutineer against his joy,
That is my heart's desire, that is my spur!

[2.1.84–88]

C'est là ce qui m'irrite. Literally, that's what scratches me.
Even conquest, though, is illusory, for no one really conquers
except "Venus herself, entire, crouched on her prey." It is
particularly as a sexual moralist that Racine diverges from the
Hippolytus of Euripides. In Euripides the lust of Phaedra is
forbidden mainly because of a specific taboo against incest
(that is also true in Jules Dassin's film *Phèdre*). In Racine the
evil lies more generally in the tyranny of sex itself, evenly
distributed among the characters, and incest is horrible not
so much as taboo but as an extreme example of a tyranny
that prevails even over the most cogent reasons and the most
lively conscience that can be marshaled against it.

We have only alluded, thus far, to Phaedra herself. We find
her magnificent, of course, because of her prodigious moral
and animal energy. What gives us pause about her is her
autonomy. Her drama almost slips through the net of the
unities because it is so thoroughly internalized. The outside
to her is an oppressive blue; frequently she fails to understand even the drift of what is being said to her; and her
eloquence responds more readily to the pictures of her own
mind than to discourse or the passing scene. Of the actual
Hippolytus in present time, finally she admits: "Alas, I look
on him as a monster, frightful to my sight." From the beginning, in fact, it has been images of Hippolytus she has feasted
upon, tableaux of the chariot in the forest, herself leading
Hippolytus through the labyrinth, Hippolytus as a younger
Theseus arrived at Crete for the purpose of falling in love not
with Ariadne but with her, Phaedra. For another reason,
then, it is fitting that she be thwarted in her attempt to touch
Hippolytus; her pursuit of his image is autoerotic.

Yet again, we are apt to be misled by associating any one

quality with a specific character; Phaedra's passionate awareness of internal corruption serves to signal its existence in
those less conscious of it: the *dénouement,* even including
her prevarication, is her universal lesson. The virtual solipsism
of *all* Racinian heroes is most evident in the conventionality
of their utterance, in their shared pool of restricted language.
It is one of our oddest naiveties to assume that an artist is at
the mercy of a medium he has inherited. Racine's tragic
vocabulary consists of some two thousand words, Shakespeare's twenty thousand. Surely the narrowness of heroic
diction must be the albatross of a flexible mind, we say—but
could not that be precisely the point? After all, very obviously the exotic selectivity of the language of Racine's
characters contributes as much to their isolation as their
royalty does. If we say that it serves on the contrary to bring
them closer together, to make them resemble each other
more closely, we have forgotten the tragic significance of the
unity of place; Phaedra and Hippolytus, for instance, are
squeezed together, on two sides of a magnetic but imperme-
able wall that is language as well as the stage.

Tragic language has very little to do with ordinary reality.
Like the nature of royalty itself, heroic diction is at once un-
compromising and euphemistic. There is terror in the very
irreconcilability of these features; unbending severity menaces
politesse, and hampers vision. In their commitment to euphemism, the speakers tend not quite to grasp the point of
scenes they are involved in: Phaedra declares her amorous
desire, and Hippolytus, thinking it to be some sort of courtly
compliment, replies nervously in kind; Hippolytus declares
his love, and Aricia classifies it, even as they separate, not as
love but as an elaborate metaphor of empire. There is a
further tendency in the direction of mutual paranoia: Phaedra
thinks that Hippolytus and Aricia are plotting against her;
Hippolytus thinks that Phaedra is plotting to instill in him
the pollution he feels in himself; and Hippolytus and Aricia
think that "the greed of Phaedra will chase us both from our
rightful thrones."

Yet in each case these verbal errors, marked equally by moral extremism and diplomatic euphemism, are confirmed not by ordinary reality but by a harsher *tragic* reality than even suspicion would warrant. Paranoia is justified because tragic experience bears out the assumption that he who is not loved is hated. Phaedra is quite right, Hippolytus *does* hate her; Hippolytus and Aricia are quite right, Phaedra *is* plotting against them; they are only wrong in thinking—nobly thinking—that in the late stages of her disease Phaedra is capable of giving attention to politics: to that noble and objective displacement of human needs that we recognize as euphemism when we analyze our dreams of empire.

It is what Phaedra calls the "heart so full of what it loves," so full of an interiorized object or mirror of the self, that radically restricts the scope of heroic language. Beauty, for example, has its reality in the heart rather than in the object, and specific physical attributes are never describable except in a distant tableau. After all, beauty among neoclassical kings and queens is invariable; it is what Roland Barthes has called a "class privilege," and goes without saying. There is very little descriptive imagery of any kind in heroic language, and this is as it should be, for if a hero were to turn aside from his problems long enough to pictorialize his surroundings, that in itself would show that he was not obsessed, and the theater of unbroken crisis would be broken. By contrast, Theramenes, who is not a hero, can pause for description:

> Before our eyes spews forth a furious beast,
> A monster armed with terrifying horns,
> And all its body clothed with yellow scales:
> A thing at once indomitable bull
> And darting dragon whose hind-quarters lashed
> And twisted down in hideous slimy coils.
>
> [5.6.31–36]

Theramenes and the other servants might be characterized as the seeing-eye dogs of royalty. They differ from their masters in that they do things and go places. Theramenes at the behest of the grounded Hippolytus has traversed the entire Aegean in search of Theseus. Ismene, by standing outside the enchanted void at center stage, has a chance to scrutinize Hippolytus much more carefully than Aricia does. Oenone is simply everywhere, full of gossip and opinion, pinning and unpinning, flattering her queen and lying to her king—she is so hyperactive, in fact, that just as she is a kinetic extension of the will of Phaedra, so she needs an even more kinetic extension of herself, an otherwise quite inexplicable nonentity whose name is Panope. By so aggressively doing things, the servant class frees the upper class for sitting still, for keeping tabs on the ebb and flow of its own blood. Heroic blood colors the face (one does nothing so often as "rougir"), retreats to the heart and freezes there, rages through the arteries, and finally stains the cliffs of Trozene. The servants bustle along the corridors of Racine like blood in the veins of his heroes, but they have no blood of their own; they are entirely sexless in a play about sexuality.

However flexible they may be in space, however, their insouciance about the constraining imperatives of tragedy makes the servants far greater fools than their masters. They are optimists, and just as paranoia, euphemism, and hyperbole are appropriate responses to a tragic world, so also the only clear intelligence in such a world must be, as Phaedra's is, altogether pessimistic. Oenone has usurped the hyperbolic privilege of her mistress when she says, farcically: "Alas, my Lord, whose grief or tragedy/Has ever equalled mine?" Notice how skillfully Racine plays cat and mouse with the "Tragical Mirth" of Shakespeare's equally walled-apart lovers, Pyramus and Thisby in *A Midsummer Night's Dream.* Characters like Oenone dispel the threat of farce because they show what language is like when it *really* slips off its moorings. To be sure, Oenone kills herself and acquires a degree of dignity, but Phaedra reminds us that a quick leap into the sea is much too easy for a real hero; it is thoughtless, and in any case, says Phaedra, Oenone deserved worse. Oenone's plunge is a blind suicide against which we measure the thoughtfulness of Phaedra's: she does not use the sword of Hippolytus, nor does she drink Medea's poison until her self-exposure is complete. There is only one path open to Phaedra, but she can choose carefully how she treads it. Oenone defines the opposite approach to suicide when she says:

> Always a thousand paths are open to us,
> And my righteous grief shall show me how
> To find the shortest cut!

[1.3.83–84]

It is misleading, then, to conclude that because they are temporizers the confidants in *Phaedra* are also realists. They too are tragic thinkers, but of a different order. They are beset with moral options, "a thousand paths," and lacking the reflective power of a hero of Corneille, for them the act of choosing becomes a game of pick-your-motto. Better this than that, rather do than don't, the apogee of which confusion occurs when Oenone, trying to persuade Phaedra to accuse Hippolytus, opines, "To save your honor you must sacrifice all, even conscience!" Honor and conscience return us to the Ladder which leads to the City of True Voluptuousness, two of the highest rungs of which, again, are Reputation and Virtue. Racine's heroes, like Pascal, rarely nitpick in this edifying way.

In a world as barren of human prospect as I have suggested Racine's to be, it is necessary finally to account for the role of his gods. This is not at all easy if we rest content with the deities whose names actually appear in the play. Apparently Phaedra is the sacrificial victim of Venus, while Hippolytus and Theseus are victimized and tricked, respectively, by Neptune. Yet despite its proper stress on the determinism of the plot, this attribution of agency is not wholly satisfying. The gods resemble instruments more than causes. The avenging Neptune is called into the fray by Theseus, while Neptune as horse-tamer is a kind of tutor hired by Theseus for his son.

Venus too, whose enmity has been the undoing of Phaedra's family for some time, is herself circumscribed and anticipated by the hostile scrutiny of Phaedra's grandfather, the Sun above ground, and of her father Minos, the avenging judge of the underworld. Venus and Neptune seem most consistently to be expressions of paternal wrath, agent-purveyors not unlike Oenone and Theramenes. Yet the play is unmistakably, profoundly religious; somewhere entrenched in its unhappiness there must be a god who is more than a servant and more than a conventional exclamation point ("Dieux!" "Ciel!").

In the preface to *Phaedra*, Racine perhaps somewhat disingenuously explains how he has chosen to observe the *bienséance* of poetic justice: legend obliges him to kill off the traditionally perfect Hippolytus; therefore he will provide his model youth with a mild tragic flaw: to wit, a politically undesirable lady. In grafting Aricia, wife of the Hippolytus described by Virgil (*Aeneid*, book 7), onto the Euripidean story, Racine shows that the sin of Hippolytus consists in rebellion against the father. We have seen that it is possible to call Hippolytus variously a "mutineer" and a "rebel." Thus, Racine's preface would have us believe, poetic justice is served. But on the other hand, as I have tried to show, in creating a world in which of necessity all men are equally wretched, Racine has sabotaged the very relevance of poetic justice, while having introduced a mode of paternal tyranny unlike anything to be found in his sources.

Racine was educated by Jansenists, a group of austere determinist Catholics who believed, with Pascal, that as a consequence of the Fall all human endeavor was vain without the intercession of divine grace. Because God's perfection was so infinitely removed from corrupt human understanding, God was inscrutable; he was, in Pascal's famous phrase, a "hidden God." In the majority of Racine's tragedies the father, like God, is absent or in hiding until the third act or later. In *Phaedra* Hippolytus undergoes a crisis of filial faith. The virtue of Theseus is maligned on all sides during his absence; Hippolytus agrees with the substance of the criticism (that his father is profligate) and yet, as he says, he must persist in filial piety; he must sustain in his mind a noble image of the father for whom he is searching in order to justify that father's absolute authority. Despite this effort, he acquires the appearance, at least, of a rebel when Theseus appears. Everyone in the play is necessarily a rebel, for the fact that Theseus lives on and on miraculously is what keeps Phaedra's son and Hippolytus and Aricia from inheriting their birthright and choosing their sexual destiny.

Theseus hoards all the glory; he is the only killer of monsters, he controls all the women and all the thrones. Not only is he a tyrant but there *has* been every reason to believe that he is dead, hidden forever in an underworld from which it is his unique gift, apparently, to be able to return at will. The general crisis of faith in the play is the failure to believe that Theseus can come out of hiding. "Can I believe," says Aricia, who betrays, one is tempted to feel, considerable impatience for *her* birthright, "can I believe that any mortal/Before his last breath can penetrate the deep realm of the Dead?" And Phaedra says, "No one views twice the mansions of the dead." Hippolytus keeps his faith; he never wholly gives up thinking that his father will return, and as a reward for his faith the father falsely accuses, banishes, and kills him. In acting out his expiatory sacrifice by keeping silence about Phaedra's guilt, Hippolytus takes sin upon himself, he absorbs it: "I can look no more except with horror on myself." The crimes he shoulders are not just those of wretched man against the father, but also the crimes of the hoarding, jealous, outrageously long-lived father against the sons.

The father in Racine's plays, and in *Phaedra* especially, has the autocracy of God but the personality of man; this anomaly must have been the chief frustration of Racine as a playwright. The writing of *Phaedra* must have been a crisis for his own faith. He had found that classical tragedy could almost wholly subvert the humanistic optimism which had come to be its hallmark as a genre—and this was all to the good—but what it could not do was suggest the alternative optimism of Christian faith with any degree of integrity. The Hidden God must either remain hidden or he must appear onstage like Dionysus in Euripides' *Bacchae*, "disguised as man," and disguised as well, unfortunately, by more than his share of the corruption which is only human. ("Gods," complains Euripides' Cadmus, "should be exempt from human passions.") The God of the Freudian unconscious and of *Phaedra*, the jealous tribal father who persecutes his offspring in competition for the mother, is not at all the perfect and unknowable God of Jansenism, and there appeared to be no way of reconciling these two conceptions in the theater. *Phaedra* is the last secular play Racine ever wrote.

Still, it is not blasphemous. As Phaedra dies she says:

> Death removes
> The light from eyes which have defiled it, so—
> Restores to daylight all its purity.
>
> [5.7.51–52]

As there is much human impurity still flourishing in the person of the chagrined Theseus, Phaedra can hardly mean human purity, though an audience may think so if it wishes. The unity of time, the day of tragedy (to which Phaedra refers), synthesizes the future as well as the past, and it is to this "daylight" that purity is restored. The "beautiful Trozene" of Hippolytus's first speech is beautiful once more: there is the sun. What remains is the purity of time and place. The action has consisted of discourse; Phaedra's carefully timed death exists apart from action as the end of discourse and also its validation. Hippolytus, on the other hand, has been unable to control his horses because he could not control his language. He anticipates his death when, in recoiling from Theseus's accusation, he says: "Such unexpected blows, falling at once,/Take all my words from me, stifle, choke my voice."

In this condition of unpreparedness Hippolytus is robbed of his last word; he dies in midsentence. Not so Phaedra, of whom Theseus has said to his son, "Better to crown your perfidy you should have robbed her of both speech and life at once."

Human purity, then, is not restored to daylight, but what does emerge untouched by the catastrophe is the dignity of language, and the light itself. When she talks of the purity of daylight, Phaedra is talking about a quality of light itself; she is creating a religious symbol of the spirit embodied in a perfect form. She is telling her audience about pure tragedy, a singleminded tragedy like her own, which sidesteps the impure divisiveness of, for instance, Oenone's hairsplitting between honor and conscience. Consider Racine's definition of what he calls "simple action" in the preface to another play, *Bérénice*:

> There are some who think that simplicity is a sign of lack of invention. They do not reflect that on the contrary all invention consists in making something out of nothing. It suffices that the action should be great, that the actors should be heroic, that the passions should be aroused, and that everything should be imbued with that majestic sadness wherein lies the whole pleasure of tragedy.

Blasphemous though it may be, the purity of unified art is still an offering, an offering to the sun and the Sun King; in its "majestic sadness" it is also an offering to God, for the greater glory of God, as a frail imitation of the original "simple action" which made "something out of nothing." The offering itself is a tragic act like Phaedra's, who says as she dies, to translate it another way, "Let there be light."

BIBLIOGRAPHICAL NOTE

Jean Racine was born at La Ferté-Milon in 1639 and died in Paris in 1699. *Phèdre* appeared in 1677.

Quotations from the text are taken from Margaret Rawlings's translation (New York: Dutton, 1962),* which has a facing French text. A more scholarly but less dramatic version is by R. C. Knight (Edinburgh: Edinburgh University Press, 1971). Also available is John Cairncross's translation in *Iphigenia, Phaedra, Athaliah* (Harmondsworth: Penguin, 1970).*

I am conscious of widespread influences which are difficult to sort out, but I have deliberately adopted certain ideas from the following works: Roland Barthes, *On Racine* (New York: Hill and Wang, 1964); Paul Bénichou, *Mind and Ethics* (Garden City, N.Y.: Doubleday, 1971); Lucien Goldmann, *The Hidden God* (New York: Humanities Press, 1964), and *Racine* (Cambridge: Rivers Press, 1972); and a collection of essays including interesting studies by Georges Poulet and Jean Starobinski, *Racine*, ed. R. C. Knight (London: Macmillan, 1969).

Other important works include Georges May, *Tragédie cornélienne, tragédie racinienne* (Urbana: University of Illinois Press, 1948); John C. Lapp, *Aspects of Racinian Tragedy* (Toronto: University of Toronto Press, 1955); Raymond Picard, *La carrière de Jean Racine* (Paris: Gallimard, 3d ed., 1956); Martin Turnell, *The Classical Moment: Studies in Corneille, Molière, and Racine* (New York: New Directions, 1948), and *Jean Racine, Dramatist* (London: Hamish Hamilton, 1972); Eugène Vinaver, *Racine and Poetic Tragedy* (Manchester: Manchester University Press, 1955); and Bernard Weinberg, *The Art of Jean Racine* (Chicago: University of Chicago Press, 1963).*

*Paperbound available.

FAUST

Fred J. Nichols

Faust is the man who—in Goethe's version of the story—sold his soul to the Devil, got all that he wanted from him, and nonetheless was saved at the end. Of the many questions that this version raises, we might focus on two. First, how did he manage to do it? Why in spite of all the harm that he does, to himself and to others, while in league with the Devil, does he nevertheless attain salvation when he dies? And if that is so, why (our second question) did Goethe choose to call his great work a tragedy?

The Faust story of course is not one that Goethe invented. There was a real Faust; he lived from 1480 to 1539, mainly in his native region, the southwest of Germany, and he did in fact become a legend in his own time. We know that a Faust book was printed at Frankfurt in 1587, a German translation done some time earlier from a lost Latin original. This work was translated into English in 1592, but the story was already known in England. Christopher Marlowe had written *The Tragical History of the Life and Death of Doctor Faustus* apparently about 1590. (This version was not a source for Goethe's treatment of the story, but he read it with great interest after he had conceived of his own Faust.) Indeed, the continual fascination the story has exerted on poets, playwrights, and novelists—and composers as well—down to our own time has made the Faust legend perhaps the most significant and most vital myth in Western literary culture after those we have inherited from classical antiquity.

What is interesting from our point of view about these earlier versions is that in all of them Faust is damned, usually ripped limb from limb, at the end of his life. The notion that it might be possible for such a man to be saved arose only in the eighteenth century and was the idea of the genial founder of modern German drama, Gotthold Ephraim Lessing. In his *Seventeenth Literary Letter* of 1759 he proposed as an ideal subject for German dramatists the Faust theme, treated in a "Shakespearean manner," and he appended a specimen scene he had written himself. In Lessing's Enlightenment version of the story Faust is saved. Goethe began work on his own version of the legend in 1773 (at the age of twenty-four), a labor that he would devote himself to intermittently for the rest of his long life, leaving when he died some fifty-nine years later a poem in dramatic form of more than twelve thousand lines.

Between Lessing's idea of a new kind of Faust story and Goethe's lengthy accomplishment, however, there is something new: romanticism. The young Goethe who embarked upon the early version we now know as the *Urfaust* was very much a romantic writer, and in particular a romantic playwright. The *Sturm und Drang* (storm and stress) movement of Germany in the 1770s can be seen as the first concerted romantic literary movement in Europe. When Goethe embarked upon his own *Faust* drama he had just written one of the greatest of *Sturm und Drang* plays, his *Götz von Berlichingen*, and it was as such a drama that he initially conceived of *Faust.*

It may be better to delay an explanation of what is here to be understood by romanticism so that we can consider what *Faust* itself proposes to us as romanticism and not read an external definition into the work. Equally essential to an understanding of the work, however, is the fact that after his move to the court of Weimar in 1775, Goethe, in reaction to his

earlier affinities, embraced classicism. In this frame of mind
he made his famous visit to Italy, and the fruit of this phase
of his career includes his great classical drama, *Iphigenie auf
Tauris* (1787). In moving from a form of romanticism to a
form of classicism, Goethe, as we now can see, went against
the grain of the whole tendency of European literature of his
time, and in his great work romanticism and classicism are in-
termingled and entangled in what becomes almost a dialectical relationship. The ways the work implies that these two
concepts should be understood, and the way they are mingled,
have an important bearing on the answer to the question of
how Faust is saved.

The *Faust* story, as Goethe reworked it, falls naturally into
two parts: the smaller world of sixteenth-century Germany
of part 1, in which the story of Faust's love for Gretchen is
located, and the greater world of part 2, ranging in space and
time from the Holy Roman Empire to ancient Greece and
forward into more modern times. The focus of this context
is Faust's love for Helen of Troy. But before proceeding to
an examination of the basic patterns of the work we must
first understand the drama's terms. In particular we must see
how its two focal characters, the protagonist and the antagonist, Faust and Mephistopheles, are identified.

We see Mephistopheles first and, although he is a devil, it
is a characteristically Goethean touch that we see him first in
Heaven. In the context of a wager evoking the story of Job,
he is defined not only as a figure of evil but also as a joker by
no less authoritative a voice than that of the Lord. MacNeice's
translation conveys the light touch of the German:

> I have never hated the likes of you.
> Of all the spirits of denial
> The joker is the last that I eschew.

> [337–39]

Mephistopheles immediately proves the point in the words
which end the scene:

> I like to see the Old One now and then
> And try to keep relations on the level.
> It's really decent of so great a person
> To talk so humanely even to the Devil.
>
> [350–54]

As a spirit of denial Mephistopheles is traditional, as the kind of joker we see here, he is not.

He defines himself in precisely the same terms, using in the German the same verb, *verneinen* (the Lord's words translated above as "spirits of denial" are literally "spirits who deny," *Geistern die verneinen*): "I am the spirit which always denies," "Ich bin der Geist, der stets verneint!" (1338). It has been traditional in Christian theology since Augustine and especially in Aquinas to define evil as nonbeing, opposed to good, which is understood as the ultimate ground of being, but what is striking here is that the defining term is a verb. Denial here is not a metaphysical condition but an action. This demon, as a principal of evil, represents dynamic negativity.

As a spirit of denial, Mephistopheles goes on to express his sense of the ultimate futility of being:

> Whatever has a beginning
> Deserves to have an undoing;
> It would be better if nothing began at all.
>
> [1339–41]

But he does perceive a pattern in all this futility. Specifically, he sees everything as going around endlessly in circles. Ultimately, nothing gets anywhere that it has not already been, and therefore all is uselessness. This view is a perversion, a displacement to a negative level, of the cyclic nature of Heaven implied by the prologue in Heaven to which the whole drama will finally return at the very end. The prologue itself opens with the cyclic movement of the repeating song

of the angels celebrating the circling spheres of the heavens.
This is a symmetry which Mephistopheles' entrance interrupts.

But Mephistopheles is a demon particularly conscious of
time, and in a final summing up at the climax of the work he
expresses his sense of time as a series of meaningless and
empty circles:

> What use these cycles of creation!
> Or snatching off the creatures to negation!
> "It is gone by!"—and we can draw the inference:
> If it had not been, it would make no difference;
> The wheel revolves the same, no more, no less.
> I should prefer eternal emptiness.

> [598–603]

The "cycles" in the first line here are merely implied in the
German. *Schaffen*, "creation," is echoed in the following line
by the term for what is created, *Geschaffenes*, but the rhyme
word, *hinwegzuraffen*, "snatch away," negates creation's
process. Mephistopheles repeats himself here, at a point
when, with Faust's death, another apparently meaningless
cycle has been completed. It is because time is cyclic that it
is meaningless, and this concept of dynamic evil sees all effort
as incapable of evolving in any vertical direction because it
must always revolve on the same plane. Hence, "You remain
forever what you are" (1807). To go round in a circle is to go
nowhere.

Before turning to Faust, we must consider what kind of
good might be opposed to this particular kind of evil. Here as
elsewhere Goethe is unorthodox in his use of Judeo-Christian
traditions. These traditional beliefs are valuable to the poet
precisely because they function so well as metaphor. Opposed
to any concept of evil as Nothing there must be Something,
as Mephistopheles himself points out. What opposes his nihil-
istic effort is the persistence of procreation, the "new blood,
fresh blood" that constantly circulates, the "thousand em-

bryos" constantly emerging from the elements.[1] Faust understands the point:

> So you, when faced with the ever stirring,
> The creative force, the beneficent,
> Counter with your cold devil's fist
> Spitefully clenched but impotent.

[1379–83]

If evil is negativity understood as a process, not so much destroying as denying, the ultimate good is creativity. Dynamic evil is most effectively defeated by creation, by the power to bring into existence that which did not exist before. Part 2 of *Faust* in particular will explore the dimensions of this notion.

Faust at the beginning is an old man who has exhausted human learning. Obsessed with "the impossibility of knowledge" (364), he reflects on the fact that it does no one any good. Even the medicine his medical skill enabled him to make killed more people than the disease it was supposed to cure. He is isolated, alone in his "god-damned dreary hole in the wall" (399), his study, and we first see him fail again, this time with the magic to which he has now turned. His impulse —a constant one—is to get out into the world of nature, to escape enclosure, and he is able to conjure up the Earth Spirit, who merely illuminates his failure. In the face of this gigantic vision he shrinks back in his littleness, a "poor worm" (498).

Characteristic of Faust is his persistent desire to fly, to escape the horizontal plane that men are confined to. Echoing Psalm 54 he complains, "Alas that I have no wings to raise me into the air!" (1074). (The varied course of Faust's progress can be gauged by noting the different points in the work

---

1. A view consistent with the tradition of the deaths of infants and children that is a persistent part of the satanic tradition, although in that tradition the Devil has not been thought of as sexually impotent. Mephistopheles' lust is sterile because, as it turns out, he is a pederast.

in which he does succeed in flying by one means or another.) Faust's disciple Wagner unintentionally points up the problem when he observes that the joy he derives from his scholarly efforts involves bringing "all heaven into your study" (1109). For Faust, this is precisely what is wrong and it is why he fails with the Earth Spirit. One cannot drag the world of nature into such cramped spaces. To be enclosed is to run the risk of being snuffed out.

Faust reacts by rejecting the word for the deed. Turning to the Bible he rewrites the opening of the Gospel of Saint John, "In the beginning was the Word" (1224). But Faust can no longer accept the limitation of the universe of language. He experiments with alternatives, replacing "the Word" with "the Mind" and "the Power," before seeing the way out: "In the beginning was the Deed." Sick of the words that have gotten him nowhere, he wants to act, and in these terms he defines his human status: "It is restless action makes the man" (1759). And in so doing he abjures the intellectual for the sensual as a way of knowing, that sensual experience which is the common experience of all men:

> And what is allotted to the whole of mankind
> That will I sample in my inmost heart. . . .
>
> [1770–71]

We should observe that Faust's restless, yearning striving toward the infinite implies an essentially linear view of things, and in particular a linear sense of movement through time. This contrasts very sharply with Mephistopheles' sense of time as cyclic. The question, then, as to which of the two will win out involves a conflict of fundamental patterns as ways of understanding, and operating in, the universe.

What is the solution to Faust's predicament? One possibility is suicide, an escape into "nothing—nothing at all" (719). Faust is about to yield to this kind of denial, raising the cup of poison to his lips, when he is awakened "back into living" by an Easter chorus, celebrating the Resurrection in characteristically unorthodox terms as a rebirth:

> He in the zest of birth
> Near to creating light.
>
> . . . .
>
> Christ is arisen
> From the womb of decay!

[790-92; 797-98]

Here we see an instance of the metaphoric value of Christian traditions, in the theme of birth.

The solution to Faust's predicament that he does accept involves a different relationship with the principle of negation: signing the traditional pact with the Devil. Faust does not reject or flee from evil, the negativity that is in things, rather he embraces it, to make it, so he thinks, his servant. You accept the evil that is in the world, and by implication the evil that is in yourself. The bargain that is made is the traditional one of promising oneself to the Devil in the next world in return for the services he can perform in this, but we should carefully note the condition that Faust stipulates as to when the Devil will get what he is after:

> If ever I stretch myself on a bed of ease:
> Then I am finished! Is that understood?
>
> . . . .
>
> If ever I say to the passing moment
> "Linger a while! Thou art so fair!" . . .

[1692-93; 1699-1700]

What is arresting here is that the clause involves the very questions of ways of understanding time that we have seen. If ever Faust wants time to stop for him, if ever he wants to halt its flow, implicitly denying thereby that time is a linear progression—in other words, if he accepts Mephistopheles's view that the process of the passage of time is meaningless—then his time is up:

The clock may stop, its hands may fall,
And that be the end of time for me!

[1705-06]

Whose view of time will triumph? At the end of this scene, Faust flies for the first time, borne off by Mephistopheles' mantle.

Faust wants to feel the sensual experiences that all men feel, therefore he falls in love. The rest of part 1 tells the story of that love and what it costs. Before Faust goes out into the great world of time and space—and his progress will be a series of outward movements—he must in his own world have human experience in its most intense form. But in any quest for experience for its own sake there are likely to be innocent victims. Here the victim is Gretchen.

Gretchen is the one important Christian character in the work. She comes from a religious context: we first see her coming from confession. Her mode of expression also sets her apart from the other characters. Left to herself she utters simple lyrics, some of Goethe's most accomplished. In several senses, then, Gretchen will be out of place to the extent that Faust, entering her world, succeeds in drawing her into his. Her world from the beginning has been encompassed by death. She tells Faust of the little sister she raised: "I brought her up quite alone/On milk and water; so she became my own" (3132-33). But the child has died. Faust, in the grip of his passion, deftly parries her religious argument with a rhetorical assertion based on his sense of the inadequacy of language:

Fill your heart with this, great as it is,
And when this feeling grants you perfect bliss,
Then call it what you will—
Happiness! Heart! Love! God!
I have no name for it!
Feeling is all;

Name is mere sound and reek
Clouding Heaven's light.

[3451–58]

Here we see Faust putting his philosophy to work. In yielding to him, Gretchen implicitly accepts his terms and the cost mounts: she is responsible for the deaths of her mother and her brother. Conscious of her guilt, she nonetheless continues to pray.

We get a sense of one of the things wrong with Faust's passion for her in an incident during the Walpurgis Night scene. In the midst of the revels, while dancing with a young witch, Faust's attention is arrested by a phantom. Faust is increasingly convinced that he sees Gretchen although Mephistopheles argues that he sees a "lifeless phantom, an image of air" (4190). For Faust, it might be argued at this point, she has become merely an image, a shape, and it is significant that he is now often away from her. It is ironic that he makes his way back to her by flying. He finds her in a dungeon condemned to death for, in her derangement, having drowned the child she has given birth to. She sings scraps of lyric; she has become in fact herself a lyric, rather like Helen of Troy:

People make ballads about me—the heartless crew!
An old story ends like this—
Must mine too?

[4448–50]

The procreation that Faust has been responsible for is blighted, and Gretchen can see her world only in terms of graves: her mother's, her brother's, her child's, and finally her own. Faust has brought all-encompassing death with him into her world. She has only her own death to look forward to. "The world lies mute as the grave," she says, and Faust can only reply, "I wish I had never been born" (4596). Appropriately, as Faust succumbs to nihilism, Methistopheles appears. Yet Faust has not expressed his despair in terms that would activate his own removal from time.

Gretchen dies gradually stifled and enclosed, her dungeon the point farthest from the outer world of nature, but her prayer saves her and it is Faust who is led off by Mephistopheles as Faust wanted to lead her off. Gretchen ends (and part 1 with her) as a dying voice, uttering his Christian name. Faust had said to her, "If you feel it's I, then come with me" (4536). She does not. It is Faust who is lost. His first intimate attempt at creation has led to an appalling and bitter tragedy, and at the end of part 1 it is he who is on the side of damnation.

Part 2 begins with Faust's reawakening, and we see him once more in the world of nature. That world is characteristically amoral. Nature spirits have pity on "the luckless man," "be he holy, be he evil" (4619–20). Faust, upon awakening, perceives more clearly than ever that life is process, and sees himself as "stirring and summoning a strong resolve/ Ever to strive for life in highest measure" (4684–85). But how does one strive for life in a universe where creation is the good? And what precisely does it mean to create? Part 2 of *Faust* explores these questions in more speculative ways as Faust becomes more conscious of his yearning for form.

A particular light is shed on the question by Homunculus, that curious artificial being created, interestingly enough, not by Faust but by Faust's disciple Wagner. We have had to return to Faust's old study, back to where it all began, to come to something absolutely novel, Homunculus, a diminutive human figure enclosed in a glass retort. Here man has engendered man by a new scientific method rendering sex obsolete, as Wagner proudly points out. Homunculus seems to embody Faust's definition of man: action is his very essence:

> While I exist I must show energy.
> I'd like to gird myself for work this minute.
>
> [6888–89]

But Homunculus is incomplete. He is artificial. He needs a corporeal genesis; he needs to be born, as he comes to realize during his travels:

From place to place I hover round
And hanker in the proper sense for birth.

[7830-31]

The philosopher Thales perceives his problem very clearly:

Having no lack of intellectual qualities
But quite devoid of concrete functionalities,
Till now his glass is all that gives him weight,
But next he yearns to be incorporate.

[8249-53]

Homunculus is pure intellect without body—and this seems
to be the limit of what man, working as does Wagner in the
laboratory he never leaves for the outside world, can create.
His problem is to attain a corporeal existence. Being pure
mind is not enough; in a sense Homunculus has yet to be
created. We begin to understand that in the universe of this
poem creation is embodying. To create is to give substance
to form.

It is the god Proteus, master of all shapes and forms, hence
in a way most particularly the god of substance, who has the
answer to Homunculus's difficulty:

In the wide ocean you must seek creation.
There in a small way you begin—
Glad to devour the smallest creatures—
Then slowly grow through valve and fin
And thus evolve to higher forms and features.

[8260-65]

The secret is evolution, a process of gradual becoming by
slowly taking on more and more complex forms, acquiring
substance by a kind of accretion. Homunculus finally learns
passion, "desire overriding," and literally disappears in a
blaze of glory. In spite of his sexless engendering he discovers
that passion must accompany true human engendering. The
notion that the most authentic form of creation is evolutionary process, matter giving body to ever more complex forms,
lies behind Faust's personal tragedy in part 2.

It is Homunculus, too, who provides us with material for considering romanticism and classicism, by moving us, and with us Faust and Mephistopheles, into the world of ancient Greece. As pure mind, Homunculus is naturally a classicist, and he knows of the classical Walpurgis Night, setting off the clear and sharply defined south against the gloomy, gothic, misty north where Mephistopheles is in his element. We should note, however, that the classical world that *Faust* moves us into consists of all that is chaotic, grotesque, and irrational in classical mythology. The gods of the classical pantheon hardly appear in this welter of peculiar beings, and it is Proteus and the Centaur who appear relatively normal. The extreme is reached in the classical shape that Mephistopheles takes on as most congenial to him, that of one of the Phorkyads, who share a single eye and tooth among them, perhaps the ugliest beings mentioned in classical mythology.

We see nonetheless in the classical episodes, acts 2 and 3 of the second part, what distinguishes romantic and classical attitudes in the poem. Romanticism subjectively creates its own world, while classicism, associated as it is with classical antiquity, is objective, clear, and bright. The subjective process of romanticism involves making a world by shattering old forms and inventing new ones more appropriate to what must be expressed. It is the force of the urgency motivating the need to express that shatters existing forms. The objective process of classicism, on the other hand, accepts the world that is already there and expresses itself by working in terms of what the old forms provide.

The interaction between these two modes of expression—and of being—in this part of the poem are complex and subtle. Romantic characters are plunged into the classical context while classical characters are transformed by romantic impulses working on them. In this sense *Faust* serves as Goethe's laboratory for testing romanticism and classicism against each other, and tracing a part of the process in some detail will shed light on the questions of form and creation that emerge as increasingly important in part 2.

The central figures here are Faust and Helen of Troy. (In this classical world the gothic demon Mephistopheles, although often present, can play only a subsidiary role.) Helen's appearance in the work comes at first merely to amuse an emperor, but Faust is so greatly taken with her beauty that he must have her himself. But to raise her in the first place he has had to visit the realm of the Mothers. Without plunging into the murky question of precisely what the Mothers represent in philosophical terms and what their origin may be, it does seem safe to say that they are in some sense the keepers of pure forms without substance:

> Formation, transformation
> Eternal Mind's eternal conservation.
> Wreathed with all floating forms of what may be
> They see you not, shadows are what they see.
>
> [6287-90]

Because of their associations with forms that are not "embodied," hence not—or not now—"created" in the sense we have seen that process to be understood in part 2, the Mothers exist wholly outside of space and time, outside of any dimensionality. "Flee from created things/Into the realms of form no lives attend!" (6276-77) Mephistopheles tells Faust, when asked how to seek them. Hence the loneliness and terror of their lifeless realm. There is no guarantee that a living being who penetrates it (something that has not been done before) can return to the world of time and space once he has so radically severed himself from it.

Why does Faust need to visit the Mothers in order to bring Helen back to earth? Having visited them and somehow gotten back, Faust invokes them as he conjures Helen back into being at the emperor's court:

> Around you weave
> The forms of life, which move but do not live.

What once existed in full glow and flame,
It still moves there, eternity its aim.

[6429-32]

Here it helps to recall certain classical ideas of death as a
process in which the body is left to decay but the soul continues to exist as a pure form. The union of body and soul
understood as the union of matter and form is an Aristotelian
idea, although for Aristotle the individual soul perishes with
the body. In most respects, however, Goethe's treatment of
forms is Platonic in origin, although his use of Platonism is
ultimately as unorthodox as his use of Christianity. If to die
is to be reduced to a pure form, then it should be possible to
raise the dead as insubstantial spirits.[2] This explains why
Faust is so enraptured by Helen's beauty when he sees her in
this scene. It is after all pure form. It is interesting that he
momentarily thinks back to Gretchen at this point.

The lovely form that once enraptured me,
That blest mirage of sorcery,
Was a mere foam-draft of such beauty.

[6495-97]

We recall that since the very beginning of his progress in the
world Faust has spoken of feminine beauty as an "image,"
and may recall as well Mephistopheles's sarcastic prediction
that Faust would soon be seeing Helens everywhere (2605).
   But Faust is making a crucial error here, because he mis-
takes the realm of form for reality:

Here is sure ground! Realities are here,
Here spirit dare strive with spirits, and prepare
For itself a double realm, wide as the air.

[6553-55]

---

2. This seems to be true in *Faust* of the dead from classical times. So profoundly is the poem permeated with a sense of evolution that even the process of death
has changed. See Mephistopheles' remark on how souls now cling more tenaciously
to the bodies they inhabit (11,623-30).

This is why, having raised up Helen, he loses her. He has succeeded in bringing her form to earth but he has not been able
to give that form a substance. She is a spirit without a body.
Hence the spirits disappear in an explosion when Faust
touches Paris with the magic key, much like what results
from the collision of matter and anti-matter, and Faust is left
unconscious but, in the next scene, dreaming.

We can now understand the significance of what Faust
dreams, interpreted for us by the newly created Homunculus,
who, as pure mind, seems to have access to the dream forms
of others. (Mephistopheles can see nothing.) What Faust
dreams of is Leda and the swan, that is, the episode of Helen's
engendering. It is Homunculus, pure intellect, who sees the
solution: to transport the still sleeping Faust back to ancient
Greece where his dream can—and does—become a physical
reality.

Faust's mission is to save Helen from time:

> And shall not I, imbued with wild desires,
> Draw into life that form the world admires?
> That eternal being, born to be divine. . . .

[7437-39]

But he has something yet to learn about feminine beauty, and
it is the centaur Chiron, the preceptor of Achilles (another
lover of Helen, who, as Faust aspires to, has loved and possessed her after death[3]), who instructs him:

> Ah! Woman's beauty is skin-deep
> Too often a mere frozen form;
> My praises only one can reap
> Whose life is a fountain glad and warm.

[7399-402]

True beauty is not merely formal, it must be generative, it

3. The name Goethe gives the child of Helen and Faust, Euphorion, is the name
of the child of Helen and Achilles in the legend about the affair they had after
their deaths.

must be capable of bringing life into being. Faust's sense of Helen's corporality is reinforced when he realizes that riding on Chiron's back he is sitting where she sat as a ten-year-old child.[4] Faust's dreaming and thinking of Helen in act 2 of part 2 recapitulate her development from conception onward.

It is appropriate, then, that Faust must move back in time to the classical past when Helen did have a corporeal existence. Having done this he must somehow move her forward to the present. The purest classical moment in time comes at the beginning of act 3, where Goethe inserts the *Helena*, the beginning of a classical play he had left unfinished years before, into his greater work, and in the scene that follows Helen as a classical figure is inserted into the romantic world of Faust's castle in Greece. She has been brought forward in a single step from antiquity to the Middle Ages. Time has been successfully conflated, but it is a problem that has not yet been resolved.

Helen, unlike Faust, is weary. "Rest is all I wish," she says when she finds herself in Faust's medieval castle near the beginning of the third act (9140). Nonetheless, Faust brings her into his world and they learn to talk to each other. He teaches her, a figure from classical epic, romantic love. He kneels at her feet. (To see the distance Helen has to come, imagine Homer's Achilles kneeling at a woman's feet.) He teaches her how to speak in dialogue rather than formal speeches, and teaches her to speak in rhyme. And with rhyme she learns how to express herself romantically, to express the pure feeling that flows directly from the heart. He teaches her to be sincere.

Yet the problem remains. How can two figures from such different periods of time exist together? Faust, one might imagine, could here be facing the temptation to wish that

---

4. One cannot help comparing Faust's effusion in part 1 over Gretchen's chair, the seat where his other love has sat, as part of a curious pattern. There, too, he imagines his beloved as a child.

time might stop, and so lose himself. But he does not. Instead he and Helen move into the timeless pastoral world of Arcadia, a world outside of time because the world of Arcadian pastoral has never really existed in any historical time. Faust saves Helen from time by moving her out of it, and here he and Helen are able at last to consummate their union.

That union does achieve a creative force. The result is song, and Goethe conceived of the scene as being performed operatically. The child of their union is the romantic singer Euphorion, whom Goethe associated—rightly or wrongly—with Byron, the Byron who went off to die in the Greek war for independence. Euphorion embodies an unrestrained romantic exuberance, acknowledging no limit to his increasingly greater flights (in this very much his father's child). Helen and Faust jointly perceive this:

> But how wilful! But how frantic!
> No hope here of curb and border!
>
> . . . .
>
> What an uproar! What disorder!

[9785–89]

Euphorion is another for whom the word alone is not sufficient; he must have the deed, even though he is aware that the consequences are likely to be fatal.

Euphorion perishes, and Helen evaporates. Time has reclaimed her and Faust has been unable to endow her with lasting substance. Again he has struggled and lost, and in this particular defeat we can perceive the limits of both pure romanticism and pure classicism. Romanticism, knowing no restraint, is not viable as a way of living: a fatal flight is the inevitable result, when raw energy is so little controlled by form. Classicism, on the other hand, is nothing but pure form. Its substance is lost in the past, and one cannot live as pure form without substance. What Faust, who is after all a romantic figure in his origins, learns from this episode is the necessity of restraint, the need to impose form and order on

310 THE DRAMATIC TRADITION

chaotic energies in a world where loss of order always leads to destruction. Heroic striving must be controlled by form.

Acts 4 and 5 tell the story of Faust's ultimate struggle. They begin with Faust's return to his own time alighting on a mountain peak—foreshadowing his ascent among mountains at the end of the drama. He wants only to work, "the action counts alone" (10,188). He embarks upon the most extensive of his projects, against a mighty opponent:

> Thus at a myriad points creeps up the sea,
> Infertile, spreading infertility.
>
> .   .   .   .
>
> And I could thus grow desperate to behold
> This aimless power of elements uncontrolled.
> But here my spirit dared a flight unknown:
> Here could I war and, warring, win my throne.
>
> [10,212–21]

His opponent is the sea, the endless, shapeless, cyclic flux embodied, the sea that is both formless and life-giving. His purpose is to create land, to extend fertility, to make more space in which men can live, grow, and plant. Having failed in his personal attempts at creation, he turns to social purposes.

His project succeeds, with the help of evil forces. Yet at the end he is reduced to being responsible for the deaths of an old, weak, and defenseless couple for the sake of a paltry bit of property so that he can "gaze on the unlimited" (11,345). His failure is that he has lost his humanity, as he himself is forced to recognize:

> To face you, Nature, as one man of men—
> It would be worth it to be human then.
> As I was once, before I probed the hidden,
> And cursed my world and self with words forbidden.
>
> [11,406–09]

Still he continues to struggle, although blinded by Care. And in a final irony, he now must depend upon the word in order to act as he directs his great project. "Only the master's word is weighty here. . . . What has been outlined must at once be made" (11,502–06).

Faust's ultimate moment, the moment of his death, is a vision. His purpose has been to extend the earth where man lives, to make a space where human activity can be about its business of creation:

> Oh to see such activity,
> Treading free ground with people that are free!
> Then could I bid the passing moment:
> "Linger a while, thou art so fair!"
>
> [11,579–82]

He has spoken the words that he himself had stipulated would end his days on earth. It is true that he has prefaced them with a conditional construction, *dürft ich sagen*: if he could see (which he cannot), then he would say. . . . But the Devil is a literalist, one who is wholly bound by legal forms, and it is enough for him that the words are actually spoken, whatever the intention and however they are qualified. Why does Faust speak them? The lines next following can be taken as an explanation:

> The traces of my earthly days can never
> Sink in the aeons unaware.
> And I, who feel ahead such heights of bliss,
> At last enjoy my highest moment—this.
>
> [11,583–86]

Faust feels that he has finally accomplished something that will last in time. In this sense he has at last conquered time. It can halt and he can enjoy a moment of relaxation, his highest moment. Mephistopheles takes this moment to be that of Faust's final defeat by time: "Time masters him and here he lies his length. The clock stands still."

Has Faust succeeded or failed? Whose view of the pattern

of time, linear and evolutionary, or cyclic and static, has been vindicated? Some of Faust's failures are obvious. He has failed in the small world with Gretchen and in the greater world with Helen. He has engendered nothing that lived and has lost them both, failing in a simple human love and in an ideal human love. On the personal level his life has indeed been a tragedy. What of his grandiose land-reclamation project? He does not see it, because he cannot, and the results are in fact ambiguous. The cost is great again on the personal level: he has lost his humanity and he must endure the bitterness of acknowledging that loss. And what he "sees" at the end is a vision that has not yet been attained. The permanence of the project depends upon the draining of a swamp that has not yet been accomplished. The work is a form whose substance has not quite been wholly provided, and we know now what happens in this particular world to form without substance. The lemurs, when Faust can no longer see them, are digging not the intended earthworks but his grave.

> The word today, from what I've heard
> Is not "intended" but "interred,"

> [11,558–59]

remarks Mephistopheles. (The German plays on *graben*, to dig, and *Grab*, grave.) In several senses language gets the better of Faust at the end. If true creation, embodying, can only meaningfully take place as an evolutionary process, then any shortcut is bound to fail.

Why, then, is Faust saved? There are two reasons. First, we should notice that he is not stretched out "on a bed of ease" when the final moment comes. Although he has learned the nature of creation and the necessity of control, he still sees ceaseless striving, "restless action"—although now action that is channeled into patterns—as the ideal essence of man:

> He only earns his freedom and his life
> Who takes them every day by storm.

> [11,576–77]

It is his preference for action as opposed to mere words that saves him.

In this we may see as well a clue shedding light on why Goethe chose a dramatic form for his work. As the course of his life suggests, he shared with his hero Faust the belief that language alone was not enough as a way of operating in the world. This is not be to understood as a denial of language but as an attempt to transcend language. Hence in what he conceived of as his great work Goethe uses words to create in the reader's mind an image of dramatic action, moving through language to something beyond it.

The same striving that defeats Faust on earth finally saves him. In this the work is tragic. It is Faust's conscious attempt to work beyond the limits of his humanity that causes the destruction of his human status. The angels who carry his soul off to Heaven make the point: "Should a man strive with all his heart,/Heaven can foil the devil." And, they go on to explain, "if love also from on high/Has helped him through his sorrow," (11,936–39) he will be assured of a future after death. Here we see the second reason for Faust's salvation. However imperfect his love has been and however tinged with lust, Faust has loved and been loved in return.

Back at the beginning of act 4, his love affair with Helen ended, the ideal shape of womanly form dissolved as a cloud, Faust has a sense of what he calls "Aurora's love," his dawn love, Gretchen. He now understands the value of that love, and sees her form also rise to Heaven:

> Like the soul's beauty now that gracious form ascends
> Yet does not melt but climbs the heights of sky and takes
> Away with it the best and inmost part of Faust.
>
> [10,064–66]

Here we see the Petrarchan notion (Petrarch's response to a tradition which Beatrice and Dante most memorably represent) that when a man loves, however impurely, a woman who is pure and gives his heart to her, when she dies and goes to Heaven she takes his heart with her. Hence the lover's salvation becomes a kind of reintegration. Part of him, "the best and inmost part," is already in Heaven. It is a question of the rest of him being drawn up at his death. Hence the importance of "Eternal Womanhood" leading on high in the poem's last words. Woman's beauty is greatest, as we have seen, when it is capable of engendering, when it is fertile, potent in further creation.

The final scene suggests as well a solution to the problem of the conflicting patterns of time in the poem. In a sense the cyclic view is correct. Like the "Prologue in Heaven," the final scene, "Mountain Gorges," is full of references to rings and circles and finally "higher spheres." Yet one can move up into Heaven from the planes of lower cycles. It is possible to "ascend to higher circles," as the Pater Seraphicus remarks (10,918). The soul who achieves salvation can rise to places it has not been before. So the linear view of time also involves a perception of its true nature, insofar as a linear process implies movement through a series of unique events. But in fact the basic pattern finally suggested is that of time as a spiral. If one strives upward each revolution of the circle can raise the active soul to a higher cycle. The concept of time in *Faust* is three-dimensional. Spiral time is the time of evolutionary cycles, and while the human intelligence cannot assign limits to the process, it can comprehend its pattern.

Faust finally reborn again undertakes his final flight. Again there is a symbolic return to childhood: he accompanies the most innocent of all, the souls of those who died at birth. Like a chrysalis soon to be transformed and emerge from its cocoon (11,985),[5] Faust sets off into an afterlife itself conceived of as an evolution, a process leading up to yet higher spheres. Meanwhile he will instruct the blessed boys. Here man, because of his earthly experience, has something to

5. Mephistopheles, at what he takes to be the end, reverses the metaphor, seeing the soul as a Psyche who becomes a worm when her wings are plucked (11,659–61).

contribute even to Heaven. And time does not end yet in
this evolutionary afterlife. Faust continues upward toward
cycles and spheres neither he nor we can as yet understand.

BIBLIOGRAPHICAL NOTE

Johann Wolfgang von Goethe was born in Frankfurt am Main in
1749 and died in Weimar in 1832. The composition and publication
history of *Faust* is complicated. The *Urfaust* was composed, but not
published, between 1773 and 1775. *Faust, Ein Fragment* was published
in 1790; the first part, *Faust, der Tragödie*, was published in 1808; a
further fragment, *Helena*, was published in 1827; and the complete second part was published in the year of Goethe's death, 1832.

I have used the Louis MacNeice translation of *Faust* (New York: Oxford University Press, 1960).* Of currently available versions this
seems to me most effectively to convey something of the poetic flavor
of the original. Unfortunately, MacNeice's translation is not complete
and sometimes eccentrically cut (my essay is of course based on a reading of the whole poem). One especially regrets the omission of the
Helena. An attractive new translation of the complete poem is that of
Walter Arndt (New York: Norton, 1976).* Extremely useful for an
English-speaking reader wishing to explore the poem in depth is the
complete verse translation of Charles E. Passage (Indianapolis: Bobbs-
Merrill, 1965).* The translation is accurate, if not really successful as
poetry, but the extensive interpretive material and commentary are the
most useful available in any English version.

Good introductions to further study of Goethe are Liselotte Dieck-
mann, *Johann Wolfgang Goethe* (New York: Twayne, 1974), and the
well-chosen collection *Goethe: A Collection of Critical Essays*, ed.,
Victor Lange (Englewood Cliffs, N.J.: Prentice-Hall, 1968).* Both volumes contain bibliographies listing the fundamental studies in German
as well as material written in English. Among the numerous more detailed studies in English, I have found the following particularly useful:
Stuart Atkins, *Goethe's Faust: A Literary Analysis* (Cambridge, Mass.:
Harvard University Press, 1958); Barker Fairley, *Goethe's Faust: Six
Essays* (Oxford: Clarendon Press, 1953),* and *A Study of Goethe* (Ox
Introduction* (Cambridge, Mass.: Harvard University Press, 1964).

There is considerable biographical material on Goethe available in
English: Kurt R. Eissler, *Goethe: A Psychoanalytic Study*, 2 vols. (De
troit: Wayne State University Press, 1963); Richard Friedenthal

Goethe, His Life and Times (Cleveland: World Publishers, 1965); the nineteenth-century study by George Henry Lewes, *Life of Goethe*, (New York: Fredrick Ungar, 1965); and Elizabeth M. Wilkinson and L.A. Willoughby, *Goethe: Poet and Thinker* (London: Edward Arnold, 1962).

*Paperbound available.

THE CHERRY ORCHARD
AND *HEDDA GABLER*

Walter L. Reed

The Cherry Orchard is a classic of modern drama that has proved hard to classify. One of the ways we respond to a play is to appreciate it in terms of its genre, and for the drama the most time-honored generic terms are comedy and tragedy. But from its inception *The Cherry Orchard*'s genre has been in dispute. Chekhov himself insisted, in a letter to Constantin Stanislavsky, that it was a comedy: "a comedy, even in places a farce," he wrote. And there is ample evidence in the play for this classification: people continually mistake one another, trip over furniture, no one dies from a position of power. But critics and directors have often interpreted *The Cherry Orchard* as tragic: after all, an aristocratic family loses its estate, the family is broken up, the cherry orchard is laid waste. Stanislavsky, a close friend of Chekhov's and the director of the Moscow Art Theater where the play was first performed, replied: "This is not a comedy or a farce as you wrote; it is a tragedy."

The debate is sometimes resolved by a compromise term like *tragicomedy*, and the play is then felt to be understood. But the question of literary genre is a more dynamic one than such a simple labeling implies. It is a question that is frequently asked—and answered—by the work itself, in ways that contribute significantly to the work's meaning. Like the farcical play within the play in Shakespeare's *A Midsummer Night's Dream*, "the tedious brief scene of young Pyramus and his love Thisbe: very tragical mirth," plays define themselves within and against the conventional categories of genre. They arouse and defeat our expectations about the kind of drama we are watching, and in this arousal and defeat they generate the new terms by which they are to be understood. *The Bacchae* of Euripides is a tragedy which questions the validity of tragedy as defined by Sophocles' *Oedipus the King*. Molière's *Misanthrope* is a comedy that only barely contains the tragic potential of its titular hero. In a similar fashion, *The Cherry Orchard* defines its theatrical mode by playing itself off against both comic and tragic possibilities, possibilities that the play itself conjures up, only to dispel.

The materials of tragic drama, as I have suggested, are latent in *The Cherry Orchard*. We witness the fall of an aristocratic family, its dispossession by a former servant, and the sacrifice of the cherry orchard, a symbolic bond between man and nature and a promise of renewal—at least to Mme. Ranevsky: "Oh, my orchard! After the damp dismal autumn and the cold winter here you are, young again and full of happiness," she exclaims in act 1. At the end of the play we hear the axes cutting down the trees. For some of the characters some of the time, at least, there is a mood of pathos and suffering that aspires to the condition of tragic experience. If no single character emerges as a hero or heroine, there is still the collective fall of the family and its isolation from the old order of society.

Of course this tragic potential is continually being subverted. The play as a whole never makes it clear that the cherry orchard is a source of redeeming value and not simply a luxury that the upper classes can no longer afford. Mme. Ranevsky's emotional apostrophe to the orchard is counterbalanced by the old servant Firs, chattering about the recipe for cherry jam. Gayev himself admits at the end, "It's quite true, everything's all right now. Before the cherry orchard was sold we were all worried and upset, but when things were settled once and for all and we'd burnt out boats, we all calmed down and actually cheered up a bit." Firs has the last word, a favorite of Chekhov's, apparently: *nedotyopa*, which is variously translated as "addlehead," "duffer," "nincompoop." It is interesting in view of what Chekhov himself said about the play as a "farce" to notice the elements of vaudeville and slapstick that deflect its potential for tragic depths. Yepikhodov is constantly bumping into furniture; Trofimov makes an impassioned speech to Mme. Ranevsky and falls downstairs; Gayev delivers an eloquent address to a bookcase. Varya accidentally hits Lopakhin with a stick. As soon as a character gets emotionally worked up, something ludicrous usually happens to him.

But *The Cherry Orchard* resists the embrace of comedy as well. Farce in its turn is undercut by pathos. The theme of the comic is the integration of society, as many critics have recognized, but although we are led to expect a number of social integrations, such as marriages, in *The Cherry Orchard*, these unions never take place. The house is abandoned at the end by everyone except Firs. To a great extent, the negation of the simply comic depends on how the character of Lopakhin is played. "You see, Lopakhin is the central character," Chekhov wrote to Stanislavsky. "He must not be played as a loud, noisy man; there is no need for him to be a typical merchant. He is a soft man." In saying that Lopahkin is not a "typical merchant" Chekhov is referring to a stock character in Russian comedy, crass, boorish, materialistic. Lopakhin is more sympathetic. He tries to advise Mme. Ranevsky on how to save the estate; he keeps lending her money and scarcely complains that she doesn't pay it back. And he buys up the estate almost unintentionally. He is not a figure we can treat simply with condescending laughter.

What these frustrations of comic and tragic archetypes point to is Chekhov's desire to get beyond the conventional resolutions that literature provides. The frustrations are not simply negative, but help to define Chekhov's theater of realism, a literary mode that attempts to reach out beyond the literary. Like so many writers in the post-romantic era, Chekhov feels that "life" can no longer be captured by the formulas of "art." He wants to bring the drama squarely up against "reality"—the reality of everyday feelings and everyday experience. He uses the phrase "real life" in one of his letters:

> After all in real life people don't spend every minute shooting each other, hanging themselves, and making confessions of love. They don't spend all the time saying clever things. They're more preoccupied with eating, drinking, flirting, and talking stupidities—and these are the things which ought to be shown on the stage. A play should be written in which people arrive, go away, have dinner, talk about the weather, and play cards. Life must be exactly as it is, and people as they are—not on stilts. Let everything on the stage be just as complicated, and at the same time just as simple, as it is in life. People eat their dinner, just eat their dinner, and all the time their happiness is being established or their lives are being broken up.

This is a call for what we would call realism, but like most manifestos of realism it is misleading in the way it suggests that reality is essentially formless, or that we know all about it before we see it. The realism of *The Cherry Orchard* is in fact carefully structured. In the first place, as we have seen, there is a consistent pattern in the failure of pattern, the failure of the conventional dramatic and social formulas for interpersonal relations. Chekhov takes a situation which makes us expect a significant event, then defeats those expectations. Act 1 is a homecoming, which should be a climactic moment. But Lopakhin has fallen asleep and missed the beginning of the homecoming, while Anya falls asleep and misses the end.

Act 2 shows a series of conflicting romances among the younger people; no romantic climax is allowed to take place. Act 3 centers around a dance in the ballroom, a ceremony of social harmony. But there are no generals, barons, or admirals in attendance as in the past, only the post-office clerk and the stationmaster. It is significant that the ballroom itself is offstage. The ceremony is interrupted when Lopakhin reveals, again quite anticlimactically, that he has purchased the estate. Act 4 is a final parting which is not quite a parting. Even Lopakhin is going off with the others on the same train. The projected marriage between Lopakhin and Varya never comes off.

Like the frustrations of the tragic and the comic possibilities, these are all negative patterns. On the positive side, Chekhov provides another kind of pattern, a structure of "real life" which shows us individual human beings trying to connect to a larger world outside themselves. In traditional drama before the nineteenth century it is the relationship of individual characters in the play to one another that is important. In *The Cherry Orchard*, however, the involvement of the characters with one another is more tangential. It is the relationship of character to world, a world beyond interpersonal relations, that creates dramatic meaning. The characters tend to engage in parallel play rather than direct confrontation. One can see this shift in orientation earlier, in Goethe's *Faust*, where both Faust and Mephistopheles relate more significantly to an external reality than they do to one another; the word *Welt*, world, is tremendously important in Goethe's play. The world of *The Cherry Orchard* is very different from the world of *Faust*, however, and needs to be considered in detail.

One of the first things we learn about the world of this play, and one of the most important, is that it is a world of time. "What time is it?" Lopakhin asks Dunyasha as they enter at the beginning of act 1. The play begins with a homecoming, a return to a place full of memories of the past, and

it ends with a departure, a facing of the future. Time is passing for individuals and for society; time brings changes that
are both painful and inescapable.

> *Anya* [*thoughtfully*]. It's six years since Father died.
> and a month after that our brother Grisha was drowned
> in a river. He was a lovely boy, only seven years old. It
> was too much for Mother, she went away, just dropped
> everything and went.

Or, in another example from act 1:

> *Gayev.* . . . At one time, dear sister, we both used to sleep
> in this room. And now I'm fifty-one, unlikely as it may
> sound.
> *Lopakhin.* Yes, time marches on.
> *Gayev.* What's that?
> *Lopakhin.* Time. It marches on, I was saying.
> *Gayev.* This place smells of cheap scent.

The idea of time emerges unobtrusively, in casual conversation. Chekhov makes us feel it as an integral part of reality,
something that is "out there," above and beyond the characters who perceive it. Every character has a different sense of
time. Lopakhin is precise, always looking at his watch. Mme.
Ranevsky wants to believe that "nothing has changed" in the
orchard; she wants to recapture the joy of the past but not
the sorrow. Trofimov, the revolutionary, has a grand vision of
the distant future: "Mankind marches on, going from strength
to strength. All that now eludes us will one day be well within our grasp." Firs wants to turn the clock back to a time before the emancipation of the serfs. Only in the aggregate of
these individual attitudes do we get a sense of the larger historical picture, and it is important that this is continuous
with an historical time in which the audience of the play is itself living, not a distant past or symbolic epoch. *The Cherry
Orchard* gives, among other things, a thick-textured repre-

sentation of the historical forces of late nineteenth-century Russia.

Time is the primary constituent of the world of *The Cherry Orchard*, but there are other "real" constituents as well— geography, for example, which is a realistic geography, Moscow and the provinces, not a symbolic geography like Athens and the fairy forest in *A Midsummer Night's Dream* or Germany and Greece in *Faust*. There is the house itself, where three out of the four acts take place. There is the outdoors of act 2, open country but with a city in the distance and the telegraph poles that connect Mme. Ranevsky with Paris. There are many allusions to the railroad, which brings people and takes them away. "We're all taking the same train," says Lopakhin in act 4. And there is the cherry orchard itself, which, according to Gayev, is mentioned in the encyclopedia.

"All Russia is our orchard," says Trofimov, looking beyond the immediate setting, and the play is about national as well as provincial geography. Beyond Russia lies France, which, for the characters in the play (and for Russia historically), is a primary source of high culture and polite society. Other constituents of the real world in the play include money—one notices how often money is mentioned specifically, or even dropped, onstage—and class distinctions, as in the allusions to the relatively recent emancipation of the serfs in 1861.

This, then, is the world of the play, a world which is not merely a projection or reflection of the characters, not simply the embodiment of a theme or the presentation of a symbol. The illusion is created that the world of the play is part of the world of the audience's everyday experience. It has been suggested that the "hero" of a realist play or novel is society itself, there being no single character who truly transcends his social environment. This formula is appropriate to *The Cherry Orchard*, but it does not then follow that the characters themselves are of no importance, merely the insignificant results of larger causes. Chekhov is a realist but by no means a determinist. We must turn here from the world of the play to the characters who inhabit it, and consider how they are presented.

The main thing that all the characters, even Lopakhin, share is their isolation. The isolation is self-imposed, however; characters isolate themselves by the kinds of things they say and do, all of which involve a retreat into artificial attitudes and objects and away from the threat of reality. Gayev provides the clearest examples. As the other characters remind us, he indulges in excessive eloquence, and he often addresses it to inanimate objects, like the bookcase:

> Dear and most honoured book-case. In you I salute an existence devoted for over a hundred years to the glorious ideals of virtue and justice. In the course of the century your silent summons to creative work has never faltered, upholding [*through tears*] in several generations of our line confidence and faith in a better future and fostering in us ideals of virtue and social consciousness.

On the other hand, as immediately after this speech in act 1, he escapes to the artificial or game world of the billiard table: "in off on the right into the corner. Screw shot into the middle." Billiards is a game at which he is presumably proficient, in a way that he is not in the realm of economic and social competition. Every character in the play has similar qualities that are artificial, contrived, or repetitive. Just as Gayev shoots for the corner pocket or keeps popping candies into his mouth, Firs always worries about whether Gayev is wearing his overcoat; Trofimov has his own stylized brand of eloquence ("What splendid things you say," Anya remarks); Charlotte, the governess, performs amusing magic tricks; even Lopakhin, the realistic merchant, goes to plays and tries to quote *Hamlet* to Varya: "Amelia, get thee to a nunnery," he misremembers in act 2.

However, it is important to see that the characters in *The Cherry Orchard* are not simply comic caricatures; it is important in reading the play not to be misled by the trivial dialogue, the silly joking, the silly weeping. These are not simply caricatures but potentially full, round characters who *reduce themselves* in the ways they act and speak, the ways in which they change the subject or pull back from painful recognitions. In the conversation between Anya and Varya in act 1, for example, Anya asks Varya whether Lopakhin has proposed marriage: "Why can't you get it all settled? What are you both waiting for?" The question is painful to Varya: "Wretched man," she says, "I'm fed up with the sight of him. Everyone's talking about our wedding and congratulating us, when there's nothing in it at all and the whole thing's so vague." Varya takes refuge in commenting on a piece of jewelry that Anya is wearing, fixing on something artificial. "[*In a different tone of voice.*] You've got a brooch on that looks like a bee or something." But this comment proves painful to Anya, who recalls their mother's extravagance with money: "[*sadly.*] Yes, Mother bought it." Anya herself escapes into something else artificial, the memory of a balloon trip in Paris: "[*Goes to her room, now talking away happily like a child.*] Do you know, in Paris I went up in a balloon." The gesture of escape is both formal and thematic.

Thus it is the *way* the characters speak more than the content of what they say that reveals the self behind their self-delusions, the insecurities and sufferings behind their chatter. Chekhov had definite ideas about the actor's delivery of his lines. He thought that the subtle intonation of the voice, the emotional inflection of a sentence, ought to be able to project a depth and realism of personality. There are approximately 175 different directions in the text of this play that specify how the lines are to be spoken—*Tenderly, Pensively, Through tears.* The numerous pauses and silences are also important in conveying the proper sense of the lines. They make the many shifts in a character's train of thought more clear and comprehensible. Characters rarely communicate with one another in any depth; instead they voice their isolated, private concerns in the superficial medium of social discourse. For example, in act 2 Mme. Ranevsky has just finished saying that giants are all very well in fairy tales but in life they might be alarming. Yepikhodov, the clerk, crosses the back of the stage playing a guitar.

Mme. Ranevsky [*pensively*] . There goes Yepikhodov.
Anya [*pensively*] . There goes Yepikhodov.

The feelings behind these words demand a deeper interpretation. Is Mme. Ranevsky thinking of her son, of her lover in Paris, or of her childhood? Is Anya unconsciously comparing Yepikhodov with Trofimov, or with Trofimov's vision of the future race? These are things the director, the actors, and the audience are left to decide.

To understand better this notion of character in the play—character as self-trivializing but not in itself trivial—it is useful to know something about the kind of theatrical production Chekhov's plays required. In fact, both the idea of character in the play and the idea of the realistic world are reflected in the kind of acting and staging that Chekhov's plays received in the Moscow Art Theatre under Stanislavsky. The Moscow Art Theatre was founded in 1898 by Stanislavsky and others partly in an attempt to create a theater where Chekhov's plays could be adequately produced. Although Chekhov was never completely satisfied with Stanislavsky's productions, he and Stanislavsky influenced each other in developing this realistic theater. Stanislavsky's major contribution to the theater of realism (or naturalism, as it is sometimes called) was his theory of acting. He felt that the actor should think himself into the character he was playing, should *become* the character in a much more intimate and spontaneous way than conventional acting styles had allowed. He wrote a number of books, among them *An Actor Prepares*, which have had considerable influence on the development of "method acting" (so-called) in the United States. What Stanislavsky was trying to get away from was the exaggerated, histrionic acting style typified in the performances of Sarah Bernhardt, who was extremely popular in Europe and had visited Moscow in 1881. Chekhov had criticized Bernhardt: "She transforms every one of her heroines into the same unusual woman she is herself."

The acting style advocated by Chekhov and Stanislavsky probably seems to us the most reasonable and convincing because it is a kind of illusion by now quite familiar and accepted. But it was a radical departure from what was then more usual in the theater, histrionic productions of Shakespeare or productions of Racine in an artificial declamatory style. In actual fact, an actor would have to be temporarily insane to believe completely that he was Gayev or Lopakhin as he played the part. Stanislavsky only intended the technique as a means of preparing the actor for a particular conception of character—the conception, as we have seen, in which the actual content of what is said is commonplace and trivial but behind which is communicated a larger, more dynamic reality of the self. In effect, the actor offers the audience *clues* instead of explicit statements. The audience is like a detective who must deduce larger conclusions about the nature of a person from bits and pieces of evidence. It is like the beginning of a Sherlock Holmes story, where the client comes into the room and Holmes reads the nonverbal clues of the client's dress and mannerisms before the client gets around to stating his business. The only difference is that Chekhov arranges the evidence so that the deductions are more elementary for the audience; the work of a Sherlock Holmes can be done by a Dr. Watson.

Thus the acting style supports the notion of character as something human concealed behind something artificial. In a similar way the staging in the theater of realism reflects the notion of a real world in and beyond the play. The Moscow Art Theatre was less original in its use of the stage than in its methods of acting. It treated the proscenium arch as the fourth wall of a room; the furniture, walls, windows and doors were all realistically rendered. These were techniques used by Ibsen and others before Chekhov. Chekhov does use this stage in special ways, however. He often leaves the stage empty, before characters enter and after they leave, to suggest the way the world exists independently of the people in it (for example, the stage is empty in act 1 as the carriages are heard driving up to the house). The room in act 4 is the same room as in act 1, except that most of the furniture is gone. The stage is left empty at the end as we hear people drive away, then Firs, the representative of the old order, appears. He lies down on the couch—not to die, as some productions melodramatically imply. He simply falls asleep, like so many characters in the play. The last sounds we hear are not human words but sounds of the world itself: first the mysterious sound of the breaking string, heard first in act 2 and puzzled over by the characters, a realistic detail which points delicately in a symbolic direction; then the sound of the axes cutting down the cherry orchard. Sound effects were another of Chekhov's special concerns in staging his plays, although he had sometimes to restrain Stanislavsky, who was even more enthusiastic about them, wanting, for example, to use the sounds of a train, frogs, and corncrakes during act 2 of *The Cherry Orchard*. Sounds are used sparingly in Chekhov's plays, but they reinforce the audience's sense of a world existing beyond the scene immediately before it.

The realistic theater of *The Cherry Orchard*, then, represents a twofold reality. On the one hand there is a stage which attempts discretely to give the illusion of a world continuous with the actual world of the audience, a world of historical change with its geographical, economic, and social dimensions. On the other hand are characters with only partially revealed motivations and various mechanisms which prevent them from coming to a full recognition of the world, of other people, or of themselves. Lopakhin, the "central character" of the play, in Chekhov's words, seems to come the closest to participating in the realities he stands over against. He seems to be the man of the hour if not of the future. It is Trofimov who offers the solutions to the problems of modern Russia when he says that everyone should work, but he remains a student, largely theoretical. It is Lopakhin who does the only work in the play: "I'm always up by five o'clock, you know. I work from morning till night," he says. His mercantile activity is not the kind of work Trofimov has in mind, but it is the best the play has to offer. This is not to say that Lopakhin is the real hero of *The Cherry Orchard*—for it is a play without a hero—but he is the character most in tune with the unvarnished realities of his contemporary world, the closest to the historical moment as Chekhov saw it. "God's world is good," Chekhov wrote in one of his letters. "Only one thing isn't good: ourselves. How little there is in us of justice and humility, how poor is our conception of patriotism. The drunken, bedraggled husband loves his wife and child, but what is the good of that love? We, so the newspapers say, love our great country, but how is that love expressed? Instead of knowledge—inordinate brazenness and conceit, instead of hard work, laziness and swinishness; there is no justice. . . . What is needed is work; everything else can go to the devil. The main thing is to be just—the rest will be added unto us."

If we move from Chekhov to Ibsen, we see another response to the theater of realism. Here realism itself is held up to criticism. Where *The Cherry Orchard* defines itself in opposition to the conventions of comedy and tragedy, a play like Ibsen's *Hedda Gabler* calls attention to the conventionality of realism and tries to reclaim, on a symbolic level, what remains of the tragic sense of life. It is in these terms that I would relate these two plays to one another. In Chekhov we see the theater of realism at its moment of perfection. In Ibsen we see the theater of symbolism struggling for a kind of Faustian regeneration. This assertion may seem to fly in the face of the evidence and the reputation of Ibsen as a realist playwright.

After all, Ibsen was a pioneer of realistic staging. He wrote a number of plays, like *A Doll's House* and *An Enemy of the People*, that were solidly concerned with the social roles and social trials of men and women. It was for such classics of realism that he was praised by George Bernard Shaw. And such a mode seems dominant in *Hedda Gabler*, with its domestic setting, its focus on the petty politics of social institutions and the institution of the family, and its conscientious use of the fourth-wall stage. But in his later plays, of which *Hedda Gabler* is one, Ibsen tried with increasing insistence to move beyond realism to a more intense and introspective symbolistic mode.

Shaw did not like these later symbolistic plays very much; neither did Chekhov. But another Irishman, James Joyce, was enthusiastic about them, so much so that he learned Norwegian to be able to read them in the original. Joyce wrote a review of one of these later plays, *When We Dead Awaken*, and in it he makes two important points which we can use for contrasting *Hedda Gabler* with *The Cherry Orchard*.

First, in regard to staging, Joyce talks about the tendency in Ibsen's later plays to "get out of closed rooms." In *The Cherry Orchard* we begin and end in the same closed rooms, almost empty of people, but in a play like *The Master Builder* we end up out of doors, watching the architect Solness climb up and fall off the tower of his new home. In *When We Dead Awaken*, Ibsen's last play, the characters are out of doors all the time and are finally swept away by an avalanche. Hedda Gabler stays inside throughout, but she is always walking over to the French windows and looking out. More important, she considers the house itself as something petty. "It was our admiration for the late Prime Minister's house that brought George Tessman and me together," she says sardonically. "And you really didn't care in the least about the house?" the judge asks. "God knows I didn't," says Hedda. Chekhov makes us feel that the house is substantial and something of value in itself; Ibsen makes us feel it as a constraint on Hedda's imagination.

Joyce's second point has to do with the conception of character. As with the world suggested by the staging, we are moving here beyond realism. "Ibsen's drama," Joyce wrote, "is wholly independent of his characters. They may be bores but the drama in which they live and move is invariably powerful." Ideas and symbols are larger than the characters in *Hedda Gabler*, larger even than Hedda Gabler herself. Words mean more than the characters intend. This is just the reverse of the situation in *The Cherry Orchard*, where the characters have *more* depth than their superficial conversation suggests. Hedda and Loevborg raise large philosophical questions; they talk about life, power, courage, truth, and art. One of the reasons Hedda shoots herself is that Loevborg has failed to live up to the role of Dionysian hero she has imagined for him: "With a crown of vine-leaves in his hair, burning and unashamed!" She is left to fulfill this mythical role herself, and in doing so she sacrifices her realistic character.

What I am suggesting is that Hedda Gabler is a character who feels imprisoned in the domestic drama to which she gives her maiden name. She has aspired to a certain level of worldly success—she still has lingering hopes that Tessman will "go quite far in time." But she has realized that her aspirations go further than this realistic world. Ibsen makes us feel the suffocating presence of the house, the fussy scholarliness of Hedda's husband, and the cloying solicitation of Tessman's spinster aunts, even as he dramatizes the cruelty and will to power in Hedda herself. Hedda's aspirations are hardly ideal in any moral sense, but they proceed from energies that lie beneath the visible surface of "real life."

In the midst of this circumscribed boredom, the eccentric figure of Eilert Loevborg reappears, a historian and regenerate dissolute who has turned his attention from the dead past to the vital future. Hedda has rejected his sexual advances in the past, we learn, just as she rejects the possibility—or the fact—of her present expectant motherhood. She prefers to "shape a man's destiny" in her imagination. Hedda sees Loevborg first as the romantic antagonist of her husband ("It'll be a kind of duel," she says of the competition for the professorship), then as a Dionysian figure whose triumphant return she can claim as her inspiration ("With a crown of vine-leaves in his hair"), and finally as a tragic hero who sacrifices himself before the world ("I am saying there's beauty in what he's done"). Hedda sees herself as a combination of Muse and Valkyrie, leading men on to creativity and battle. But Judge Brock disabuses her of her vision of Loevborg's suicide, and shows her how completely she is trapped in his cynical "triangle," a hypocritical liaison in which, he says, no "compulsion" is involved. Hedda finally realizes that she can only act out the imagined heroic role on her own. She takes the remaining pistol, an object by now charged with symbolism, and turns it on herself. As she closes the curtains of the rear room before her final act, she creates for herself a symbolist stage within the realistic stage occupied by the other characters. When the curtain is opened, we are left with a portentous tableau that violates realistic expectations. As Judge Brock says, using the same words Hedda had used earlier in the play, "But, good God! People don't do such things."

The heroism of Hedda Gabler is deeply problematical—her suicide is a dubiously symbolic gesture—but it clearly aims at rejecting the world of historical and social interdependency that a play like *The Cherry Orchard* tries faithfully to represent. This realistic world, in its turn, rejects the aspirations of the symbolic. In *The Cherry Orchard* the character who talks of suicide in Yepikhodov, the bumbling clerk. "I'm a cultured sort of person and read all kinds of remarkable books," he says, "but I just can't get a line on what it is I'm after. Shall I go on living, or shall I shoot myself, I mean? But anyway, I always carry a revolver". Chekhov discredits the heroic gesture that Ibsen tries, however precariously, to redeem.

Like the older opposition of comedy and tragedy, however, the opposition in Chekhov and Ibsen between the theaters of realism and symbolism can be seen, from a higher level, as two sides of a single dialectic, a dialectic which depends on a confrontation of character and world. In the theater of realism, character and world are kept apart. Characters are defined by their social and economic bearings, and their consciousness rarely is allowed to penetrate into the world they inhabit. In the theater of symbolism, on the other hand, the minds of the characters and the world they inhabit are made to coalesce. As far as the theater itself is concerned, the main difference between these two modes is the attitude they assume toward the dramatic illusion, the illusion that the audience is seeing "real life." In realism or naturalism this illusion is encouraged, allowing the audience to move imperceptibly, with little imaginative dislocation, from the world of the play to the world they themselves live in, and vice versa. In symbolism (also called "expressionism" in the theater) the dramatic illusion is actively *dis*couraged; "real life" is denied and the play transcends marked boundaries. The work of art becomes itself the locus of a transcendent reality, a higher truth. The theater of realism looks outward, like a window, onto the real world, trying to deny its contrived "artistic" nature. The theater of symbolism looks inward upon itself, transmuting the real world into symbolic substitutes. The artificiality of the theater is thus intensified to become artifice in a more positive sense, even as it acknowledges its involvement in the raw materials of what society has agreed to call the realistic world.

BIBLIOGRAPHICAL NOTE

Anton Pavlovich Chekhov was born in Taganrog, Russia, in 1860 and died in Badenweiler, Germany, in 1904. *Vishnyovyy Sad* (*The Cherry Orchard*) was produced in 1904 by Stanislavski's Moscow Art Theatre.

There are some ten different translations of *The Cherry Orchard* currently available in inexpensive or paperbound editions. The most readable and the most successful in conveying the comic, social dimensions of the play is Ronald Hingley's version, available in paperback together with *Uncle Vanya* (London: Oxford University Press, 1965).* (This translation was the basis of a superb production by England's National Theatre in 1974). David Magarshack's version in *Anton Chekhov: Four Plays* (New York: Hill and Wang, 1969)* also reads easily and well. Too many of the other translations present the dialogue in the play as thoroughly disjointed, giving *The Cherry Orchard* an inappropriately Beckett-like air.

The following works have been useful to me in my consideration of *The Cherry Orchard: Chekhov: A Collection of Critical Essays*, ed. Robert Louis Jackson (Englewood Cliffs, N.J.: Prentice-Hall, 1967),* especially A. Skaftymov's essay, "Principles of Structure in Chekhov's Plays"; Francis Fergusson, *The Idea of a Theater* (Princeton: Princeton University Press, 1949);* David Magarshack, *Chekhov the Dramatist* (New York: Hill and Wang, 1960); Constantin Stanislavsky, *My Life in Art* (New York: Theatre Arts, 1948);* J. L. Styan, *Chekhov in Performance* (Cambridge: Cambridge University Press, 1971); and Maurice Valency, *The Breaking String: The Plays of Anton Chekhov* (New York: Oxford University Press, 1966).

Henrik Ibsen was born in Skein, Telemark, in 1828 and died in Christiana in 1906. *Hedda Gabler* was first performed in 1890.

There are a number of inexpensive translations of *Hedda Gabler* available, most of them quite good. The problem is to render from the Norwegian the precarious balance of Hedda's heroic aspirations, without making her speeches sound overly melodramatic on the one hand and without making Tessman and his household seem implausible on the other. Michael Meyer's translation, in *Hedda Gabler and Three Other Plays* (Garden City, N.Y.: Doubleday, 1961)* seems the most successful in this respect, although the versions of Una Ellis-Fermor (Harmondsworth: Penguin, 1950),* Eva Le Gallienne (New York: New York University Press, 1955),* and Rolf Fjelde (New York: New American Library, 1965)* are strong contenders.

The following works are helpful: Muriel G. Bradbrook, *Ibsen, the Norwegian* (London: Chattto and Windus, 1946); *Ibsen: A Collection of Critical Essays*, ed. Rolf Fjelde (Englewood Cliffs, N.J.: Prentice-Hall, 1965),* especially an essay by Caroline W. Mayerson, "Thematic Symbols in *Hedda Gabler*"; James Joyce, "Ibsen's New Drama," in *The Critical Writings of James Joyce* ed. Ellsworth Mason and Richard Ellmann (New York: Viking, 1959):* James McFarlane, ed., *Discussions* *of Henrik Ibsen* (Boston: Heath, 1962); John Northam, *Ibsen's Dramatic Method* (London: Faber, 1953);* G. B. Shaw, *The Quintessence of Ibsenism* (New York: Brentano, 1913);* Herman J. Weigand, *The Modern Ibsen* (New York: Holt, 1925);* Raymond Williams, *Drama From Ibsen to Eliot* (London: Chatto and Windus, 1952).

*Paperbound available.

THE CAUCASIAN CHALK CIRCLE
AND *END GAME*

Edward Mendelson

Observed in broad outline, the history of European drama is the history of increasing fidelity to the details of ordinary speech and daily events, the history of an ever more precise and accurate "realism." The characters in the drama of ancient Greece neither looked nor sounded like their audiences—who wore no masks and seldom sang in choruses. The psychological and political depths of Greek drama lay beneath a rigidly schematic mode of presentation. The drama of the Renaissance, even when it conformed most enthusiastically to what it took to be the classical "unities," modified the ancient schemata, and conformed more closely to the details of the perceived world. Renaissance *dramatis personae* look and dress like their audiences, although, like their classical predecessors, they sound a lot more grand. By the end of the nineteenth century almost all European theaters presented actors whose onstage conversation sounded almost exactly like that of their audiences offstage, in settings that might have been copied from the audience's homes. But this history of increasing realism ends in an abrupt reaction which occurred all along the border separating the nineteenth from the twentieth centuries. The impulse toward realism—or what might more accurately be called *concealed artifice*, that is, the illusion of simple rather than complex equations between events onstage and events in the world outside—yielded, on some fronts without a struggle, to a renewed impulse toward schematization, abstraction, and a whole repertory of dramatic techniques that may be summarized in the term *exposed artifice.* All art is schematic, but writers like Chekhov and Ibsen, who approach and resist realism from different directions, conceal the schematic quality of their work—their artificial selection and shaping of events from the flux of experience— behind a surface that pretends to have the texture and detail of daily life. Modernist writers several decades later, writers like Brecht and Beckett in their radically different ways, insist on presenting the schematic artificiality of their work, on its visible surface as well as at its structural depths.

Realism and its modernist opposition, different as they appear, have closely related historical origins which this essay might usefully explore. We need not look back as far as Greece or Rome. Dante's world makes an adequate starting point. For in Dante the transition is most dramatic between a medieval world view of a coherent universe whose transcendent meaning is fully perceptible only to the mind of God, and a Renaissance (and modern) world view in which individual perspectives become (at first *faute de mieux*, then triumphantly) adequate means of perceiving a world made up of physical and psychological facts. In Dante the personal, individual voice speaks with the immediacy of recent self-discovery while remaining in its universal context. But the balance in Dante between a divine universal perspective and individual secular perspectives was never again achieved. Soon after Dante, a crucial set of developments in intellectual history, already begun in small ways, would take on overwhelming momentum: the world would submit to rapid demythologization, and almost all belief in transcendent meaning would yield to the scientific search for theoretical and practical meaning (as Faust would "put nature to the question"). At the same time, the human psyche, which is the means of perceiving the world, would become increasingly a center of attention in itself. The European Renaissance studied the secular nature of the external world through experiment and exploration, while it simultaneously explored the internal world of motive and emotion. Hamlet's attention to his own mental state, to the detriment of his ability to act on the political world outside, is the inner counterpart to the Renaissance experimentation on the outer world of nature which Goethe will personify in Faust. As intellectual attention shifted from the mind of God to the world (and the mind of man), and as the world became increasingly accessible to human understanding, philosophy and the arts focused their attention alternately on the *object* of that understanding—the social and natural world—and the mind which was the agent and *subject* of it. For better or worse, a world of fact is not necessarily a world of serene scientific detachment. As in revolutionary France, the Feasts of Reason accompany a Reign of Terror. A world without transcendent meaning can become, in Nietzsche's phrase, a world without judgment, purpose, order, or God—a world in which an observer, like Faust, may come to find meaning only in the moment of experience, for he can find no meaning either in the past or in the grandiose structures of philosophy.

If the prospect of a world whose significance lay only in the immediate moment was despairing for some, and wildly exhilarating for others, it became at last the comfortable justification for nineteenth-century realism. For Chekhov to find a serious subject it was unnecessary for him to look back into history, as in *Hamlet* or *Macbeth*, or into myth, as in *Phaedra*. He needed only to look closely at events in the ordinary world around him, a world of facts without transcendence. But realistic drama attended only to observed fact; the other aspect of perception, the observer himself, remained unexamined and unaltered. Attention to the observer—the parallel strand in intellectual history to the strand of increasing realism—had not disappeared, although it had gone underground in the byways of European romanticism. Writing at the historical edge between realism and modernism, Proust noted, with something of an air of discovery, that "every impression is two-ended, one half embedded in the object, the other half—which only we can know—extending into ourselves." It is the latter half that becomes the focus of modernism. In some phases of modernism the author's goal is to *change* the observer, as in the political purposes of Brecht's plays, while in other phases the purpose is limited to a steady, reflexive *observation* of the observing self, as in the increasing isolation and claustrophobia of the world of Beckett's novels and plays.

The historical background to the focus on the observing mind, rather than on the observed object, includes the eighteenth-century development, and nineteenth-century refinement, of the concept of *dialectic.* Dialectic is central to both Brecht, who acknowledges it, and to Beckett, who does not. The term itself is of course an ancient one, referring until recent centuries simply to argumentation or logic. But in the eighteenth century the term began to take on its current usage, in which it refers to a process that is both mental and historical: the process by which a *thesis*, as a result of its own inherent limitations or inadequacies, passes over into its opposite *antithesis*, these counter-ideas, forces, structures then progressing into a single larger *synthesis*, which produces its own antithesis as the progression continues. (The common attribution of the thesis-antithesis-synthesis triad to Hegel is more a matter of legend than of fact, but its origin is less important than its influence.)

Something of the same function that sacred myth served in the ancient world, and that sacred history serves for orthodox Christianity and Judaism, is served by the concept of dialectic in modern thought. That is, dialectic has become an acknowledged or unacknowledged means of organizing personal and historical experience: it is of course the structural basis of Marxism, which applies the process to the material world of political events, and, in a more concealed fashion, it gives structure to the Freudian myth system as well (the mythical being called the Id, for example, gives energy to its antithesis the Superego, which in turn controls and shapes the Id until the Ego—another mythical being—is synthesized.)

Dialectic also provides the theoretical framework for Brecht's politically purposive theater. Brecht used a variety of names for his special repertory of dramatic techniques, most often *epic theater*, but he finally more or less settled on *dialectical theater*. Although he at one point called his methods merely a shift in accent from—rather than an antithesis to —the methods of naturalistic drama, it is clear that he considered the naturalistic drama and the epic theater as opposites. Naturalism, in Brecht's view, provided the illusion of reality in a manner designed to dull its audience's critical faculties; the audience was supposed to identify with the characters on the stage, to accept the stage action as the inevitable consequence of unchanging human nature. Dialectical theater was to *influence* reality as well as represent it: instead of inviting identification, dialectical theater would invite criticism, would call social contradictions to consciousness, would leave the audience aroused to change the world for the better.

From his conversion to Marxism at around the age of thirty, in 1928, until his death in 1956, Brecht constantly thought of himself as a propagandist. Orthodox propaganda makes notoriously bad literature, but Brecht was too much a rebel ever to be orthodox or doctrinaire, even toward causes in which he believed. He maintained a lifelong distrust of all authority, although he accepted the direct authority of the East German government when he returned to Berlin after wartime exile, in order to see his plays produced in a state-supported theater. Even more shrewdly than his character Azdak, Brecht always made sure he knew how to find the exit: he left his copyrights in West Germany, he kept his money in a Swiss bank, he obtained an Austrian passport before settling in East Berlin, and, though an atheist, on his deathbed he prudently called in a Lutheran minister. The most ambiguous aspect of his political life was his running battle with the regime whose support he accepted. Although he never risked open dissent, he usually managed to evade most state control over his theater. Around the time of the Berlin riots of 1953 he wrote (but did not publish) an ironic poem saying that the government had lost the support of the people—it would perhaps be best to dissolve the people and elect a new one.

Where a realist like Chekhov observed the world of each of his plays from a single unchanging perspective, Brecht always used multiple perspectives and mutually contradictory approaches in a single play. *The Caucasian Chalk Circle* tells the same story three times, in three different ways, and the arrangement of the stories is effectively a dialectical one. At issue is the just use of things, persons, and ideas. First land, then a child, then justice itself is each in turn placed in the hands of "those who are good for it," instead of those who might claim it merely as property on the narrow, inhumane grounds of simple legality. The play begins with a prologue titled "The Struggle for the Valley," a formal, stylized representation of a dispute between two collective farms or *kolchos* over ownership of a valley that had to be abandoned in wartime. Are the old residents, the goatbreeders, to resettle, or are the neighboring fruit growers to replant the valley with vineyards? The peaceful solution of this dispute, in which the fruit growers gain the valley, occupies the prologue. This is presided over by an efficient and unsentimental expert from "the capital," for the prologue is a propaganda text, an account of rational Soviet problem-solving. But for all the ease with which the prologue settles its problems, it leaves some disturbing undertones which must be resolved. (The girl tractor driver, for example, seems a faintly chilling figure, whose presence raises the possibility that rational justice may be somewhat heartless.) The prologue's static quality is especially strange in the context of the work of as lively a playwright as Brecht. It is, in fact, saved from dullness only by brevity: the naively rational and featureless society it describes (a future society, incidentally: Brecht wrote this postwar scene before the end of the Second World War) is one that no one in Brecht's audience would want to live in for long. The scene is the dramatic equivalent of the socialist-realist statues that portray a musclebound Soviet worker about to marry a tractor.

But the prologue's flatness is surely deliberate. It is a schema, i.e., a model of experience, which is corrected and transformed in the play within a play, the singer's story of the chalk circle, which follows it. Although the singer's story is evidently "artificial"—it is partly narrated and partly acted, with no naturalistic illusion, and is set within the distancing frame of the prologue—it is also far deeper and more emotionally compelling than the tidy example of propaganda art which frames it. Brecht begins with a schema that would be fully acceptable as "official" art: bland, simplistic, without personal conflict or idiosyncratic character. He then opposes this schema with an antithetical kind of writing: subversive, obscene, noisy, and various. (A Soviet critic once wondered in print how to defend the presentation of a conflict which, "against all the rules of agricultural cooperatives and against existing Soviet legal practice . . . is decided with the help of a ballad singer.") The singer will not alter his story for the sake of official convenience. When the expert asks the singer "very confidentially" to make his story shorter, the singer, without explanation or excuse, simply answers "No."

The singer's story has a structure that is virtually unique. As the bare style of the prologue has its antithesis in the exuberant variety of the singer's story, so the singer's story itself is divided into two antithetical stories which are synthesized at the end of the play. The two stories cover the same period of time, but instead of being intertwined as plot and subplot, with alternating episodes of each, they remain entirely separate until the final minutes of the play. During most of the second story Brecht pretends almost to have forgotten about the first. The first story tells of Grusha's flight from the capital with the child who was abandoned by the governor's wife in *her* flight from political chaos. While Grusha is raising the child and making it her own, the child is suddenly retrieved by soldiers and brought back to the capital. At this point the story stops abruptly, and returns to its beginning, to the times of political chaos, and takes up the story of Azdak. At first Azdak attempts to denounce himself for unwittingly helping the Grand Duke in *his* flight, but is instead named judge by the soldiers who hold the only real authority in the midst of political upheaval. As Grusha had taken up the child left behind by its mother, Azdak takes up the obligation to serve justice which was left behind by the Grand Duke. At the end of the play, when the Grand Duke recovers power, Azdak (retained as judge in recognition of his unwitting help in the Duke's escape) presides over a trial in which the governor's wife seeks to recover her child—the family estates are bound up with the heir—but Azdak finally grants the child to Grusha, the "true mother."

Azdak and Grusha could hardly appear more antithetical. Grusha, far too unimaginative to be anything but selfless (though cautious), determined, chaste and direct, willingly suffers indignities and danger for the sake of the child whom she has made her own. Azdak, cowardly, lecherous, drunk, self-contradictory, sits on the statute book when he judges a case. His rulings leave poor thieves in possession of their plunder, rich farmers in terror of further loss. What Grusha attempts through direct and simple acts, Azdak achieves through contradiction and illogic. But despite appearances, each desires the same end: that possession should accrue to responsibility, that persons and things should go to those who are best for them: "the children to the maternal, that they thrive . . . the valley to the waterers, that it shall bear fruit"—and the court of justice to the merciful, that those who suffer may be relieved.

Azdak's inverted justice is appropriate to the time of upheaval in which he becomes judge. His rulings conform to no statutes: he is merciful more than just, replacing the old legal dispensation with a new dispensation of miracles—in which the poor are fed and the rich punished for their "lack of faith." Azdak's rulings so grossly violate justice that they become comparable to double negatives in grammar: they are positively merciful despite their double contradictions. Not only does he violate legal ethics by taking bribes from plaintiffs, but he then compounds the "injustice" by ruling against those who have bribed him, in favor of those too poor to be able to offer money. His small gestures toward the redistribution of wealth serve a justice larger than any laws. In some notes to the play, Brecht wrote that Azdak "is utterly genuine, a disappointed revolutionary posing as a human wreck, like Shakespeare's wise men who act the fool. Without this the judgment of the chalk circle would lose all authority."

Grusha and Azdak achieve their synthesis and resolution in the end. When, during the trial, it appears to Grusha that Azdak will rule in favor of the governor's wife (whose lawyers have paid him healthy bribes), she shouts at him, "You don't know any more about justice than I do." She is right. As Azdak casually agrees, "There's something in that." Both know, without being able to tell the other, what is best for the child. When Azdak asks Grusha if after all she would not prefer that the child be returned to its first mother so that it might become rich, she is unable to answer. But the singer tells the audience her thoughts, her knowledge that riches do evil and that power is a destructive burden. Azdak tells the silent Grusha, "I think I understand you, woman." And he does.

When the singer speaks what Grusha thinks, but cannot say on her own (as in other emotionally intense moments in the play), the stage action is of course far from naturalistic in style. The action of the main characters cannot be part of the same represented "world" as the action of the singer who tells their story. The play holds different styles of action and representation onstage at the same moment, in a technique Brecht (admittedly borrowing from fashionable concepts of the time) called "montage." In place of the naturalistic "growth" of action which Brecht found in nineteenth-century drama, he used disjunct scenes and methods, and as many disparate elements as possible within the confines of a single play.

Ibsen uses only one or two metaphors in *Hedda Gabler*, and once or twice recalls the myth of Dionysus. He makes gestures at creating symbolic worlds, but they are worlds with little mythic or symbolic depth. Brecht, in contrast, throws in everything, and finds depths beneath everything. Grusha, Simon, and Michael often echo Mary, Joseph, and Jesus (the husband must come to believe that the mother is a virgin). When Azdak kneels to an old woman whom he calls "Mother Grusinia" (Grusinia is the Caucasus), he echoes the worship of the Virgin in her Mater Gloriosa aspect. The story of the chalk circle is Chinese in some details, from the story of Solomon in others. Azdak himself recalls the saturnalian Lords of Misrule, the Roman slaves elevated to brief authority during festivals in which all laws are overturned. The style of narration is Japanese, Azdak's song of chaos is from the Egyptian, and Brecht's staging of Grusha's wedding to a peasant derives from the stateroom scene in *A Night at the Opera*.

The intended effect of all this recollection and allusion is to make it impossible for the audience to imagine that the characters are persons exactly like themselves—and to make it thus impossible for the audience to lose its critical faculty in the course of *identifying* with the characters. Or so Brecht hoped. (He was fortunately a better playwright than theorist: when he learned that an actress in *Mother Courage* had made audiences weep, he was outraged and rewrote the part; but they still wept.) At the center of Brecht's dramatic theory is the principle of *distancing* instead of identification, a constant and conscious separation of character and audience,

which Brecht called the *Verfremdungseffekt* (usually translated "alienation effect," but "distancing effect" is better).
Instead of identifying, Brecht wants his audience to remain
detached and "alien" from the action onstage—in order that
they might study it, learn from it the significance of the conditions in the world outside the theater, and ultimately make
conscious political acts on the basis of what they have
learned.

Brecht attempted to achieve his distancing effect through a
variety of stage techniques: printed slogans, stagehands doing
their work in full view of the audience, above all "narrative
acting," Brecht's term for a technique in which the actor,
rather than "living the part," remains evidently an actor who
tells the story of his character. In *The Caucasian Chalk Circle*
this technique is extended to narration in its most simple
form—when, for example, the singer tells Grusha's thoughts
during the trial. The technique distracts attention from the
lives of the characters to the artifice of the play, and from
there to the real contradictions in society that the "unreal"
play exposes. In *The Caucasian Chalk Circle* in particular,
Brecht wrote that the "main contradictions" included these:
"The more Grusha does to save the child's life, the more she
endangers her own; her productivity leads to her own destruction. That is how things are, given the conditions of war,
the law as it is, and her isolation and poverty. In the law's
eyes the rescuer is a thief."

For Brecht the condition of the social world and the people
in it is dynamic, "dialectical," subject to change through the
press of opposing forces. Naturalistic theater, Brecht said,
wrongly presented human beings as unchanging, as directed
deterministically by their unalterable personalities to an inevitable end. Epic theater was to be concerned less with the
end than with the process, and it is the process of change that
its audience is supposed to maintain, outside the theater,
among the contradictions of the social world. Change may be
inevitable, but, Brecht insists, the courses of change, the de-

cisions to be made by conscious actors on the field of history, are subject to choice and decision.

The vital processes in Brecht's work, the rapid shifts of scene, tone, and method, the thrusts toward a plausible and better future, help make his plays the exhilarating triumphs they are. But they have their quiet antithesis in the static world of Beckett, especially in the world of Beckett's later plays. To move from *The Caucasian Chalk Circle* to *Endgame* is to move between worlds whose differences seem irreconcilable. But the visions of Brecht and Beckett are inevitable adversaries. Each claims, implicitly or explicitly, to be the true successor to naturalism, but the limitations of each vision seem almost unavoidably to summon the other into existence. Brecht demonstrates to Beckett the real complexity of the external world that the latter's vision can only remember from a faint and distant past. Beckett calmly reiterates to Brecht the fact of the unbreakable kernel of privacy at the center of even the most socially conscious individuals, the pit of self that neither generates light nor admits it. In Brecht's world lovers marry, children grow, the conscious self can lose its isolation in a resolving dance. In Beckett's world, age declines into isolation, speech into silence, flesh into dust. *The Caucasian Chalk Circle* is wide-ranging and shrewdly hopeful; *Endgame* is narrow and constricting in both its setting and in the range of possibilities it offers.

The room that is the only setting of *Endgame* is descended from the closed rooms of French classical drama, but at least in classical drama there was a peopled world outside the closed room, no matter how inaccessible that outside world might be. In *Endgame* the whole range of action is tightly restricted to a single room, whose two high windows and single door may be a shorthand notation for the eyes and mouth of a human head, the private room from which no one escapes. The world outside *Endgame* is either a dead featureless plain or a becalmed silent sea. The light is gray, without

distinctions of day or night. "There's no more nature," Clov
says. Outside is a world without beings or events; within,
only varieties of inability and limitation. Hamm is blind and
cannot stand; Clov cannot sit (and, like Alceste, keeps saying
he will leave but never does). Nagg and Nell have no legs, and
live and die in trash cans. Hamm, like the human mind, has in
himself no means of motion or action, but depends entirely
on Clov who, like the human body, can "never refuse" the
orders of Hamm. Only at death does the mind no longer need
the body, as, at the end of the play, Hamm, his "reckoning
closed and story ended," releases Clov at last.

Many events take place in *The Caucasian Chalk Circle*, and
when Brecht's play ends its world has substantially altered.
And Brecht hopes the world outside will alter even more. At
the close of *Endgame* little has changed; and the opening
tableau repeats itself. Where Brecht throws in every available
literary and political recollection and allusion into his work,
Beckett excludes almost everything. The goal of Beckett's
work is the most minimal possible notation of experience—a
goal Beckett actually achieved in a notably short play titled
Breath, whose notation of human life consists of a birth cry,
inhalation, exhalation, and a death cry, all these sounds
made beyond a stage, littered with rubbish, where light
first rises and then falls. Early in his career Beckett stopped
writing in his native English and changed to French because
he found himself too fluent in English: it was too easy to say
too much. (It may be worth noting, in case anyone should be
tempted to read an author's life into his work, that where
Brecht's political vision of courage and change was the product of a personal character that was too often ready to move
with the currents of the moment, Beckett's vision of futility
and limits is the work of a man who voluntarily risked his
life for the authentic causes of the French Resistance during
the Second World War.)

Endgame is a work that approaches the conclusion of Beckett's course toward isolation and stasis, but does not reach it.
Outside the room that is the world of the play, there may

perhaps be a child, a "potential procreator"—though he is only a potential one, and may be only a reflexive memory of Clov as a child (if, as the play implies, it was Clov whom Hamm, in the story he tells in the middle of the play, once agreed to take into his service). On the whole, inside and out, little happens or exists in *Endgame*: all that is certain is that "it" is coming to an end. Just what has occurred to bring affairs to this pass is never made explicit. There was nature once, but there is none now, none "in the vicinity." The situation within is stark enough: we know only that Nagg and Nell are Hamm's parents, that Clov is Hamm's adopted servant. We can guess that Hamm is short for *hammer*, Clov a typographical variation of the French *clou* or *nail*, which itself varies into Nell and into the German *Nagel* or Nagg. (Outside, in addition, was once Mother Pegg.) Are these names arbitrary, or do they have some indicative meaning? Beckett gives no answers.

In *The Caucasian Chalk Circle* there are no mysteries, and all questions have answers. Dialectical argument proceeds to synthesis and resolution. In *Endgame* the potentially dialectical pattern of question and answer gets nowhere. Clov complains (or merely asserts), "You've asked me these questions millions of times." To which Hamm exclaims (but does not answer), "I love the old questions . . . the old answers, there's nothing like them." Clov said earlier, "All life long the same questions, the same answers." Much of the dialogue of the play consists of questions with no answers at all. Things do not exist in Beckett in active relationships, as they do in Brecht, but in a stasis that can only decline and end. The dialogue reads often like the conversation of an unhappy family that will always be unhappy, with its bursts of resentment and a few comfortable memories, its fixed inescapable relationships, its verbal shorthand in referring to old wounds. But Hamm loses his parents and dismisses Clov. All that remains at the end of the play, Hamm says, is his old handkerchief, an "old Stancher" of wounds that at last stanches the play.

The isolation which Hamm finally enters, the isolation of

a world with "no more nature," is the extreme case of Cartesian dualism between spirit and matter. For Beckett the separation of body and mind is absolute. There is then no purpose in speculating what has "happened," outside the house, to bring events to this sorry pass. Nothing at all has happened outside; all that has occurred is that the separation of the mind from the body has reached its inevitable consequences: the mind, detached from the body, is detached utterly from the whole physical world of which the body is a part. At one point in the play Hamm recalls showing a madman the beautiful fertile world outside a window—"All that rising corn! . . . All that loveliness!" But the madman drew back appalled: "All he had seen was ashes." The madman's situation is now Hamm's own. "It appears," Hamm says of the madman, "the case is . . . was not so . . . so unusual" (Beckett's ellipses). To Hamm and his extensions there is effectively no nature, because there is no means of perceiving nature. The dialectic has faded into futility because nothing remains to *oppose* the individual mind—to oppose, shape, and ultimately to build a new synthesis. The "potential procreator" can be nothing more than potential.

If Beckett's plays were a precise description of their author's vision of the world—as some readers naively assume—they would be self-pitying and humorless. But they are not. Beckett's often manic comedy is a reminder of the contradiction his plays imply but do not embody (unlike Brecht's, which deliberately *embody* contradiction). What stands behind Beckett's world and ultimately gives it value is the unnamed alternative vision to which Beckett gives a contradictory response: the loud, various, changing, industrial and political world, full of noise and events, the enemy of self-awareness. *Endgame*, taken as a whole, is the dialectical antithesis of such a world. It presents the psychological state—never very far from the world of social events and relationships—of privacy, futility, silence, repetition, decline, and decay.

Beckett's progression into silence and vacancy (somewhat

reversed, incidentally, in his most recent work), is mirrored by Brecht's maturing into a theater of range and coherent vitality. Brecht's earliest work expressed an anarchic individualism, but as he developed his theories of epic or dialectical theater, he increasingly devised ways of presenting the world of relations, a world where politics, philosophy, history, and the interconnectedness of human events are consequential and real. Like Beckett, though, Brecht knows that a chaos lurks outside the vision of his plays, a world of social chaos and mere cruelty which Azdak describes in his "Song of Chaos." For Beckett the waiting chaos is a chaos of vacancy and silence which inspires no songs beyond a fragmentary chant of desperation, like Hamm's last: "You cried for night, it falls: now cry in darkness."

Beckett's vision is private in the most extreme possible way, Brecht's extremely public, but the two are not finally exclusive. Each may be understood in a dialectical relation to the other. The person who reads Beckett for pleasure—normally, perhaps, the sort of person who is unhappy everywhere but prefers to be unhappy alone, who imagines every day as an ending or defeat—should force himself to read Brecht instead, in order to learn the uncomfortable truth that there is a world outside the confines of his own selfhood, a world to which he is responsible whether he chooses to be or not. On the other hand, the person who reads Brecht for pleasure—an optimist who finds the personalities of others more interesting than his own, who faces each day as a new beginning, the essentially healthy man or woman who, having experienced happiness, wants others to share it—should read Beckett to learn the depths and intransigence of the isolation of others, the isolation that must be overcome if anything is ever to be shared or communicated. Neither the Brechtian nor the Beckett-enthusiast may care much for the other's vision, but each needs the other if he is to understand the difficulties his own vision tries to ignore. Their reconciliation can never remain stable. It can at best only echo the reconciliation

achieved by Azdak through his own contradictions: "a brief
Golden Age that was almost just."

BIBLIOGRAPHICAL NOTE

Bertolt Brecht was born in Augsburg in 1898 and died in Berlin in
1956. He wrote *Der kaukasiche Kreidekreis* (*The Caucasian Chalk Circle*) in 1943–45. The play was first produced at Carleton College, Min-
nesota, in 1948, using Eric Bentley's incomplete translation.

Bentley's effort has been supplanted by two excellent complete
translations: the lively and intelligent version by James and Tania
Stern, with verse translated by W. H. Auden, in Brecht's *Plays*, Vol. 1
(London: Methuen, 1960),* and the accurate and sensitive version by
Ralph Manheim in Brecht's *Collected Plays*, Vol. 7 (New York: Random House, 1975).* The latter collection also includes Brecht's extensive notes on the play, some of which I cite.

Useful books on Brecht in English include Martin Esslin, *Brecht: The
Man and His Work* (Garden City, N.Y.: Doubleday, 1960);* John Fuegi,
The Essential Brecht (Los Angeles: Hennessy and Ingalls, 1972); and
John Willett, *The Theatre of Bertolt Brecht* (New York: New Direc-
tions, 1959). Also valuable is *Brecht: A Collection of Critical Essays*,
ed. Peter Demetz (Englewood Cliffs, N.J.: Prentice-Hall, 1962).* John
Willett's translation of some of Brecht's notes, interviews, and essays,
Brecht on Theatre (New York: Hill and Wang, 1964),* is indispensable.

Samuel Beckett was born in Dublin in 1906. *Fin de Partie* first appeared in French in 1957; Beckett then translated the play into English as *Endgame*, and made some minor changes from the original
(New York: Grove Press, 1958).*

Beckett studies expand at an ever more rapid pace. This list can in-
clude only some of the wider-ranging books. See, for example, Ruby
Cohn's two books, *Samuel Beckett* (New Brunswick, N.J.: Rutgers
University Press, 1962) and *Back to Beckett* (Princeton: Princeton Uni-
versity Press, 1973); John Fletcher and John Spurling, *Beckett: A
Study of His Plays* (London: Eyre Methuen, 1972);* Hugh Kenner, *A
Reader's Guide to Samuel Beckett* (New York: Farrar, Straus and
Giroux, 1973);* and Michael Robinson, *The Long Sonata of the Dead*
(New York: Grove Press, 1969).* A useful group of shorter studies is
Beckett: A Collection of Critical Essays, ed. Martin Esslin (Englewood
Cliffs, N.J.: Prentice-Hall, 1965).* Stanley Cavell has an exceptionally
intelligent essay on *Endgame*, "Ending the Waiting Game," in his *Must
We Mean What We Say?* (New York: Scribner's, 1969).*

*Paperbound available.